STORM THE GATES OF JERICHO

ABRAHAM

STORM THE

JERI

L. FEINBERG

GATES OF CHO

Marzani & Munsell New York, N. Y.

DESIGN: F. NEWFELD

Canadian Publishers
McClelland and Stewart Limited
25 Hollinger Road, Toronto 16

FIRST EDITION
LIBRARY OF CONGRESS CATALOG CARD
NUMBER: 65-28156
PRINTED IN THE UNITED STATES OF AMERICA

Contents

ACKNOWLEDGEMENT

The quotation on page 176
is from Gordon Allport,
The Nature of Prejudice, Addison-Wesley Publishing Co., Inc.,
Reading, Massachusetts.

To Ruth, with love

Introduction

No priest, pastor or rabbi in North America has ever published a book like *Storm the Gates of Jericho.* Whatever page you scan, you will find unmistakable signs of a completely unafraid, undiluted personality.

The author recounts with searing beauty the destruction by Hitler of the Lithuanian ghetto that bred the Jewish piety of his parents; he lampoons with both savage and subtle irony the shams of the professional clergy (including his own); he laughs with wry self-pity at the anti-Semitic pretensions of fundamentalist Christian theology; he leaps with unflagging vigor to the barricades against fascism—but always with a deep sense of the tragedy of life and compassion for the human being.

As a cleric, he looks upward—quizzically, yet prayerfully, not expecting much—to God; as a Jew, he looks backward to the stubborn traditions of his own people; as a child of this "psychological" age, he looks inward without flinching at his own alienated ego; as a champion of social justice, he looks outward to the poor and mistreated.

"Jericho" is not an autobiography. Rabbi Feinberg admits that what happened to him has no importance in itself. The book is intensely personal—but the incidents narrated have been chosen because they led to, or arose from, ingrained convictions about some of the major controversies of our era. In fact, "Jericho" thrusts to the core of the issues that have plagued Western society from the dawn of this combative twentieth century, when the author was born, to the present hour. Abraham Feinberg is a committed man. *Time* magazine once wrote of him: "He never crossed the street to avoid a fight"— often as a minority of one. He lived in a state of war with himself, with his environment, with his God!

The villain of this personal drama, Feinberg's prime enemy, emerged in January 1933, when Feinberg was on the bright road to Broadway stardom as romantic tenor Anthony Frome, "Poet Prince" (after his sensational resignation from Temple Israel, one of the most lucrative and glittering rabbinical posts in New York). That enemy of Nazism, embodied in Adolf Hitler.

At the rabbinical college, he had encountered the readiness of reactionaries to drape their contempt for the common man in the slogans of anti-communism—and to exalt Mussolini because he ran Italian trains "on time." From boyhood, Abe Feinberg's experience as a Jew had exposed his abnormally sensitive nerves to the stench of race-hate and the brutality of naked power. Now he saw the full flowering of evil, and thenceforth he accepted no respite from its challenge.

Back again in a New York pulpit, from countless platforms, on radio, through the press, with tongue and pen, he flayed Il Duce's bombs in Ethiopia, Franco's "rehearsal for World War

Two" (he will not set foot in Spain while Franco rules it), the flirtation of Western tycoons and politicians with Hitler, the susceptibility of public opinion and "respectable" leaders to German "gemutlichkeit." In Denver, Colorado, he stood up against "America First." In Toronto, one of his earliest non-synagogue affiliations bore the then prestigious name Canadian-Soviet Friendship (it was soon after the Battle of Stalingrad).

Feinberg's passionate crusade against fascism was Canadian only in geography; in significance, it continued the endless war he had begun as a skinny youngster in an Ohio mining-town, carried to the Cincinnati seminary, and then to pulpits in Niagara Falls, Wheeling, New York and Denver. The embattled preacher became one of Canada's most controversial figures, but the issues he chose for battleground were as American as the Stars and Stripes, and no less symbolic of Western democracy. The foe bears an assortment of labels: discrimination against the Negro, anti-Semitism in all its guises, sectarian public school religion, re-militarization of Germany, ecclesiastical throttling of divorce reform, birth control and sane abortion laws, puritanical authoritarianism about sex, installation of nuclear arms, the "balance of terror" cold war with the Soviet Union, United States intervention in Viet Nam and the Dominican Republic, orthodox clerical power-play in Israel, or the anti-Jewish teaching of the Crucifixion story—to Rabbi Feinberg they all wear the faceless mask of fascism. But he now had a new weapon: television.

The "war-record" of Rabbi Feinberg has not run its course in the pages of "Jericho." Although he retired from the active rabbinate in 1961—some years earlier than usual, to write the book—his silver-topped head, dynamic speech and militant posture still send excitement out to audiences throughout North America despite failing eye-sight, and his pen can arouse a fever of delight or wrath. One day he roiled the citadels of quiet neutrality by leading two picket marches—1,000 men and women each time—around the auditorium where Governor Wallace of Alabama (whom he dubs "a magnolia Hitler") was addressing an International Lions Convention, all the while chanting "We Shall Overcome." Deluged with obscene threats after he insisted on "color-blindness" at an anti-apartheid rally, smeared by a tabloid as "paid agitator and Communist" after heading a white-Negro protest against race restrictions, attacked by financial interests for endorsement of a boycott of South African imports, railed at by devotees of Wm. F. Buckley, Jr. when he supports the Student Non-Violent Coordinating Committee—the writer of *Storm the Gates of Jericho* is still a stormy petrel.

On June 10, 1960, Feinberg presided at a huge mass rally of the Toronto Committee for Disarmament, which he had helped to found. The speaker, Rt. Hon. Philip Noel-Baker, was the first of a series of distinguished leaders invited to Canada to solidify public opinion against the nuclear arms race. Among them were Dr. Linus Pauling, Canon Collins, Dr. Benjamin Spock, Jerome Davis, Jacquetta Hawkes and spokesmen from the Soviet Union, Nigeria and India. A national organization, the Canadian Campaign for Nuclear Disarmament, made Feinberg its Vice-President and best-known voice. It circulated a petition signed by 125,000, on a "financial shoe-string," demanding that Canada refuse to install nuclear weapons on its soil. From Montreal to Victoria, British Columbia, the author of "Jericho" addressed mass-meetings directed to that crucial goal of non-membership in the nuclear fraternity, "God created us equal; the five-star generals will cremate us equal." Meetings were held in border cities with "ban-the-bombers" (Feinberg rejoiced in the epithet: "That's just what we are!"). He and his wife joined up with the San Francisco-Moscow peace marchers in silent vigil on Moscow's Red Square; he paraded with a placard around Parliament Square in Ottawa and argued with Ministers for Foreign Affairs; he walked in the vanguard of a pre-Easter peace demonstration to Toronto city square, quipping that "the only thing 'red' about me is my wife's beret"; he hailed Bertrand Russell and milled with the great protesting throng in London's Trafalgar Square. The apathy of church and synagogue in the Cuban crisis stirred his ire; the indifference of the average citizen did not daunt him; the government's boondoggling with fall-out shelters and civil defense he mocked as a tragi-comedy; he lifted the redemptive principle of co-existence with the Soviet

Union into a nation-wide political philosophy.

The fight was lost. Canada accepted nuclear installations, and is now, in Feinberg's phrase, "fifth wheel on the Pentagon juggernaut."

But the meditative scholar will not forsake the field of action and the war for peace. From the steps of Toronto City Hall he spoke in the rain to a large gathering of marchers: "For North Viet Nam, bread—not bombs; for South Viet Nam, ballots—not bullets"; on the grass of a playing-field at University of California, in Berkeley, he sat with 10,000 students and applauded the 36-hour teach-in by opponents of the Johnson policy in Viet Nam and the Dominican Republic, and over his signature and others, resolutions urged Ottawa to "stop being a carbon-copy" of the State Department, and in Washington on August 6th, 1965, he knelt beside Rev. A. J. Muste and Joan Baez in front of the White House, pleading for an end to the war.

In the meantime, his courage has grown into a legend. He does not quail at jeering, leather-jacketed hoods in Toronto, pickets and scurrilous hand-bills in Vancouver and Rochester, over-zealous cops on the Peace Bridge at Buffalo, early-morning death-threats and poison-pen letters, the raised eye-brows of "respectability"— or a fascist hate-sheet proclaiming that his bid for Canadian citizenship was rejected because the F.B.I. had sent the R.C.M.P. a dossier on his machinations as "The Kremlin's Number One" agent. (Actually, the author did not even *apply,* being intensely proud of his United States birth and citizenship.)

"The Red Rabbi" however, is the favorite smear-tag of the neo-fascists. It is a slick, 12-page pamphlet published by World Service, hate-propaganda outlet for the National States Rights Party in Birmingham, Alabama. A venomous little sheet, it is being distributed in some sections of the United States, and especially in Canada, not only to discredit the author's pro-peace leadership, but to advance the cause of resurgent, international anti-Semitism, which clearly wants a beachhead along the northern boundary of the United States. (Rabbi Feinberg is their natural target.)

If the Church of England can have its "Red Dean" of Canterbury, Judaism can afford a "Red Rabbi." This was pointed out by Rabbi Jacob Weinstein, President of the Central Conference of American Rabbis, who regards the author as an authentic contemporary voice of the great Hebrew prophets. Ontario's Attorney-General finds no clause in the Criminal Code, "unfortunately," to justify government action. Feinberg himself will not "contaminate a court of law" by slapping a slander charge on professional hate-experts, who have foraged for libellous material in the morgues of every newspaper in New York back to 1928 (and are using the "Red Rabbi" brochure to advertise "The Protocols of Zion."

As a student of Nazi ideology and militarism *Storm the Gates of Jericho* has been a moving experience. Rarely has a book given me such deep insight into the psyche of the Jewish people, such identification with its agony and idealism. Were I a rabbi or Jewish communal leader, I would want everyone in America to read this beautifully written testament of a man loyal to his heritage—if only for the first chapter, on "Grinkishok." Yet the man is also scrupulously honest—and he does not silence his intense dislike of the values set up by "bagel-and-lox" suburbia and the ram-rod rigidity and intolerance of orthodox "pot-and-pate" (dietary laws and head-covering) Judaism.

There are many such paradoxes in this wide-ranging, colorful book. Here are some notable examples: a boyhood reminiscence of sex so poignant that one reviewer compares it to Thomas Wolfe—and then a demand that sex be deflated, with less "fixation on the pudenda"; a poetic response to Jesus the man of sorrows which every Christian will rejoice at—and then a knock-out punch at the anti-Semitism of "Christ Crucified"; a passionate plea for civilized good-will between Jew and non-Jew—and a devastating exposé of Brotherhood Week; childhood yearning for the serene bosom of the Catholic Church—and bitter condemnation of its deals with Hitler and the ambivalence of the Ecumenical Council, coupled with an adulatory private-audience portrait of Pope John, who should have risen to the Papal throne "thirty years earlier"; restless pursuit of a true God

—and nagging doubt that He is both all-mighty and all-good; a flair for oratory that won him acclaim in a poll as one of Canada's "Seven Greatest Preachers"—and disillusionment about the worth of sermons so profound that it drove him from the plush New York pulpit of Temple Israel ("Temple Sinai" in the book) to the stage of the Paramount Theatre and the "razma-taz" of Broadway, as famed love-songster Anthony Frome, lyric tenor, "Poet Prince" of radio; a healthy zest that could savor the bistros of Paris — and a solemn sense of utter nihilism before the furnaces of Dachau; love of life that illuminates every page of "Jericho"— and yet a feeling of solidarity with the massive suffering of mankind, in the final chapter on "Death."

Storm the Gates of Jericho was first published in Toronto, 1964. It has appeared on Canadian best-seller lists. The author derived the title from the Biblical Book of Joshua, which relates how the Israelite priests brought down the walls of Jericho, which blocked the road to the Promised Land—by a miracle: the blowing of trumpets.

"We can't wait for a miracle to blast *our* road-blocks to freedom and peace in the atomic age. We must *storm* the gates of Jericho—ourselves!"

No reader can finish any chapter in this book without being warmed by its literary skill and challenged by its honest, forthright radicalism. Many reviewers have found it "fascinating." I agree.

Charles R. Allen, Jr.

Charles R. Allen, Jr. is the author of Heusinger of the Fourth Reich: The Step-by-Step Resurgence of the German General Staff *(Marzani & Munsell) which has been critically acclaimed and published in more than a dozen languages throughout the world. Five Nobel Prize winners—among them Bertrand Russell, called the work "brilliant . . . one of the most important books in the growing literature of the Cold War." Mr. Allen is presently at work on a book detailing the sensational story of the Nazi war criminals still walking around freely in Western Europe, Africa, Latin America and—* North America.

Foreword

SOME years ago I had a corneal transplant. Both eyes were bandaged; the surgeon ordered complete immobility from toe to head. Clearly, the most practical response was the comatose unconcern of a vegetable. But neither psychology nor prayer could counteract the genes; I don't vegetate easily.

Therefore I decided to exploit the situation rather than anaesthetize myself against it. Instead of battening down the hatches of consciousness and withdrawing *from* the world, I would use my dark imprisonment for a journey *into* a world – my own. That *herpes simplex* infection in my left eye was giving me time to inch through the tangled brush of remembered experience and discover what had made me what I am.

Gradually, the undifferentiated blackness of all that I could "see" grew luminous; the hospital bed became a magic carpet and my spirit soared upon a safari into self – the only realm whence no one can be expelled. Province by province, day by day, I traversed the sovereign realm of the past.

The ground covered during those sick-bed explorations is the geography of this book. The incidents are true, although often disguised in name, place, and detail. But they have meaning only insofar as they record commitment to the passions of this combative twentieth century, on whose threshold I was born. In itself my encounter with men and things would scarcely be worth describing; the issues it involved may kindle some excitement.

This volume is not a collection of sermons. I have tried to ferret out and obliterate every trace of pulpit posture or pronouncement. Sermons are made to be heard, not seen in print. I promised myself long ago that I would never foist a tidbit collation of tiresome homilies on friends who might feel obligated to buy it (if not to read it).

I do not pretend to answer riddles; for some of the problems posed in these pages there are no answers available to the current human species. There is no continuity of theme; only the anecdotal beginnings of the chapters fall, naturally, into chronological sequence. Therefore, the reader may choose to peruse them at random.

Michel de Montaigne once said that he dared to speak the truth all the more as he grew older. Perhaps his courage was fed by waning life expectancy. With each passing hour, he had less time to live and less to forfeit. As yesterday bites into tomorrow, it cloys and curbs the appetite for toadying compromise. At the most crucial crossroad in human history, a grey head like mine may, and *must*, stick out its neck (thus reversing the alleged trend of anatomical evolution toward a shorter one).

A Canadian Senator once called me a "radical." That was his

crowning indictment. To me it is a compliment I hope I deserve; rather that than the accolades vouchsafed by a populace which heaps reward on priapic sex-kittens, slavering aspirants for public office, and lupine purveyors of pablum!

Consummation of this project would have been impossible without the counsel of friends. I am especially grateful to Miss Claire Pratt, of McClelland and Stewart's editorial staff, Professor John R. Seeley, Brandeis University and Massachusetts Institute of Technology, Professor Emil Fackenheim, University of Toronto, and his wife Rose, and Dr. Franc Joubin, for their critical examination of the manuscript.

I owe an incalculable debt to my family, dead and living, for tolerance of foibles, unhesitant partnership in causes lost the moment they were launched, and the durability of their faith; to the United States, land of my birth, and to Canada, land of my recent labours, for the pivotal boon of freedom; to colleagues of every creed for the inspiration of example and, I trust, their pardon of the abrasive candour of these revelations; to Judaism and the Jewish people for the love and loyalty they implanted in a son who hopes he has not been recreant to their heritage.

Grinkishok

"GRINKISHOK." It clatters like an empty milkpail flung from a truck, but the clanging syllables are softened by immersion in a deep well of sentiment.

One summer I worked in an enamel-ware factory. Drab skeletal iron frames of pots and pans were placed on a caterpillar-belt between a double spray of hot liquid enamel. When they emerged at the other end, brilliant-hued and shiny, it was my job to cart them to the cooling-room for inspection. "Grinkishok," too, became poetry under the multi-coloured brush of my imagination, for I never spoke the word without tenderness. Grinkishok was the birthplace of my parents.

Like thousands more scattered over the territory bound by the Black and Baltic Seas and the Vistula and Dnieper basins, Grinkishok was a *shtetl** where Jews lived – if one could term their dismal existence living. It protruded like a tiny wart from the dun plain of Lithuania, by a sluggish little river near the East German border, on the edge of the Pale to which Czarist Russia restricted its Jews, and only a few versts from the capital city of Kovno, now Kaunas, in the province of that name.

Grinkishok surely had nothing to commend it beyond Shnipishok and Pushelat, other *shtetlach* nearby, or those in Poland, White Russia, and the Ukraine. All were linked together by the *shadhanim,*† cantors, and itinerant preachers who wended an impecunious path among them; by the trade fairs and pedlars; by long, curled earlocks and the long, straight caftans worn to distinguish Hebrew sages from short-jacketed Gentile illiterates; by the implacable enmity of the Russian Orthodox Church and the Czar, who vowed to starve one-third, drive out one-third, and convert the remainder, and by the universal yearning to go to America.

Of course, the "Grinkishoks" differed in size, ranging from a ten-family hamlet to a big commercial centre of a thousand. And they differed in degrees of poverty. Polish Jews often traded in grain and lumber; those of Volin ate white bread on weekdays. Fertile Bessarabia yielded much wine and corn; the Roumanians jested about their constant diet of *mameligeh.*‡ The *Litvaks* § had a proverb that "if barley soup's a meal, then my village is a commonwealth," although they actually were glad to yoke body and soul together with black bread, herring, and potatoes – except on Sabbath Eve, when a fat fowl, a morsel of unsalted fish, with white tablecloth and candles, were considered the proper expression of welcome and hospitality to the Sabbath Queen, even if one's table be bare the rest of the week, or he require communal assistance.

According to Jewish legend, God showed Adam the whole world He had just created. The straggling, mud-road shacks of some

* A small town or village.
† Matchmakers.
‡ Cornmeal cereal.
§ Lithuanians.

shtetlach, however, were so wretched and desolate, the Jewish inhabitants were so terrorized by the *mouzhik* * who slept alongside his pigs and could be aroused to avenging fury by the priests of his God, that "Adam never set foot there. . . ." Grinkishok, one of the tiniest of the *shtetlach*, numbered itself also among the most forlorn.

In my boyhood perspective two things were certain: first, whether Adam visited Grinkishok or not, God not only visited, but dwelt there, among His people to whom He had given the Torah centuries ago on Sinai, and who now studied and obeyed it with such devotion that Lithuania boasted the nickname "Jerusalem"; second, not only were my parents born in Grinkishok, but their parents before them, for many generations, back to the seventeenth century, when a pair of ancestors fled from the Chmelnitzki massacres in Poland. And their forbears had fled from a mediaeval German mob incited by a swilling feudal lord who owned his Jews as chattel and needed a scapegoat; and theirs from Rhineland cities cleansed of Jews by sword-swinging Crusaders on their way to the Holy Grail; and theirs from Spain, whose good Catholic sovereigns Ferdinand and Isabella, at the behest of the Holy Inquisition, drove into exile the Jewish grandees, scholars, and merchants who had helped make Toledo and Granada the envy of all Christendom but declined to make Christ their Lord.

I often wished I too had been born in Grinkishok. What stories to tell my pals about thatched houses, terrible snowstorms that buried people alive, and big fur hats.

Spiritually, I *was* born in Grinkishok. The mudholes, the box-like wooden dwelling-places, the saline scent of herring, the *bes-Hamedrash* † where males pored over the Bible commentaries and Talmud, the Friday-afternoon bustle of baking and *mikvah*,‡ the susurrus of prayers in the *shule*,§ the desperate hope for freedom in golden-streeted America – I knew it all from the kitchen-table talk of my parents and an occasional *lantsmann* || who strayed in with

* Peasant.
† House of study.
‡ Public bath.
§ Synagogue.
|| Home-towner

precious greetings. And I made it my business to learn Yiddish, so that I could chat with and write to Mom and Pop in their own tongue. At certain moments of introspection I lived as a Grinkishker – beyond Bellaire, where my body was born, beyond the banks of the Ohio and the rolling hills – in the cradle of my parents.

This longing for a pre-natal Grinkishok – was it a deposit of the love I felt for mother and father; a subconscious escape from the frustrations of a dark-complexioned, spindly legged, over-sensitive Jewish boy in a small American riverfront town; the expression of a profound and ever-present pity for the homelessness of the Jewish people; the self-delusion of a kid on the other side of the tracks who craved and created a dream world; or just a ragtag remnant of racial memory?

Grinkishok has, in actuality, become a ghost town. On a September morning in 1941 a Nazi machine-gun extermination squad reached Grinkishok. With extroverted efficiency, scientific dispatch, and the enthusiastic co-operation of local Lithuanians (perhaps for a bonus of sugar, salt, or vodka), the Nazis discharged the duty of obedient soldiers, saluted Hitler, and left the entire Jewish population of Grinkishok writhing in blood on the village square, after prodding them with bayonets into digging their own mass grave. With the exception of one daughter of Uncle Avram-Itza, who was sturdy enough to be useful as a slave-labour drudge and survive for emigration to the United States, all my kin – uncles, aunts, cousins, patriarchs, and babes – were obliterated.

The synagogue is now a nondescript pile of rotting timbers, and no trace can be found of the communal institutions which embodied the *shtetl*'s spiritual solidarity. But a squalid cluster of pious Jews in a dreary Lithuanian wilderness will be immortalized in the lamentations of its far-flung children, in the lore of its scholars, in the imaginative literary reconstruction of its folk life, in the rhythm of the Jewish heartbeat.

Grinkishok was more than an accidental dwelling-together of sundry individuals! It was a historically fated habitation of the eternal Jewish spirit, a candle of compassion and intellectual gentility that flickered through the all-enveloping darkness of mediaevalism and Czarism to be snuffed out by the goose-stepping minions of a nation that sighed over Bach, stuffed its stomach with beer and butter, and perfected the technology of massacre.

The grimy *shtetl* of my parents shone as one of the brightest gems in the *Keter Torah*,* to which a Jewish settlement accorded greater reverence than to any crown of kingship. In early spring the thawing ice pockmarked the single "street" with puddles of stagnant water – but they reflected the colours of God's heavenly Throne. And the ill-shod feet that stepped into them carried nostalgia for Grinkishok to pavements of distant cities, to schools and marts and laboratories, and to the dream-packed inner world of a lad whose soul had "come from Grinkishok."

There were awkward times, especially as a high-school teenager, when I hesitated to wrap Mom's peanut-butter sandwiches in the Yiddish newspaper or to mention the outlandishly foreign name "Grinkishok" as "origin of parents." But, deep down, Grinkishok was my certificate of admission to the oldest aristocracy in the Western world.

Were Grinkishkers the Chosen People? I am not privy to God's list of favourites and can provide no dogmatic answer. Few of them would have shared my qualms. At every reading of the Scroll of the Law, the benedictions thanked God for having selected them to receive the Torah and teach it to mankind.

The role to which the Grinkishker thought himself summoned constituted a kind of knighthood. He was to become a suffering servant, bearing wounds and stripes the better to embody Divine mercy and justice.

I do not argue that the sallow, stoop-shouldered, intimidated starveling of Grinkishok consciously engaged upon such a high commitment. It was enough to eke out a minimal livelihood and avoid the heavy hand of the oppressor. His occasionally contemptuous spiritual superiority to the uncircumcised *mouzhik* may have

* Crown of the Law.

been a technique of compensation whereby he rose above the indignities heaped upon him.

Nor do I contend that the inhabitants of and emigrants from the ghettos of Eastern and Central Europe hewed faithfully to their contract. Being human, they were prone to meanness, unethical corner-cutting in shop and marketplace, petty malice, gossip, unappetizing social gaucheries, hypocritical self-righteousness, preoccupation with the externals rather than the eternals of religion, and the temptation to judge themselves by profession and others by practice. Litvaks, in fact, had a notorious itch for *pilpulism.** The ancient Talmudic debate about the propriety of using an egg laid by an inconsiderate hen on the Sabbath had many echoes in the study halls of Grinkishok.

But all this palaver dwindles into *schmoos*. The ultimate test of a people, I believe, is how it meets descent into a terrestrial hell of man-made agony, how it confronts the inevitability of physical extinction and the possibility of moral collapse.

Lithuanian Jews in Nazi-occupied Europe were subjected to such a trial – day after day, month after month, under the most barbaric, sadistic, and calculating rule of repression that criminally insane men could fashion. Had the corrosive impact of such causeless martyrdom torn their religious and moral disciplines into shreds, they might be forgiven.

What, however, is the story?

The record is available, in an account written on the spot by Rabbi Ephraim Oshry, religious leader of Kovno from 1940 to 1944, and one of the six per cent of Lithuanian Jewry who emerged alive from the holocaust.

A rabbi's primary function in the old world crystallized around erudition – knowledge of the intricacies of the Torah. As the most scholarly and authoritative personage in the community, he resolved all questions of ritual observance and religious conduct, from the usability of a diseased chicken which might be *tref*,† to a family quarrel.

* Hair-splitting.

† Non-kosher.

Rabbi Oshry compiled the dilemmas under Nazi occupation submitted to him by the remnant of Jews in Kovno and surrounding villages like Grinkishok, together with his verdicts. The Hebrew volume, entitled *She'elot U'tshuvot Mi-Maamakim,* * is one of the terrifying, and edifying, documents of our age. In the midst of travail such as no human group has ever encountered, Lithuanian Jewry concerned itself with the duty of preserving the Law of God in a world whose animal savagery might have been expected to centre the human mind wholly on sheer physical survival. Even diabolic Nazi dehumanization could not quite crush the little Litvak's faith that he might walk in the holy way of Torah.

Since the Law forbids utilization of burial shrouds by the living, the Jews of Kovno asked Rabbi Oshry whether they might cover their shivering limbs with the clothes of the slain. He decided that preservation of life was more urgent than veneration of death.

They asked about *mezuzot,*† of which Nazi restrictions had cut off the supply. Inmates of the ghetto being in effect prisoners, his judgement released them from the *mezuzah* requirement.

They asked how to deal with one especially abominable Nazi contrivance set into motion on August 27, 1941. The Germans rounded up all the dogs and cats and shot them in the most-revered synagogue. Then they dragged multitudes of Jews thither and forced certain dignitaries to cover the dead and bleeding animals with sacred sheets from the Holy Scrolls. Those who witnessed, and those compelled to execute, the horrible deed, had committed the grave sin of *Hillul Hashen.*‡ The Rabbi ordained that the participants must fast, and the spectators also if they were not too far gone from hunger and sickness. The entire community would do penance by charity.

They asked if young men may not be enabled to escape into the woods and join the partisans by the purchase of baptismal

* *Inquiries and Responses from the Depths.*
† Receptacles for Biblical verses affixed to the doorpost.
‡ Profanation of the Holy Name.

certificates. A document of Christian baptism does not constitute apostasy, the Rabbi conceded. Yet the illusion would be thereby created among Gentiles that these young men had repudiated the God of Israel. Rather than such a false show of weakness, let them perform the act of *Kiddush Hashem*.*

One heroic Jew asked concerning a cross tattooed on his left arm, exactly where the *tephilin* † are worn by males for morning worship. At daybreak, on his way to slave labour at the Kovno airfield, he had been caught praying with the *tephilin*, and German ingenuity had come up with the cross as his punishment. Rabbi Oshry advised him to cover the cross and to pray at home whenever possible – if necessary at night.

They asked permission to purloin wool from the Germans for *tzitzit*.‡ None could be obtained otherwise, and many who realized the imminence of death would go more calmly with the sacred garment on their bodies. Thievery had become the daily and national occupation of the Germans. So the property taken by them, Rabbi Oshry declared, might be repossessed.

They asked exemption from the legalistic Talmud ban on contraceptives. A Nazi edict had ordered pregnant Jewish women to be killed on sight. ,The Rabbi's affirmative reply went beyond birth control to abortion.

They asked whether beards may be removed – ordinarily a misdeed tantamount, for some patriarchs, to effacing the sign of God's presence. Bearded Jews, especially the rabbis, had been picked as a special target for German fury. This, too, was granted.

After liberation and the emergence of a handful from their cellars, they asked Rabbi Oshry to instruct them in the burial of human remains – heads, limbs, organs scattered throughout the ghetto, and putrescent corpses piled up like cordwood in the concentration camps from which the Nazis had withdrawn before they could burn the dead. From sheer exhaustion of body and spirit, the

* Sanctification of the Holy Name, or martyrdom.
† Phylacteries.
‡ Fringes worn by the very pious.

tattered remnant could not muster the strength for the gruesome job. German prisoners of the victorious Russian armies were therefore assigned to the task of burial, under the watchful eyes of the survivors, so that every possible rite of purification might be performed.

They asked, and obtained, re-interment in a Jewish cemetery of a young girl saved by a Christian neighbour in whose care she had died.

They asked Rabbi Oshry to define the status of young Jewish matrons and teenage maidens whom the "pure Aryan" Nazis had regularly and by force set aside and defiled, with the official concordat that they were later to be slain. A married victim of this inventive animalism who had miraculously lived to rejoin her husband was riven by shame – as was the husband when he discovered the official Nazi stamp, "Prostitute for Hitler's Soldiers," tattooed on her body. Does the Torah allow him to resume marital ties with her, or must he obtain a divorce? The Rabbi not only proscribed divorce; he declared it a *mitzvah* * to forget the past. Furthermore, there was no need to remove the degrading words devised for the debasement of the righteous women of Israel. Instead, the inscription on their limbs symbolized spiritual incorruptibility, which had outlasted unavoidable physical pollution.

The questions and answers marshalled like a chorus of ghosts by Rabbi Oshry are a monument to Grinkishok and her devastated sister-villages and cities strewn across Europe. I saw another in Paris – a stark, inscribed concrete wall, a metal tank resembling a gas chamber circled with the names of death camps, an underground crypt preserving the charred ashes of Jews from every concentration camp where they had been slaughtered. I saw another in the Ardeatine Caves on the outskirts of Rome, ignored by guided tours, perhaps because so many clients are German. The stone coffins of three hundred and fifty Italians, Gentile and Jew, bludgeoned to death in reprisal for resistance, contain, in symbol, the mouldering bones of my kin in Grinkishok.

* Commandment.

In Jerusalem, on a hilltop near the mountains of Judea, I visited a great, square white structure called *Yad V'Shem*.* In the lobby, panelled walls are covered with crayon or pencil drawings by martyred Jewish children; each carries the creator's name, birthday, and date of death. In the museum, across the barbed wire of an artificial barracks, I read a Hebrew sentence from the Book of Daniel: "A time of distress such as no time has ever witnessed since the existence of any nation," and poems, essays, and hand-printed bulletins, often expressing faith and hope, written by boys and girls in the doomed ghettos of Warsaw, Vilna, Kielce, Slobodka, Bialystok, and Kovno.

The archives are reached by a spiral stairway to chilly, fluorescent depths several levels down. In these vast subterranean chambers, from floor to ceiling, are thousands of massive steel cabinets, electrically operated vaults, each with neatly indexed label and code number. Twenty-one million items, original or microfilm, all pertaining to the Nazi era, are here: statistics, correspondence, snapshots of torture, thousands of movies filmed by German executioners for their private amusement, such "comic" scenes as aged Jews wrapped in prayer shawls, holding Torah Scrolls and forced to dance while burning kerosene is poured on their heads, and directives issued by Nazi officials, who had triplicate memos made of all administrative proceedings. Like those signed by Eichmann and submitted at his trial, they had supposedly been destroyed.

Here, too, has been assembled every traceable object associated with the individual six million persons lost to Hitlerism, who, under a special law, are now posthumous Israeli citizens, although the compilation of names has not yet been completed. Would I find in those vaults a broken comb, a stubby pencil, a scrawled note, a hair of a kinsman who had stayed behind to die on Grinkishok's village green after my parents fled to America? My fingers yearned to riffle through them, but I knew that many of the dead had left nothing to testify that they had once breathed and walked on earth.

In Holy Blossom sanctuary, the congregation consecrated a

* "A Hand and a Name" or Memorial Authority.

Martyrs' Memorial Window, an attempt to portray in stained glass the tragedy, torment, trauma and, to a degree, the moral triumph of the six million. The Window is tear, token, warning, shrine – my tribute to Grinkishok. True, I never saw or knew the *shtetl* "in the flesh." But a map was drawn on my heart – and I can still read it.

About Mothers

"MOTHER FEINBERG" she was – to the iceman, the "five-and-ten' clerk, the doctor, the loafers around Duffy's poolroom, the Negro washwoman, the Irish cop on his rounds, and the Italian ditch-digger next door. She sewed for weddings, baked for circumcisions, sat up with the sick and dying, and helped purify female corpses, in accord with strict rabbinic instructions, for Jewish burial. She explained husbands to their wives, children to their parents, and estranged business partners to each other. She organized the Ladies Auxiliary of Agudas Ahim * congregation, and pressed it into service, from the

* League of Brothers.

support of a Jerusalem orphanage to clothing the brood of a destitute junkman. When a Ram-Cat Alley Negro coal-miner couldn't get a job, or a "ginny" with a foreign accent got mistreated in school, Mom went straight to the Mayor's office and told him in Yiddish idiom that he should be "ashamed in his white throat."

Mom spent a good part of her life standing at the kitchen sink, even after my sisters got big enough to help with the dishes. She raised ten children; a maid never entered our household. My mother steadfastly refused a seat at the table, preferring to serve all of us first. A kid's running nose dispatched her in haste to Dr. Long, who often showed up fragrant with strong drink and eager to help "Mother's babies," but I do not recall that she ever went to bed during the day except to have a baby, or at night until everyone else was asleep.

I can still see her – an apron around her small-boned, short, plumpish figure, a faded grey outdoors shawl around a fine nose and work-chiselled features, scrubbing the floor, scurrying on tiny feet to kitchen stove and sink and washtub and my father's little shop, searching for us desperately along the bank of the forbidden river while the Feinberg boys crouched wet and shivering in the bushes – earthy, elemental, happily enslaved to all-mastering love.

In *Franny and Zooey*, Salinger has his heroine glow with exaltation describing a method of incessant prayer. The prescription was to keep praying, even without faith, and with the lips alone; gradually, the words get synchronized into the heartbeat.

Mom's prayer did not need to travel from lips to heart; it was already there: "God, Thou hast given me my work; help me to do it well." Had one exclaimed, "'God,' you say! Who is He? Why do you believe in Him?" she would have been shocked into stone. Such a question belonged outside her realm of discourse. Faith in *Der Aibersten* * was in her bloodstream, and no less vital to her existence. A Divine decree made her the wife of a man without taste or talent for business, and the mother of ten, each of whom was a unique domain of duty and must receive the affection of an only

* The Most High.

child. Indeed, she gloried in her destiny – a rich, rewarding, and literally restless mission.

My mother died in 1934. To this day I mourn her immolation, and marvel at the moral strength with which she bore it, without a syllable of complaint against a destiny in which a dish of ice cream from Agostino's candy store was a lingered-over luxury. Hers was not the bovine placidity often confounded with stoicism, but rather the tension of a coiled spring.

One day I ran home with my upper lip cut through by a broomstick in a game of shinny. After rushing me to Dr. Long for the stitches, she furiously slapped my brother Allen, who had missed the can and hit me, screaming that a *meeseh meshuneh* * should take him, and then pressed him with tear-wet face to her bosom. Years later I realized that a Yiddish curse resembles the mediaeval church anathema in thoroughness and ingenuity, but does not even pretend to believe in itself. It was the peculiar realm of women, because it offered them the escape men found in synagogue.

Mom could not armour herself with the strict Orthodox dogmatism that takes, and gives, refuge in a ritualistic straitjacket. On a visit to me in New York, when asked by a prospective dinner-host whether she would require kosher food, she replied that she was sure the Lord would forgive her son Abe an infraction of the dietary laws, and therefore herself as well.

She had the sturdy skepticism that knows life, yet loves it. When Liberty Loan orators lauded the "war to end war," she thought they should take such *meshugass* † to Mose's infantry regiment in France. She exacted a promise that I would permit no *hesped* ‡ over her grave. "I have heard enough honey about hypocrites and thieves," she said.

It was in the late autumn of 1929, when I told Mom I had decided to leave the rabbinate, that I encompassed the grandeur of her self-sacrifice.

From the hour when School Superintendent Jackson himself strode down Union Street to tell Mom "Abe must go to college," she

* Unusual death. † Insanity. ‡ Eulogy.

had held my will to its course and sustained my resolution never to take a factory or store job like the older boys, none of whom went beyond grammar school. Now the golden grain of her years of struggle was spread for harvest. I had become co-rabbi of the second largest Reform Temple in New York City; my aging senior would soon retire; the monthly cheque I sent home was a mild foretaste of the financial help and kudos I would soon be contributing to the family. We had merely to await the ingathering – and Mom would *kleib nahas* * and be blessed with a tittle of the comfort that surrounded the parasitic mommas of New York.

Intellectual revolt had cut deep into the fibre of my faith. I could no longer withstand the inroads of big-city sophistication; discontent and guilt were tearing at my self-pride; the commercialized synagogue turned my stomach. I went home to tell Mom I could not go on. She had no inkling of my spiritual malaise and would not, I knew, understand its roots; I dreaded the shock and hurt surprise I was about to bring her.

Before Mom spoke, so softly each word plummeted into my heart, the droop of her mouth and the grey in her hair told me things were not good. Father earned practically nothing; he was getting too old to peddle. There had been much sickness. The Carnegie steel mill was gone. Coal mines operated only two or three days a week. Houses were crumbling into ruins because their owners couldn't collect enough rent to repair them. Many stores were empty; others the banks had taken over. The 1929 stockmarket bust a few weeks before had set off an even worse panic than 1907, when the family had almost starved.

She said I was like Joseph in the time of famine! Without my monthly cheque God knows what would have happened. With what she could spare from it, she even helped rag-pedlars who could not buy food for their children. "Is that all right, Abeleh?" I told her I did not mind at all, but I had a macabre vision of Bellaire's Jews feasting on my carcass. The gratitude she conveyed to me in letters

* Gather joy.

after each cheque seemed so pathetic it had always discomfited me. Now I almost wept.

To gather courage, I walked over my old treadmill route, up and down Belmont Street. I bumped into one-time schoolmates, chatted with Gentiles for the first time since entering the gilded ghetto of Manhattan, and inquired after old acquaintances dispersed across the country because they could not make a living in Bellaire. Even the corner drugstore where I used to buy chocolate-nut sundaes was empty. I looked down the side street that led to the rickety old ferry boat, and across the river. The Wheeling Steel furnace was cold and the huge plant a rusting skeleton.

Hands in pockets, I sauntered with dry-tongued, sporadic whistling through the city park. Tufts of grass sprouted from the Civil War cannon, the benches cried for paint and new legs, the edges of the flowerless plots were overgrown. In the centre circle I slumped down on the pedestal of the bronze World War Memorial doughboy leading a charge with hate-twisted face, clutching a rifle in one hand and raising the other over a long list of names on a plaque. "Mike Hogan" – he had once doused my head in the nearby fountain. Nothing was ever found of Mike save an identification tag, but his mother didn't know, and was going to France with a Gold Star contingent, at government expense, to pray at his grave.

On my way back, I passed the nickelodeon where my first love, Dorothy Caldwell, used to sell tickets. It had given way to a movie palace with an organ and uniformed attendants. But gilt was chipping off the lobby decorations and the single usher, in frayed pants, stood idle, cracking his knuckles.

Birdie, my oldest sister, was making sandwiches in the kitchen when I finally dragged myself home, and cousins and aunts and uncles had gathered to do me honour. "Come on, Abe, show us how you speak to them New Yorkers. You're the big one of the family!"

Pop was deep in anecdotes about Grinkishok, or listening avidly to the compliments the clan paid me. He had long ago given up being angry about my flight from orthodoxy. In fact, Mom said he was very proud of me now, though he would never admit it. His laughter had an artificial ring. His ingrown eyes beseeched me for affection, and I longed with my whole heart to give it. In the frustration of my high-spirited "umbrella-man" dad, I beheld my own.

Finally the guests departed. Mother went into the kitchen to make tea. We all carried the chairs back from the parlour to the kitchen, and sat there. Sally and Mose were missing. Sally liked college immensely, Birdie said, and was doing her best on the tiny stipend I sent her. Mose had been managing a chain grocery store in Columbus, but war-gas had finally consigned him into a government hospital. Allen was out of work for the time being. So was Sam. Jack still had his old job in the glass factory. Sylvia taught a country school in a little coal town, riding down and back on the dinky narrow-gauge train. Her pupils still wouldn't believe she was Jewish; Jews are black, and ugly! I burst into raucous laughter and reminded them of Pop calling limited service "liniment service" during the war.

"Liniment service! Hah! Hah!" I noted Sylvia's wan and wistful beauty.

One by one, father, brothers, and sisters went upstairs, and Mother and I were left alone. She still wore Woolworth's ten-cent glasses! I poked fun at her. "*Nu,* I can read by them! Why pay more?" She poured me a third cup of tea.

I heard the cat scratching at the door and let her out. I washed my hands. I found some soda crackers in the breadbox. I wound my watch. I paced about.

"Abe, you don't look well."

"Oh, it's nothing."

"You look very sad and old."

"Do I? Hah! You can't be young forever, sweetie!"

"Are you happy?"

"As much as anyone ever is."

I slipped down in my chair and pressed my spoon on soggy cracker crumbs in the teacup.

"You are not happy – as – a – rabbi?"

Her right wrist was trembling; it had not quite recovered from a fracture. My thumb bore down hard on the spoon.

I turned my head towards the steam-peeled wallpaper. Grasping her right hand with the left, to steady it, Mom slowly put on her glasses and opened the Yiddish newspaper as if to read.

"Then quit being a rabbi! For us don't be unhappy! You'll do fine, whatever you do; only like it!"

I tried to control a thumping heart and a tongue that stuck to the roof of my mouth. I met her eyes, now raised from the *Tageblatt*.

"We'll see. Maybe I'll study singing. What about my cheque?"

"Suppose we didn't have you! *Gott vet helfen.*"

Replacing the spoon in the saucer with slow deliberation, I picked up bits of cracker from the tablecloth and crushed and sprinkled them one by one into the cup between thumb and forefinger. Then, both hands on the table, I pushed myself upward, stood beside "Mother Feinberg" and touched her shoulder, and a tear tumbled into my mouth....

Father was feeding the chickens when I stepped outdoors early the next morning.

"Hello, Pop! Is that the same pipe? Gee, it stinks!" I slapped him on the back. His face suddenly billowed into smiles. I had never done that before!

I heard him chortle as I sped out, and down the alley, to a steep path that led up the hillside. Thirteen years before, I had been lifted up that path by a new-found mission – the resolve to be a rabbi.

My shoes and feet were a New Yorker's. It did not matter. At every curve I filled my lungs and watched the fog drift away under the rising sun. When I reached the top, even the heaps of coal slag gleamed with a glint of gold.

I lay face down on a familiar knoll and let my body sink into the earth. Tiny shafts of grass reached out between the rocks and tickled my nose. I sang. A robin hopped about me and cocked his head. I sang. Branches shook themselves awake in the morning breeze. I sang. And my song went swirling off down the valley. I turned over on my back and sang at the sky.

Ballads dripping with Broadway sentimentality that I always disdained, from "A Yiddishe Mameh" to "Mother Machree," even a long-forgotten "Mother's Day" lyric which my high-school class had parodied for its graduation theme – I sang in full-throated homage to her who had borne me in her pain and sustained me in my own.

In later years, at Mom's grave on another hilltop whence I could descry the river far in the distance winding down to the Mississippi, I recaptured the echo of those songs, and realized they were the first expression I ever gave to the deep love I bore my mother.

We were not a demonstrative family. Each one kept his own counsel; communication about anything deeper than work, study, play, food, hand-me-down clothes, and diapers and thermometers was rare and painful. The traffic lane on which words endearing and intimate might pass and bring their warmth was clogged; things we longed to say to one another withered within the breast.

Even when my brothers boarded the train for the First World War draftee training-camps, each in turn, at the tomb-like depot, I was almost afraid to shake their hands, and they said nothing. An embarrassed peck on my mother's forehead, a quick, nervous flight to an unseen seat on the far side of the coach, and the prospective paladin of a world to be made safe for democracy vanished. I managed to mumble a few feeble words of cheer into my blouse – and that was all! After watching the hindmost baggage car disappear around the bend, we slouched homeward, each one without a word, knit to the others by inexpressible melancholy, and threshing about in the dungeon of his own nameless fear.

What the psychologists call relating to others has always presented me with a thorny problem on the level of fundamentals. Whenever a conversation draws near to basic issues like God, or dying, or one's ideals, I am reduced to ironic frivolity or a self-mocking quip. The more deeply the subject resides below the subliminal borderline, the less I can say about it. Even the familiar household circle of wife and children can harden into a rampart beyond my power to breach with words.

On the pulpit or platform the barrier vanishes. Communication ceases to be on an individual plane; I address myself to an idea, a cause, and inhibition falls away.

Is my ineptness in personal verbalization a holdover of introverted pride from those years in Bellaire? How often I ached to hold my mother in my arms and assure her of my love! Instead – and I remember with consuming guilt – a churlish accent wedged into my voice. Why? Perhaps each one kills the thing he loves. Perhaps I shrank from a compassion that would surely have unmasked and unmanned me, whereas harshness protected me from dissolution. Perhaps, in the secret places of my heart, I resented the humility and eager acceptance of hardship which fashioned Mom into the image of a drudge rather than the gracious, beautiful queen she had the right to be. And I instinctively fled from pity, in dread of pitying myself.

Perhaps I lashed out with inarticulate anger at the extremity of sacrifice for which Jewish folklore has throughout generations praised the "typical Jewish mother" – an almost masochistic urge to erase herself. When I came home after school and stumbled upon my mother scrubbing the floor instead of greeting her brood neatly dressed and fragrant, I forgot her uproarious, breast-heaving sense of the comic, and that she could laugh until breathless exhaustion plopped her on a chair, tears pursuing each other down her cheeks. Instead, sadness welled up in me and turned to bile; she had stripped herself of self-esteem. Hating the poverty which had brought my mother to her knees and clenching an impotent fist at fate, I vented my impotence on its victim.

Was my Mom wrong-headed, sublimely mistaken? I have often thought so. My brothers and sisters would not give a nod or ear to such a judgement. In their view, our mother was a figure of heroic dimensions and self-fulfilment. By negating a private goal, she achieved a greater one, without qualm or querulousness. Religious precept and Jewish folk-practice undergird that verdict, and I should now be the last to denigrate it.

None of us merited such boundless maternal offering of self; in that sense, an injustice was perpetrated. And some of us were harmed by it. Parental anxiety can blight as well as build; innumerable lives have been throttled by the "silver cord" of a mother's all-shielding care. Excessive and obsessive concern for another's well-being can destroy both subject and object. I have seen hollow sepulchres, drained of the will or capacity for life, who had emptied themselves without stint in chains to a "dear one" – and "dear ones," as a result, transformed into malingering tyrants. If self-sacrifice became a universal practice of all human beings, nothing would be left whole except an intellectual abstraction, a moral principle, ruling over a dominion of zeros.

In a profoundly thoughtful discourse on love, C. S. Lewis names three kinds relevant to my mother and me: Need-love, which cries to the lover for solace and attention, Gift-love, which longs only to suffer and to serve, Appreciative-love, which simply adores, and gives thanks that the beloved one exists. Responding to the clamorous need of husband and children, Mom gave her total self, and thereby shaped it into a thing of art whose outer form, now gone, embodied an inner spirit that is mine to contemplate while I have the mental competence to remember. In retrospect, I have stepped back to observe it, as one seeks perspective before a natural landscape or a masterpiece of painting. The colours and contour of my mother's life, to me at least, did not glow with brightness and sunshine, but with each year that passes over her grave on the top of a high hill they spell, all the more clearly, the portrait of a rare and radiant spirit.

The New World and Nissen Nisselewicz

I WAS a very restless sleeper. A touch of the pillow peopled my mind with terrors and fantasies.

One May I bolted supper and sped down to the meadow for a peep at the carnival which every spring brought to town. Having passed circulars for the advance man, I had an admission ticket instead of a hole under the fence. One show fascinated me: Nemo, half-man, half-turtle, snared in the wilds of Madagascar with a bloody human arm in his mouth. Every few minutes the portly barker, decked out in checkered vest and grey derby, would bend over the pit, wave a long desiccated bone (the arm), and draw a blood-curdling groan from its depths.

I never saw the freak; he cost fifteen cents. But I held nightly vigil, rooted to the spot, before the yellow tent and lurid canvas picture. And, finally, tight and tense in bed, I quivered under the blanket; the Turtle-man crouched in the corner, clung to the skylight rope, clawed at my undershirt, cavorted around the bedpost.

It was during that febrile week that my mother told me about her romance with Pop in the old country, when I slipped down to the kitchen where she was waiting up for Birdie and begged her for the story to avoid telling what kept me awake. . . .

Sarah's ancestors were rabbis and *hahamim** for generations. Her eyes matched the blue tint of a spring sky, and "the time" was approaching. No one stayed single in Grinkishok; even an orphan girl got a nest-egg dowry from the charity fund so that she could wed. And for a maiden of family, a boy stuffed with knowledge had more worth than one stuffed with gold.

"What matters it if a *lamden*† be poor and unaccustomed to bargaining in the marketplace? Let him dwell with us, as is the custom. And let his wife preserve him from want; through study of Torah he brings the Divine Presence into the world." Even as a child, Sarah received such admonitions from her father, Rav Tzvi Hirsch Abramson.

She also heard it said that "love is fine, but love with noodles is even better," that "poverty may be no crime, but it is also not a virtue," and that the morning prayer of males in the synagogue praising the Lord "who didst not create me a woman" expressed a Jewish man's delight in the yoke of the commandments, from many of which females were exempted, rather than gloating assurance of superiority.

Sarah neither doubted her father's wisdom nor ceased to dream about the bashful master of the Torah who would lead her to the *huppah*‡ and to God's footstool. In the meantime, Rav Tzvi crooned to the Deity in the dim shadows of the study house and, as the rabbi,

* Wise sages. † Scholar. ‡ Marital canopy.

curled a thumb about the debatable syllables in Holy Writ and led the *pilpulists* in prayer, while mother Rachel bent over stove, market-table, and crib, and beamed with pride in a learned husband. That was the Grinkishok fashion.

Nissen Nisselewicz, a Grinkishker by birth, was well regarded by the abstruse logicians of Yeshiva * in the large town of Ponevez. Like other boys of promise, he had read Hebrew at five, translated the Bible into Yiddish soon thereafter, studied Rashi and other commentaries at ten, was being fed as an honoured guest, if not always to satiety, in Jewish households, and could expect a rich and doting father-in-law. But, instead of the student's drooping eyes and shambling gait, he had a fiery glance, a resilient step, and a habit of tilting back his handsome head and humming, even while the teacher explained a complex problem in the Talmud.

Grinkishok's ghetto buzzed when Nissen the scholar became Nishke der Singerl.† Even unlettered men like Yankele der Bal-Agoleh ‡ and Itche-Mayer der Shuster § raised their eyebrows. Who but an idiot prefers cantor to rabbi? Nishke merely laughed. Let others quibble in a labyrinth of syllogisms in a sunless dungeon; he would praise God with song, not ply Him with riddles.

On the Day of Atonement eve, Grinkishok's beruffled maidens stretched their necks over the railing of the women's balcony and rolled unpenitent eyes towards the Ark of the Covenant and a white robe, whence the plaintive plea of Kol Nidrei pierced every cranny of the *shule* and, God willing, of the celestial spheres between earth and God's mercy. That is, all but Sarah! She sat as one transfixed, not because aloof disdain was more fitting for a comely virgin who bore the rabbi's name, but because *Hazzan* || Nissen had pierced her heart.

Marriages were arranged by parents and Reb Jacob the *shadhen*, a pollinating agent of remarkable importance for Jewish survival. The older girls whom Sarah knew had not even seen their

* Rabbinical Seminary.
† Nate the Little Singer.
‡ Jacob the Wagon-Driver.
§ Isaac Mayer the Shoemaker.
|| Cantor.

husbands until they stood together under the *huppah*. Fervid whispering under the stars and hand-in-hand walks down shaded lanes jeopardized common sense. Rebecca offered a fat dowry? Abraham was a Talmudic prodigy? Hannah came of rabbinical stock? What had love to do with it?

Sarah unburdened her affliction to my Aunt Katie who, being homely and the younger, had sharpened her wits in their mother's fish store. Within a week Nissen confessed to Katie that he had been gazing for months on the Rav's daughter. Sarah and her swain exchanged stammers during the usual Sabbath-afternoon stroll, and Grinkishok was agog.

The great bearded head of Rav Tzvi gave no sign, however, and his sons would have nothing to do with a feckless troubador who placed song and laughter above the sacred folios of rabbinic disputation. And Sarah lay awake nights. And Reb Jacob bemoaned the moon-calf stupidity of woman.

One evening the Rav summoned his neighbours to a family council – in itself an emergency signal, for the chieftain of a Grinkishok clan did not incline to consultation. White-faced, and with tight-knit brows, he patiently outlined the portents that beset him. His sons would soon be eating the flesh of swine and polishing the boots of swinish men in a filthy army camp; the *kehillah** was under heavy pressure to fill the conscript quota. Who knows, the Rav's boys might even be kidnapped off the street for twenty-five-year military service by the Czar's special procurement officers, and lost to Judaism forever! His daughters were being jostled on the highways. He had noted a baleful gleam in the glance of the local priest who, on the previous Passover, as everyone knows, had muttered about ritual murder until the missing Gentile child, thank God, was found lost in the forest. When he, the Rav, expostulated with the chief of police the day hooligans defiled a sacred Scroll, that one shrugged his shoulders. *Mouzhiks* milled in drunken, stinking clusters around the bulletin announcing the White Father's latest ukase – the infamous May Laws of 1882 which severely restricted Jewish

* Jewish community committee.

residence and opportunity for livelihood. The clerk had to read it for them; like nearly all Russian workers and peasants, they were illiterate, but they well understood that the Czar would protect them from the *Jhid* Christ-killers. Dread news was trickling in to Grinkishok from itinerant *schnorrers** about pogroms. Only they dared to breathe who had a passport and ticket to America.

In the candlelight Rav Tzvi's face grew more gaunt and ashen with each word that punctuated the respectful silence. Finally he arose from his chair and looked steadily from one to the other of his family. "We shall voyage to America. It is not the will of God that we die of hunger or the knout. Much hardship awaits us. But fear we have not. One thing only do I ask, that my marriageable daughter shall not venture to a distant land unwed. Therefore, I consent that Sarah stand under the canopy with Nissen, son of Boruch Sholom, if he will accompany us to America as her man."

Thus Alexander the Third, Czar of all the Russias, was *shadhen* to my parents.

It was a commingling of moods, that wedding. Sarah's brothers still resented the events that gave their sister to "the singer." Rav Tzvi and Rachel were torn between gloomy contemplation of their bedding, rolled up in bundles for the voyage, and the joyous realization that their eldest daughter would have a man at her side. All the elders of the synagogue had brought their wives to sob and envy.

Above the mêlée and the shouts of *mazl tov*†, like two eagles in flight over a gorge, the hearts of Sarah, daughter of the Rav, and Nissen, son of Boruch Sholom, took wing. "Be thou consecrated unto me with this ring according to the Law of Moses and Israel." The next day they sat, bound flesh to flesh, life with life, in a third-class coach to Hamburg.

After twenty-seven days in the steerage, they arrived in Baltimore, where some years later Rav Tzvi built a *shule* on Lombard Street. Although my father's name was Nisselewicz and his Grinkishok brothers retained it until Hitler's "final solution," he changed it to Feinberg on the invitation of Velvel Feinberg, a friend of his

* Beggars. † Good luck.

father, already deceased, who had bribed the immigration officer for a permit to meet them at the pier. Was not the Czar looking for Nissen Nisselewicz? He was a marked man, refugee from the *priziv*!* Besides, "Feinberg" was easier for Americans to pronounce.

During Mom's idyll of young love in Grinkishok one word swung back and forth like a lantern that night in the kitchen: *priziv*. Russian was seldom heard in our home, and Lithuanian never. Culturally the *shtetl* of my parents had subsisted on itself; Gentile communications media could besmirch only tradesmen who, unlike my father, were forced into contact with *goyyim*.

The word *priziv* intrigued me for another reason. Pop's traumatic recoil from the Czar's barracks, as recounted by my mother, opened a tiny crack in the wall that separated him and his son, by giving me a clue to his moodiness. Our relationship had little of ease, much less of intimacy and, on my part, more fear than affection – except on Jewish festivals. At these times Pop was gay, almost debonair. How he grinned and scintillated when recounting incidents on the twenty-seven-day honeymoon, particularly his disguise as a girl in order not to be separated from Sarah, and how the Captain was dissuaded by her tears from putting him in irons. But moments of hilarity merely highlighted his normal attitude of morose self-absorption.

A portrait deeply etched on my memory is that of Pop sitting tense in a rocking-chair that scarcely moved at all, brow clouded, right elbow crooked up, head in palm, eyes intent on space – sitting for hours, wordless, or softly crooning a melancholy chant. Particularly on a late Friday afternoon when Mom might be on the floor scouring with brush and soap at his feet, I almost choked in a wave of something close to resentment and not far from hostility.

He had an uncontrollable temper and hands swift to do its bidding. The suppers were legion that I missed because I had fled my father's violence and would not return home until he went to bed, at which time Mom, although she brooked no complaint against her man, would have a cold plate and warm hug waiting for me.

* Military draft.

His most condign punishments were meted out for indecorous conduct in synagogue. An open palm often swooped down on my cheek like a bird of prey when I squirmed or fingered marbles in my pocket, especially during the silent Eighteen Benedictions. In my humiliation and pain I would stifle a scream and run to the toilet.

During the tedious Reading from the Torah one Shabbas, I sneaked off to pitch horseshoes in an empty lot. By the time I dawdled back to *shule,* it was being emptied of worshippers, the Service having ended. At home, I reckoned, Pop would be pleasantly diverted, what with washing his hands, breaking bread, and bidding all *gut Shabbas.* No sooner did I slither hopefully unnoted into the front room than he turned without a word and struck me to the floor, with such paroxysmal fury that a nephew whom he had just brought over from Grinkishok was emboldened to remonstrate. *"Oncle, vest em hargenen."* *

That episode did not encourage affection for my dad or develop a predilection for Orthodox Judaism. And when I saw my mother run out on a rainy Saturday to give a customer his repaired umbrella and collect the tawdry fee because my father would never work or handle money on Sabbath, I railed inwardly at a selfish, complacent creed which helped keep us poor and heaped burdens on my mother. Respect for my father's loyalty to tradition chastened me only after years of strife with these early impressions.

For a longer period than I like to remember, I often paced the house in a fit of rancour. Father let his shoes drop to the floor when he undressed; I cursed such nerve-jangling insouciance. His pipe and cheap tobacco assailed my nostrils, his recurrent winter cough undid my sleep; I even worked myself into jealousy of the chickens for whose feeding and care he showed solicitude. And I took to comparing Pop's insensitivity with Mom's refinement.

The seed bed of discord was not of his planting. Its ground resided in the wide gap between two clashing worlds: Grinkishok and Bellaire. Nathan Feinberg (né Nissen Nisselewicz) was shaped by a Lithuanian ghetto-prison rooted in the millennial privation and

* "Uncle, you'll kill him."

parochialism of the Jewish people, where survival meant separatism in language, lore, law, and manners. And he had been catapulted by the compulsion of need into another planet, under merciless economic pressure, to squeeze out a meagre subsistence. He had neither the time, talent, nor energy for making himself over. I could construct a bridge of romantic fantasy to Grinkishok; I could not insist that my father adapt his ways to Bellaire. The obligation to understand was mine, not his.

For example, he objected strenuously to my whistling. I cultivated and complicated that lowly art to the point where it was possible for me to entertain soldiers at Fort Thomas, Kentucky, as a seminary student in Cincinnati during the First World War. Had I probed the cause of his intolerance, I would have discovered that, to a Grinkishker, whistling was the mark of a besodden *mouzhik* who used it to shepherd beasts in the field.

As to his distaste for business, so sharp that he often deputized me to obtain picture-frame glass on credit at the wholesale house, it emerged from his breeding; he had been designed for the pages of the Talmud, not for a bookkeeping ledger. The common Gentile assumption of Jewish commercial astuteness has more irony than truth. My naïve father, like thousands of other Jewish immigrants, was a babe in arms compared to a canny Yankee like Calvin Coolidge.

Priziv, the ill-omened word spoken by Mom the night Nemo chased me from my bed, guided me to my dad for the first time. When she mentioned how much Pop hated army service, I asked her if he had ever been in it. Her reply enhanced the mystery. "Ask him about his finger. You know! The one what is bent."

For a long while the sight of that finger had piqued me. The next afternoon after school I sidestepped gingerly into the umbrella shop, and proceeded at once to the subject, knowing that a moment's pause would drain off my courage like sand in an hourglass.

I pointed to his right hand. "Pop, why is your finger bent?"

"In the Japaner war. I got a medal." His eyes fairly danced, and mine lit up with relief at his puckish mood.

"But, but – Pop. You came to America before that, didn't you? That was 1905!" I watched him narrowly, and edged towards the door. The twinkle vanished, but no flame darted from his eyes.

"Well, I'll tell you. I did it myself. When I was a boy in Russia. So that they wouldn't take me for the army. See? The finger you shoot with."

"You mean . . . you didn't want to be a soldier . . . Pop?"

"No – I didn't." His deep-set eyes looked straight ahead, not at me, but beyond, into the wall. "Russia treated us very bad. The *goyyim* robbed and beat us. They broke your uncle Isaac's arm. On *goyyische* holidays we wouldn't walk in the streets. One Easter, when they were in their church, a Jewish house went on fire. The bell, who could ring it. They would have killed us maybe. So we used buckets. Houses burned, everything, ours too!"

"Didn't . . . didn't the police help you?"

"The police?" A smile slowly crawled around his lips. "Animals! In Grinkishok you couldn't even go to school. Taxes and bribes! Even the few kopeks we made from the *mouzhiks* they took. Did *you* see them carrying away the bedpost of Samuel the horse-trader? I *did* see it! On the floor his children would have to sleep. Animals! Animals!" He spat. "For such a country to give your life? Reuben the baker's son! When they came to get him he was hanging. With his belt he did it!" The voice trailed into a murmur; my father lowered his head. Then a torrent of words came forth.

"A month before my turn, grandfather took to the chief of police a lot of money. Every relative gave something. Barefoot they went! *Nu,* what did the drunkard do, *a schwarz yor** on him? He put the rubles in his pocket, and promised he would leave out my name. When the names went up, mine – mine was first." He halted, and his voice was again as one from a tomb. "I went into the kitchen, I found a knife. I stuck it into my finger."

My heart began to hammer, at first with embarrassment, then with scorn for the Czar. When a chuckle startled me, I saw that my father was fumbling nervously at his worktable.

* A black year.

"*Nu*, so today I'm in the *goldene medina.*" * He rattled Yiddish to himself, as though I had disappeared. "*A klog zu Colombos* † for finding America. Well, it's better than Grinkishok. But what have I? Only troubles and more troubles! The umbrella man! All these black years, and still the umbrella man! A cripple, a fool without pants! *Golem!*"

As his voice trailed off in a hissing stream of imprecations, he gripped an umbrella rib at each end, broke it over his knee, and stood up straighter and taller than I had ever seen him.

"Life is a burden and a weariness. Like the pack one peddles, it grows with each step. Only when evening comes will the pack be loosened and the water of many fountains bathe our feet. Oh God of Israel, in Thy Law alone is salvation. Our oppressors will flee before Thee, and Thy Chosen People will inherit their portion!"

I turned around so abruptly that a racked umbrella caught my sleeve and rattled to the floor. I had to get outdoors before the tears convulsed me.

That encounter became a sluice-gate through which a detergent flood coursed for months and laved my mind. The new image of my father began to take shape with the first briny tear that dampened my face after that scene in his workshop. A tired little man with a scraggly beard and a parcel of broken umbrellas, who spoke broken English, became a tragic little man with broken dreams who spoke the universal tongue of the broken spirit.

Why did he take to fixing umbrellas – he with that divine voice for prayer to the Divine? Persistent pumping elicited the piecemeal clue from my mother. The enigma was really not complex, and years later, when I stood on my own exposed hillock of individualism, its denouement had logic and inevitability.

Pop was a man of fiery spirit. Truckling did not come easy, particularly toward the kind of congregational leadership cast up by the wave of escapees from Russia which swamped American communities during the last decades of the nineteenth century. He took his bride Sarah from one mushroom settlement to another, always

* Golden land.

† A curse on Columbus.

augmenting progeny and problems. All the while, he wanted only to study Talmud and assault the gates of heaven with sacred chants. Pausing in Bellaire, his cup of woe had filled; he was too disheartened for another move or further effort to please what he characteristically called "a bunch of horse-thieves." So a graduate of famed Ponevez Yeshiva, who might have burnished the precious lamps of Jewish song and scholarship, directed his hand to patching umbrellas.

What deduction can be drawn from my father's ill-starred career? The most damning charge against it is that it garnered no wealth or power. Also, it pushed no one aside or down, converted none's misfortune into gain. Indeed, to humble lives it added light and laughter. An arthritic old lady wilting away from neglect in a dank kitchen would detain him an hour while he regaled her with courtly gestures and shy compliments. Like many thwarted men, he showered smiles on the stranger and unconsciously used his own for scapegoats.

The flint of a son's hard look at his father, even when that look is timid and transient, can spark an inclination to belligerence toward the revered canons of society. A boy who fights his dad may become a man who fights everyone. Is it possible that my militant opposition to the status quo, my so-called radicalism, was actually germinated years ago when I found it easier to resent my dad than to communicate with and love him? Understanding dawned on me only when I began to see how closely I resemble him.

Did not his refusal to budge from rigid religious orthodoxy grow from disillusionment? When carnivorous America would not let his heart sing, it dried up the juices of spiritual vitality, made him brittle and unyielding; a sacrosanct Sabbath, even at the cost of bread for his children, became a bastion of pride.

He did demand, often harshly, irreducible obedience to a father. Was that patriarchal tradition in essence wrong? In today's television soap operas the father-image, once glorified as the paternal miniature of an all-wise god, has been chipped down to a slightly comic, bumbling oaf, seldom heard from, and overshadowed by a wife who has a good job and knows the score. The result is often progressive anarchy, a household bereft of a final court responsible for decisions. In this unhinged, bewildering world, I cannot be entirely without nostalgia for the days when a personal God laid down the law from heaven and a father laid down the law in the home.

Child guidance began as something parents were expected to administer; it has become a set of rules for parents to submit to. The child psychologists change the tune so often that this year's panacea may become next year's anathema. When our son arrived, the cry was against overprotection; we must not croon, cuddle, or coddle. Then the pendulum swung back to "emotional security." Our daughter came during an armistice interval when all the camps seemed to be paralysed in a stalemate.

I propose that a boy or girl could do with some good, healthy neglect – for instance, in the area of organized activities. Among the children's rights so frequently listed, one of the most valuable, and least mentioned, is time to do nothing – just fiddle around and daydream. Some of my richest boyhood hours were frittered away whittling a twig or chewing a blade of grass on a hillside.

Should dad be a pal? Certainly I do not recommend the closed circuit that barred me from companionship with my father. How much more felicitous adulthood would have been for me had I found the strength and will to soften my own rebellious temper, and melt his reserve and talk to him about the nagging problems of God and sex and being a Jew in a Gentile world! But artificial cameraderie is not the answer. Calm, self-assured headship of the house has higher rating than a hockey stick or baseball bat. Children realize more clearly than parents that a generation separates them, but they are too tactful to say it, or too young to know how. More than a pal, they want a father whom they can respect, imitate, admire, and safely take orders from – a delicate balance of strong hand and soft heart.

Pop died at eighty-two under unusual circumstances. The war had just ended. My youngest sister, Sally, who returned to Bellaire to have her baby after her husband was shipped to Okinawa, waited for his homecoming while he waited for a berth on a transport. Meanwhile, cancer had done its ravaging; when I reached home, the doctors said my father should have died weeks before. They could not understand what kept his body and soul together. I peered at the twisted face from the bedside, and thought I knew. His grandson David! Pop had been playing with him in the house like a big brother, in endless delight, passionately adoring the child, and simply would not die until David had his own father back to look after him!

Through the mediation of a friend in Washington, I got Sally's man flown home on compassionate grounds in a swift bombing-plane. It was twilight of a Friday when Al doffed his trenchcoat and stood with me in the room. "Pop, Al is here!" "Pop, David's dad is here!" I repeated, perhaps a dozen times, until my father opened his eyes wider and wider and, seeing, smiled and, smiling, sank into eternal sleep.

After the funeral, Sylvia told me our father's mercurial acerbity had mellowed into a wonderful tenderness after Mom's death; he had taken her place. And throughout the week of mourning, people of every age and creed told me how much they had loved "Pop Feinberg."

Huck Finn versus Heder

HUCKLEBERRY FINN would have been at home in the riverfront town of my boyhood. It was a vestigial stronghold of Mark Twain's barefoot paradise of juvenile rusticity. The "Beautiful Ohio" of the old ballad was bountiful as well, and we had the appetite to accept the dalliance she offered: a rowing-race behind the foaming sternwheel of a steamer in a skiff rented from blear-eyed houseboaters to whom a few cents meant a pail of beer; a cool dive into the swirling ripples around the stone pier of the B. & O. railroad bridge; a meander through the bulrushes in an ungainly john-boat with a tree branch, a bit of string, and a "minny," tadpole, or worm, hoping that scaleless (and therefore non-kosher) catfish would not take all the bait; bellywhopping a railroad-tie like a cork in the trail of a chugging packet, or paddling it across the entire width to Benwood, West Virginia; sliding down the slippery mudbank into the creek that oozed limply through a cleft in the hills at the sycamore-tree swimming-hole and feeling the water purl and giggle around us; noodling for turtles with bare hands and shooting at river rats with an air gun; roasting potatoes filched from family larders; watching the jet-black stevedore heave boxes of freight from the steamboat just landed at the dock and coaxing the captain to tell us about Cairo and New Orleans; counting the chicken coops and rooftops carried downstream on the spreading waters of the annual spring flood; shouting encouragement, from the banks aswarm with people in their go-to-meetin' clothes, to the sailboats with banners on their masts at regatta races; gazing with a restless, not-yet-understood, goose-pimply hunger at the gaily costumed dancers on the showboat lashed to the landing for a week's engagement – all this, and more!

Some of us swam without a log clean across the river. Jim Diggity said he wasn't afraid because the charm around his neck had been blessed by the priest. Jim also wore a bag of asafetida to keep away germs. The stench was so strong that I told my mother no germs could live near it. She said it was all foolishness. I didn't dare tell her about the charm.

Bellaire straggled up into hills gashed by creeks and runs, from a narrow strip of level bank along the river. By well-worn paths, which avoided the eerie old smallpox "pesthouse," we explored the hills for pawpaws, blackberries, an unguarded apple orchard, or a penned bull to enrage with a slingshot. Being agile and wiry, I could almost wriggle into a snake hole. What a triumph it was to writhe from thorny depths with a cap full of luscious, shade-grown dewberries and watch hulking Nino Lucchesi and Husky Tobachnik stiffen with envy! That compensated me for legs so thin I wrapped rags under my stockings. And I can still smell the pungent dampness of the densely wooded, leaf-carpeted glens where we picked violets, buttercups, and sweetwilliam. The Feinberg dog, usually a frisky terrier, often flushed a mole or rabbit. Whitey had rheumy eyes so sad I thought of him as Jewish. He also had a charmed life, and for years eluded the dog-catcher, to whom "man's best friend" was only an expendable cur unless he wore a two-dollar tag. But one day Whitey collided with a streetcar, and we buried him on a hillside under a hand-made Star of David.

The town itself spread a varied menu: the Masonic Band in the block-square city park, the circus disembarking in the railroad yards, vagabond medicine shows where two ham-fisted Irish boys boxed for a quarter, and a tall man in a sombrero exhibited jars of tapeworms; the crowds craning necks at Halley's Comet; firelit election parades and William Jennings Bryan speaking from the second-storey porch of the Globe Hotel; home-talent minstrels with our postman as interlocutor; playing casino with real cards for decalcomania transfers; streetcar rides to Wheeling, and the sheer ecstasy of driving the flour company's horse and buggy; Hallowe'en depredations that brought Levi Lustig the miser out shaking with wrath, croaking threats to call the Marshal, and venturing a melancholy forecast of our future; unloaded banana cars on the siding and prehensile fingers that foraged in the straw for fruit fallen from the bunches; curbstone contests on summer evenings, to see who knew the most automobile brands or railroad names from boxcar initials; school operettas in Armory Hall; the station of the narrow-gauge railroad from downriver on Saturday morning, when the train disgorged hundreds of farmers with an itch for calico, sugar, hardware, and whisky – and boots whose cow dung announced their approach yards away; paradisial nickelodeons, a blind and tireless piano-thumper to raise our hair, and us kids getting in free for supplying appropriate shouts and hollers behind the screen; Old Home Week, with coloured lights strung across Belmont Street, barbecues, booths, flivver races, a tug of war between policemen and firemen, confetti so thick it had to be shovelled away, and "Bill and John" contests, when I complained to my mother that the name "Abraham" would never put a button on my cap or entitle me to be counted in anything!

There were shadows on the sun, however, and I could already sense the portent of irremediable change. We sometimes found a stream choked off by garbage and rock-dumping; the river edge got slimy with oil and stank from the white bellies of rotting fish killed by factory chemicals; and one summer the Board of Health forbade us to swim in the polluted creek. Calliope and steamboat whistles grew rare. The hilltop tollgate, a painted schedule of tariffs still visible on the worm-eaten gatepost, was converted into a stone-front gasoline emporium. The Grand Army of the Republic section in Fourth of July parades was noticeably beginning to disintegrate. The hand-drawn hose reel and kingly fire-engine stallions gave place to a motor truck – all spit and polish, and we hung around the station just to touch the brass nozzles – but it could not prance or wildly gallop or strike sparks with hooves.

There were hazards. Some boys did not survive them. A wire-bound raft caught in a vortex swirled two of our gang from a quiet cove during a flood and fell apart in mid stream. A loaded bobsled ran its course down Winding Hill past the brewery into a freight engine. The creek ice was sometimes not thick enough for safe skating. The freight-train-hopping feat – a ten-second dash beside the boxcar, a firm grasp of the iron bar, a leap to the ladder, and then the roof, with hair and shirt flying in the wind, yelling at space – emptied a few sleeves. Occasionally a panicky kid was trapped on the railroad-trestle short cut to the hills. Several of my prank-pals even went to the county-seat reform school for thievery; they were the real dead-end kids whose slovenly mothers forbore even to fine-comb their heads for lice. Had the law caught up with every trifle swiped at Woolworths or the candy store, few of us would have been spared to become constructive citizens.

One afternoon we rigged up a skiff with potato-sack sails and set out squinting into the sun. A sudden gust whipped the burlap into a balloon and the forward jerk snapped the oars out of our hands. Five miles downriver, a jutting log pinioned us to the top of the government dam, while we sat frozen, afraid even to shout lest a vibration send us over the concrete wall, until workmen reached us by pulling a john-boat hand over hand along the dam's edge – just as the *Ohio Queen*, largest packet on the river, turned the bend and her waves began to rock us loose.

Still, my mother's anxiety seemed unreasonable. She counted a nail too high a risk for the privilege of going barefoot. She tucked my chin into an old fringed shawl when I went out to sell papers on a rainy day. She screamed every time I scrambled up into the ice wagon for a few chipped pieces to suck. She hugged me publicly on our return from a jaunt to the hills. And the Feinberg boys had to be sure their hair was innocently dry before going home after a splash in the swimming-hole at the sycamore tree.

Gentile kids weren't treated like babies! Only the Zweigs and Kolitzkys and Plotkins! Mrs. Diggity even played catch with her boys! Of course Jim never could learn to spell; he was two years behind in school, and my father sneered at his dim-witted *goyyische kop*.* And I noticed with cautious disdain the way he and other Gentiles looked ahead in a vacant adenoidal stare. Yet I envied them – most of all when Jewish kids sat in *heder*.

Heder is Hebrew for "room." In the small-town American and Canadian Jewish communities of a half-century ago, it meant the one-room Hebrew school where a *melammed* † drilled Jewish boys of East-European stock after public-school hours in reading and translating *Humash*.‡

The *melammed*? A watery-eyed, parchment-pale cadaver whose coattails flapped and waggled as he shuffled with outspread feet, who smelled of the beeves dedicated to Jewish ritual propriety by his knife, and who revenged himself on destiny by pulling our ears.

And what a destiny it was! The silk-lined German Jews uptown had very few children and no inclination at all to give them Hebrew lessons. Could anyone imagine Sydney Florsheim bobbing up and down to the singsong of the Hebrew alphabet, with a thin

* Gentile head.
† Teacher.
‡ Five: the first five books of the Hebrew Bible.

white line down the middle of his well-plastered hair and a clean white handkerchief in his pocket? The Russian Jews downtown, on the contrary, had nothing but the children and the inclination. Izzy Kravetz's father, who worked on the iron-crusher in Kolitzky's junk-yard, took an oath one Day of Atonement that he would not put meat to his lips, even on Sabbath eve, until he paid the monthly *heder* fee of five dollars – and he might well have become a permanent vegetarian!

Fees did not end our *melammed's* problems. If Old Man Pleshner, the only rich man in *shule*, who bought up enamel-ware "seconds" for New York jobbers and gave a gold-embroidered scroll cover to the synagogue, didn't like the "Reverend's" cantillation or suspected that the "Reverend" thought him an ignoramus, he pointedly turned his back to the altar during prayer – and in a few weeks the "Reverend's" brood, now deprived of Pleshner's pittance, were perched atop a pile of furniture on their way to another martyrdom in the next town.

Heder lasted from four to six, in the basement of the *shule*. The material fabric of that House of God was as stark and unadorned as the Deity who dwelt therein. A barnlike rectangular wooden shack on which the grey paint of many years had peeled and blistered and curled into tiny ridges by the extremities of a variable climate, was fronted by a weed-covered plot of ground, through the centre of which a brick path zigzagged feebly in all directions. A wobbly fence, lacking a few staves, supported a gate that hung on one hinge. Wind, rain, and sun had almost erased the Hebrew characters announcing the name of the congregation. Yet they marched through time and circumstance down the warped plank above the door: AGUDAS AHIM.

The basement also housed the *melammed*'s family. I often found a pungent diaper on the bench, and an infant toddled away from his toilet at my feet while I crinkled my nose into the Pentateuch. And the tea! As soon as the *melammed* growled the order, which he did without even glancing at his wife, I twisted about on the bench so that I could see. For the tea-sucking oblation always fascinated me, and it never changed: a tiny loaf of sugar snapped in two between the teeth, but never touched by the more fastidious lips, then a low, leisurely puff across the tea's surface, then a half-sighing intake of the breath, and finally the tea following it with a gulp down the gullet. I took to comparing the sound with the guzzle of a hog at swill in Farmer Hadley's pen, the belch made by a puddle of dirty rain water as it disappeared into a clogged street sewer, the snort of a horse's nose buried in a haystack. But none matched the gurgling crescendo of that tea ritual. It had a timbre all its own.

My favourite soldier hero was Andrew Jackson. I never tired of reading about his defiant ultimatum to the British officer who ordered him to clean his boots: "I am a prisoner of war, and I demand to be treated as such!" A day came when the smell of sweet anise in a certain gulley out on the hill tortured my nostrils. I wiggled by imperceptible stages along the hard bench of the *heder* and bolted for the door, stopping just long enough to double my fist in the air and shout: "I am an American, and I demand to be treated as such!"

Heder did have its reward. On the Sabbath nearest his thirteenth birthday, a *heder*-boy stood up in the midst of the congregation, donned a virginal prayer shawl over a new blue-serge suit, twitched up to the altar, and shrilly parroted the Hebrew cadence of the Blessings over the Law. Then everyone bustled forward to congratulate, kisses smacked, and the father invited even his business competitors to dip sponge cake in wine in honour of the Bar-Mitzvah who, now an adult in the ranks of Israel, stood like the wooden Indian of Lane's Smoke Shop and fingered a shiny gold watch.

The limelight, and even the watch, were nothing. A Bar-Mitzvah boy no longer attended *heder*. That *was* something! And he could proceed to forget what had been dinned into his head, save on Holy Days or some special family occasion, when his father would take him to *shule* and buy him the privilege of reciting the blessings.

Still, the ceremony moved me. Becoming thirteen in the synagogue was an initiation, as in the Fred Fearnot Athletic Club. Had I not sworn to keep its fair name unsullied and undefiled, in a pirate's cave over a rickety table we had commandeered from somebody's backyard? At thirteen, however, I would join a club God Himself had organized. It would go on until the end of the world. I would have to obey its rules all my life. Just like the boys in Grinkishok!

The streams of thought springing from *heder* always trickled into the mud roads of that ancestral village. The erstwhile omniscients of Agudas Ahim who scolded the *melammed* for using his hands instead of a strap had had their own youth throttled in the larger and more ravenous *heders* of Grinkishok and Bialystok and Warsaw. The pathetic *shlemiel* gyrating over me had stepped from Grinkishok to *heder* with no more alteration in his gesture and being than he would have suffered in skipping from stone to stone across a stream. And the Holy Testament over which I lowered my eyes had rounded the shoulders of generations in the ghettos of Russia and Poland.

My father told me in a mellow moment of reproof for truancy that, except for timid rays that filtered into his *Yeshiva* through holes in the window shades, he had often spent months a stranger to the sun, that he had studied at night by the skimpy light of a wax candle and had frequently lunched on a piece of black bread and salt herring. I sat in *heder* but two hours a day; a gas bulb spread a rhythmic, blue-white, soft glow over boy and bench and book; and whatever the family's budget, there was always enough wholesome and sweet-savoured food on our table.

The difference between *heder* and public school sat heavily on my heart. How clean and bright Central was with its broad stone steps and great lawn! And Principal Thorpe's pants looked like straight parallel lines below his trim shoulders and crisp moustache. And the teachers did not shake their heads up and down in a cacophany of lamentations, but sideways like pink birds. There were no sickening odours. There was singing every morning, and physical exercises in the aisles, and "Happy Birthday" tunes, and romping at recess in the open air with healthy Gentile kids who dressed up for Sunday School and ate butter with meat and didn't blush during Christmas programs or hold their lips tight for Christmas carols or substitute other words for Christian hymns, and had never heard about their ancestors being butchered and driven from one country to another like cattle.

But the crushing sight and sound and smell of *heder* could not quench the grandeur of the Book we read there and the dreams it launched. Israel's story was not all darkness and defeat! Solomon the Magnificent once ruled in Jerusalem and, on the plain of Jezreel, the Lord of Hosts sounded a trumpet-call to war! The arm of Samson the Avenger froze the blood of the Philistines, and with his modest sling David the Shepherd Boy brought Goliath to the dust! Joseph the Dreamer delivered a nation from hunger; Joshua laid waste with fire and sword the land of God's enemies. And Abraham, whose name I bore, was the first to know the Lord as One!

On a late afternoon during the festival of Succot, the dingy *heder* cubicle was flooded with a white brilliance, and I stood before the Tabernacle in the wilderness of Sinai and, like unto Moses addressing God face to face, I intoned the sacred text. Even the odour of boiling noodle soup and *gefillte-fisch* could not banish the perfume of frankincense and myrrh, and the smudgy lapels of the *melammed*'s threadbare black coat blazed with the silver sheen of the breastplate of the High Priest and lay upon me.

"Loafer! Bomm! Tremp! To sleep? For this you go to *heder?*" No sooner did the *melammed*'s nasal cries smite the air than the joint of his iron forefinger dived like a hawk in a semicircle against my cheek, the knifelike nail of an alien thumb stabbed the back of my earlobe, and every nerve on that side of my body throbbed with the familiar pain. But my eyes were not affrighted, nor did the Holy of Holies depart from them. For I was the High Priest of Israel!

The contrast between Huck Finn and *heder* demolished neither my pride nor joy in being a Jew. For me, Jewishness had, and still has, excitement. If a man wants to be an individualist, what can provide him a better start than this unique thirty-five-century-old people laden with reminiscence, quick of sympathy and cleverness, inured to the ways of mankind yet eternally protestant?

Some years ago I was invited to preach at Sunday Church Service. Near the close of his introduction, the pastor paid me a most gracious compliment: "If the Rabbi were not a Jew, I would take him to be a true Christian!" In my preamble, I returned the tribute: "If your minister were not a Christian, I would deem him fine enough to be a Jew!"

That retort would have shocked Jews who slough off their identity as a senseless burden. Having no cohesive principle, "stuck with Jewishness" by Gentile rejection or an ineradicable tribal bond, they consume their own marrow with self-loathing, self-pity, and envy of the born Gentile.

Such negativism cannot be bemoaned as psychologically abnormal. Jews are and have been klieg-lighted by history. A speck of ferment, and always in the centre! We are "a problem" – therefore a pesky nuisance which ought to remove itself for the peace of mind of people who like to skirt problems. We are an ever-present opportunity for Hitlers who inflate us into a "menace" for their own self-inflation. We are many things: Western civilization's nay-saying Number One minority; target of unregenerate prejudice, and therefore an obdurate guilt-symbol in man's conscience; a mystery whose stubborn endurance seems to nullify all the rules; a maverick immune to a precise pigeonhole, being neither a nation, religious communion, or race, and yet all three. From Moses and Jesus to Marx, Freud, and Einstein, there is scarcely a dynamic process which does not involve the questing, exigent energies of "that peculiar people."

Sometimes I too get weary of the spotlight, and wish the Jew were permitted to cease being a "problem," that the world would leave us alone, forgetting both our vice and virtue. After all, we number only one-half of one per cent of the earth's human population. Why can't we be demoted to the role of ordinary human beings, from whom nothing more is demanded than reverence for motherhood and innocence of murder? Why do Gentiles expect so much of us? We are neither better nor worse than they. Jews are wonderful and terrible, good and bad, brilliant and stupid, material and spiritual, vulgar and cultured, beautiful and ugly, gifted and commonplace – in brief, people.

After a "Fighting Words" television panel on which I lambasted the choice of *A Merchant of Venice* for required school reading because its superficial classroom interpretation perpetuates an anti-Semitic syndrome, a dozen Gentiles phoned to tell me they suddenly recognized the source of their persistent, hitherto-unacknowledged "feeling" about Jews: in Shylock. Yet that oft-recited and seldom-assimilated defence by Shylock, "Hath not a Jew . . .," almost redresses the balance. The Bard in all likelihood never saw a Jew; his native insight alone gave mounting eloquence to their humanity. Yet a widely read young college student asked me during a bull session if Jews ever get cancer.

In former years, before my television appearances familiarized smaller Canadian towns with the fact that rabbi and beard are not inseparable, I often amazed Rotary, Kiwanis, and church audiences. "We didn't recognize you when you got off the train! You don't have a beard!" Their disappointment was legitimate. Conventional pictures of the "Jewish type" have always provided him with a patriarch's hirsute appendage. After centuries of drama-packed history, the portrait still imitates what the Gentiles think Abraham should have looked like, although goatees and bristles can be observed in far greater proportion among CBC playwrights, poetasters, bohemians, ban-the-bomb marchers, and baronial military regiments.

The persistence of such a stereotype is one of the relatively minor Jewish hazards. Major hazards are more numerous. *Es is schver tzu zein a Yeed* . . . It is hard to be a Jew. Of all Yiddish colloquialisms, that wry shrug enjoys the widest circulation.

Sometimes I try to imagine having been born into a non-Jewish household. My lot would be sweetened with the dividends of majority status; a smoother road, a softer bed, a safer voyage. Am I indulging in sour grapes or deceiving myself with a rationalization when I renounce the dividends, and announce a strong preference for the firing-line to assure Jewish survival and self-realization?

Even the double standard – the higher one for us, naturally – can be palatable as a compliment and congenial as a challenge. Take, for example, Israel's invasion of the Sinai Peninsula in October 1956. John Foster Dulles had habituated the United Nations to endure his finger-wagging homilies as persiflage to gild his unremitting pursuit of America's self-interest. Yet he insisted that Israel stretch her neck to the knife on the altar of appeasement. While Hungary still echoed to the rumbling of Soviet tanks, President Eisenhower called on Israel to withdraw from Sinai because Jews worship God and submit to ethical precepts; Muscovites are excused by their barbaric conditioning. When I heard that dual-standard admonition, I muttered "Thanks!"

I cudgelled my memory for an applicable Yiddish fable: Once a plague raged among the animals. King Lion decided to hold a trial and find out who was responsible. The bear, the wolf, and the tiger confessed that they tore asunder, mutilated and killed animals and humans without mercy. The verdict exonerated them. Such was their predestined function! At last Judge Lion reached the lamb. She began to wonder. What wrong had *she* done? Suddenly she remembered. On one occasion, because she was dying of hunger, she ate some straw sticking out of a shepherd's shoe. That was it, then! Without further ado, the lamb was pronounced guilty. "For her sin," growled the lion, "has this terrible disaster befallen us all."

Eisenhower's *noblesse oblige* pitch was King Lion roaring at a gnat – but the gnat in this instance *does* have an ethical obligation. The Jew *has* to do better than Gentile nations unrefined in the crucible of thirty-five centuries. He can take hold of that destiny with either of two handles: first, "I can't do anything to end it," or, "What can I do to fulfil it?" The former is cynical commentary on a Christendom unmindful of its Christian stewardship; the latter is nerve-tingling response to an aristocratic tradition.

If happiness is heightened consciousness of life, as though the pores and petals of the spirit were always open, how can a Jew's existence be drab or dull, since history dumps him into the periods and places where it is made?

At the same time, we are saved from priggishness, and nervous breakdowns, by a deflationary sense of humour. Freud credited Jews with a unique talent for self-mockery. "Where can one find a people that makes merry so unreservedly over its shortcomings?" he asked. Being a Jew by birth, like so many practitioners of the science he founded, and having suffered grievously for the adventitious detail, he had reason to discover the therapeutic value of a wit that punctures the blown-up bubble of narcissism about one's "mission." How could Jews have lasted without the liberating gift of laughter, especially when the joke was on them?

Jewish irony even took it out on the sacrosanct rabbi. Witness that famous yarn about the rabbinical applicant for an important pulpit. An obliging friend gave him a fulsome recommendation: "He can be compared to Moses, Shakespeare, Demosthenes, and even God!" After a year the congregation was sadly disenchanted, and the President dispatched a complaint to the rabbi's sponsor. "How could you describe him in such flattering terms?" The reply came at once: "Who has deceived you? He *is* like Moses, who knew no English; he *is* like Shakespeare, who knew no Hebrew; he *is* like Demosthenes, who spoke with pebbles in his mouth – and is God a man? Neither is he!"

The slapstick comedy of a man slipping on a banana peel is undoubtedly close to the childhood reflexes of the human race. For a hyper-intellectualized Jew, however, it has less "release" value than a barbed Yiddish subtlety that only he can understand.

The *heder* world which required this protective safety valve of irony has lost its isolation and intensity in pluralistic and permissive North America. At the same time, by osmosis, it has interpenetrated the free-wheeling, hospitable culture of the environment. The conflict that split my affections with civil war a half-century ago has been softened. I now live in both worlds.

My family and I yell our throats hoarse at a hockey brawl – and I rejoice that my son also plays the more cerebral and traditionally Jewish game of chess. The Stratford (Ontario) Shakespearean Festival revitalizes the uninhibited grandeur, the zest for life, the flowering dynamism of the First Elizabethan Age; the *Dybbuk*, a mighty drama of religious folk-superstition in Eastern Europe, proffers no less catharsis to my spirit. Who can touch the nerve of gaiety like Stephen Leacock? But a reader of Yiddish will equate no humorist anywhere with Sholom Aleichem.

The tongue that Shakespeare spoke is the vessel of my thinking. Am I the poorer for drinking from the Hebrew and Yiddish fountainheads of my fathers' wisdom? Should we not be delighted to admit into our common talk such international and untranslatable words as *shlemiel*, *shlimazl*, and *nudnik*?

Quebec pea soup, Winnipeg goldeyes, and Ontario cheeses can be a gustatory pleasure. But to the Jewish cuisine something is added. Our housewives probably did not invent *gefillte-fisch* – but they did popularize it.

The dietary laws observed by orthodox Judaism limited the cook's ingredients and stretched her artfulness. When ritually slaughtered kosher meat was hard to come by, culinary arithmetic multiplied the potential of dairy foods, fish, and chicken, which could be killed in accordance with approved technique by any rabbinically licensed layman. The skills thus derived from the spur of handicap have made the Jewish table a delight, if often a digestive peril.

During part of the last war, I served as civilian chaplain in a ski-troop training-camp high in the Rocky Mountains, near Denver. For combat exercise, recruits were issued K-rations – a tin of expertly chosen, vitamin-rich foods, concentrated to give maximum vitality on a gruelling mountain march. On its uphill march through the centuries, the Jewish people also had K-rations – like *kishke* (entrails stuffed with a paste of flour, chicken grease, and fried chitlings), *kugel* (pudding, usually of raisin-sweetened noodles), *kashe* (fried barley), *kreplach* (three-cornered meat dumplings in chicken soup), *knishes* (chicken-liver patty), not to speak of *strudel* (a rolled apple-nut pastry), *tzimmis* (a prune-carrot-potato mélange), and garlic-laden salami, a bedtime snack not recommended for insomniacs.

The richly seasoned gamut of Jewish cooking is a gastronomic microcosm of the Jewish psyche. Like the Huck Finn – *heder* axis of my boyhood, that psyche is enriched by the intuition and awareness of a cosmopolitan people that has been everywhere and yet in no place "for ever and ever." One needs a strong stomach and stable metabolism to transmute such hardy menu into sinew, and a strong mind and keen wit to mould the certain hazards of Jewish life into zest for living. It *is* hard to be a Jew – and it's fun!

Black and White: The Power of Race and the Race for Power

My life-long battle against racism began when a raffish gang of roughnecks from "out the crick" saw a carnival game of "hit-the-nigger" – pitching baseballs at a black man's skull. The next afternoon at the sycamore swimming-hole, an ebony lad nicknamed Skeets was making his way dog-fashion back to shore. The gang decided it would be amusing to play the game on him, and forthwith pelted his head with a steady rain of stones. I roused myself from terror and ran for help. By the time I hailed a brakeman from the freightyard, Skeets had been drained of strength by panic and, thrashing and dodging, was gone.

That night, on my tear-wet pillow, I remembered how I had been saved from drowning, at the same spot, the preceding summer, by Dude, the Negro garbage man's boy. Dude had burrowed into a suck hole where I was floundering down for the third time, and carried me out on his shoulders. Years later, I learned that Dude died under falling slate in a coal mine.

Before Skeets, my contact with the race problem was random and tangential: speculation about the bizarre dining-habits of the Fu-Manchu "Chinee" laundryman who, everyone said, ate rats; slightly begrudging acceptance of Negro classmates; suspended judgement of the shoeshine boys in the barbershops who, Jim Diggity said, had a terrible smell; and a vague feeling of kinship with people set apart as "different" and therefore inferior.

The Negro kids from the flood flats at the lower riverbend could never shove the Jim Diggitys out of my heart – but I was not going to despise them either. Our B. & O. Bridge gang was a polygot of every church and "old country" in town, as indicated by the name-calling expletives – "hunky, dago, wop, sheeny, mick" – that would spice a quarrel. Why couldn't "coon" or "nigger" be added to our loose alliance? But I didn't make a fuss about it. The morning after Skeets drowned, however, my mind was made up.

In High School, Harrison Gaines, star centre of the All-Ohio-Valley champion football team, became the centre of my race consciousness. "Modest," "handsome," "soft-spoken," "clean-minded," "manly" – sportswriters never stinted his praise, especially when Bellaire won the big Thanksgiving "classic" against Wheeling. He carried himself with an air of jauntiness, on tiptoe as though ready for a sprint, and his pearly teeth gleamed with frank, generous joviality. So I thought, until, during noon recess, I saw his lips tremble while he dangled twitching legs over a lonely window ledge. Soon our eyes met in swift glances that sought a message we were both afraid to decipher or acknowledge.

The Ram Cat Alley "niggers" hated Harrison. "*Who* does he think he is?" Dude's older brother sneered down the torso of a stogie. The whites shunned him with courtesy and competence – except on the athletic field.

Balmy summer evenings offered little for me to do and no place to go. My feet marked a rectangle, up Belmont Street, across and down, again and again, beside the arc lights that marked it as Bellaire's principal thoroughfare. Bellaire's famous Saturday hero made the same round, like a fellow prisoner in the courtyard. At first I quickened my step and fled with a nod and a half-strangled "Hi!" Finally, I touched his arm and inquired about his mother, who sometimes brought umbrellas to my father's shop.

From that time on we paced together – the Jew-boy with the physique of a starving Armenian and the black-boy Tarzan – talking aimlessly, almost absentmindedly, about everything and nothing, while my heart ached for "furriners fit only to lug a pick and shovel," for white-trash cess-pool cleaners who pasted shacks out of tarpaper and driftwood in the swamp below the creek, for the magnificent, gentle creature at my side whom frustration was gradually reducing to flaccid nervelessness, and for myself.

One night an incident in front of the Marx Dry Goods store lifted me from self-pity to flaming anger. The Marxes were German Jews, prominent in the Temple uptown, and very proud of their son, studying to be a Reform rabbi. Although quite well-to-do, they lived conservatively above the store and often sat outdoors on campstools. I could not pass by without a chat. Mrs. Marx had carefully modulated and precise diction, a college diploma, unusual for middle-aged women in those days, and genuinely concerned, albeit voluble, interest in my future.

Harrison would begin to hum softly and swing his arms when we approached the Marx stoop. While I bowed like a jack-knife and gripped my hat and twisted one leg around the other, he stood stock still and then jerked away. Having never learned how to say goodbye, I dashed headlong down successive dead-end conversational by-ways with the Marxes before tittering away to find Harrison whistling into a drugstore window. He never mentioned the Marxes.

At last Mrs. Marx mentioned him. "Why are you seen so much

with Harrison Gaines? It doesn't look nice for a naturally refined Jewish boy like you to go around with a . . . a . . . darky!" My lips had no chance to quaver; they sputtered. "He's a f-f-fine fellow, a real g-g-gentleman, the b-best I know."

Harrison did not whistle that time. When I caught up with him gazing fixedly into space, he raised his head and looked at me. Since then, I have never quite eluded those deep-brown eyes.

Thirty-five years later, from the creaky wooden pulpit of a Negro church in Toronto, I saw the eyes again. The dispirited hymn-singing (not Negro spirituals, regrettably) released my mind to identify persons I knew: a tall, soft-spoken West Indian, desiccated by a decade of truck-loading drudgery; two buxom young girls with wide-open faces hired by the day as cleaning-women; the assistant pastor, a shipping-clerk helper who conducted Bible meetings three nights a week; a dozen teenagers who quit school for messenger and factory jobs because "it's no use studyin' for somethin' you won't never get"; a housewife sitting like a ramrod in a feathered hat because her husband was a Pullman porter; a delegation from a newly formed youth club attending church for the first time since childhood – to hear someone "wake up the old fogies." All were linked by that Harrison Gaines look of the disinherited.

Reverie turned to acute discomfort when the minister introduced me in a dulcet Jamaican accent as "leader and champion of the Negroes of Canada." I corkscrewed up from the chair and forward to the reading-desk. "Reverend Dawson's a dear friend of mine and I appreciate what he said about me. But you folks don't need a rabbi to fight for you. Stand up! No man's a slave until he rivets the chains on his own soul!"

By that time, adolescent compassion for Skeets, Harrison, and Abie the "sheeny" had finally sparked a personal crusade against race hate, which was, to me, an apocalyptic, pandemic perversion. My crusade ranged wide.

During the Second World War, Japanese-Canadian citizens were deported by Order-in-Council from British Columbia homes and their economic subsistence destroyed by forced sale. At a mass-meeting of protest, I called this a high-handed piece of Nazism by a government allegedly engaged in war against it.

A Negro boy was ejected from a publicly advertised and licensed skating-rink. A statement from my study reminded Canadians of other Negro boys not ejected from military cemeteries in Holland and dared the Mayor to explain the difference.

Immigration procedures clearly discriminated against the Chinese, who are deprived of family by restrictions on wives and children. I inquired why Canadian missionaries deem yellow-skinned people of Tientsin worthy to share an everlasting domicile in heaven while the Canadian government considers them unfit for a fleeting abode in Toronto.

Little Black Sambo, a children's book which perpetuates Negro minstrel-show comicality, was for me a scared coloured kid sinking under an overhanging sycamore tree. Although my demand for its removal from the public-school reading list aroused patronizing levity in some quarters, I insisted that Canadians must protect young minds against the virus whose end-product is a concentration camp and genocide.

The exclusion of Negroes from Toronto apartment houses gave me the opportunity on Race Relations Sabbath to welcome Toronto's black-skinned people as guests in the Temple sanctuary and social hall, and to help organize delegations and lobbies for a Fair Accommodations Act, patterned after the Fair Employment Practices Act I had sponsored years before.

When the Sharpeville Massacre and Montgomery boycott touched off a chain reaction of moral shock in Canada, I measured the wide gap between preachment to Johannesburg and practice in Toronto – with a bow to churchgoers convinced that Jesus is a segregationist on Sunday mornings, good people who welcome tubercular Hungarian whites and fend off healthy West Indian blacks because "the Canadian climate might give them tuberculosis," bank managers who honour Jewish cheques but never hire Jewish clerks, real-estate agents in hopefully posh residential areas who forget all the techniques of salesmanship on learning that the client prays in a synagogue, Jewish apartment-house owners who whine that one coloured tenant will reduce their profit, and otherwise keen-witted Jewish social climbers who can't discern that snobbery toward the Negro makes them brother to the Nazi.

Hair-triggered indignation embroiled me repeatedly in hassles – with a politician who prattled about brotherhood and restricted himself to Aryan summer resorts, a personnel executive who dubbed critics of individual free enterprise "Communists" and then refused the individual Negro a job in accord with merit, a college-educated clubwoman who, seeing no unreason in the denial of a decent neighbourhood to a coloured child, was horrified by his delinquency, and a vociferous upholder of Canada's British founding-father tradition stricken with moral glaucoma in front of a television screen documenting the fetid squalour of an Indian reservation.

Preoccupied with Skeets and Harrison, I was tardy in apprehending that Canada's 185,000 Indians are a forgotten minority, a moral blot concealed by common consent of the Canadian people. A visit to Lake Temagami's Bear Island reservation left me ashamed and contrite; I was a neutral, silent newcomer in a land hospitable also to human decay, destitution, and despair. A slum is no less a slum because it sprawls over a vast acreage of wind-blown wilderness, dotted with Johannesburg-style shacks in which a white man would hesitate to install his riding-horse. Housing, hygiene, medical care, and particularly education of the young for skilled labour or a trade are there so primitive that I asked an official if the unconscious motivation of the whites for this pittance might not be punitive – to chasten gentle savages driven from their hunting-grounds, and purgative – to compensate for and cleanse themselves of guilt.

Obviously, a dismal dole to generation after generation of dependents who, like the Southern Negroes, are then exhibited as shiftless and morbidly drowsy, was simpler than preparing them for mature status beyond the reserve as and among Canadian citizens. It cannot, however, revive the cliché that Canada has no special race problem.

Politically unarmed, a splinter group, the Indian can be delegated to a bureaucratic department or survey, swept under a bright, hand-woven, native rug, with scarcely a demur, even from unremitting opponents of South African apartheid. Does this comparative indifference to the Indian derive from his proximity? Indians are close enough to be overlooked. Yet the Boers used less guile snatching the land from black men than the North Americans did to expropriate the red men, and a white enclave embedded in a huge black mass might reasonably be expected to evince more dread than a white majority whose ragged remnant of surviving aborigines is cooped up and cowed.

Does South African policy disclose a diabolism more deep-dyed than Canada's unconcern with its native population? The former is all the more reprehensible, Canadians say, because buttressed by law, and even religion. Grotesque Dutch Reformed Biblical exegesis even erased the adjective "black" from the description of the "comely beloved" in the Song of Songs. By the same logic, anti-Semitic practices in the Soviet Union which contravene the specific constitutional law of the land cannot be coupled with Nazism, which laboriously spun out genocide as the core of its legal and ideological structure. But Canada's treatment of the Indians, in essence and principle, might be said to resemble Verwoerd's Johannesburg or Hitler's Berlin. It is a product, not of blind, emotional prejudice, but of bland, indifferent legislation, unimaginative officialdom, and popular irresponsibility. The shabby Bear Island teenagers with nothing to look forward to but handouts of sodapop and chewing-gum at the white man's fishing-camps are wards of the state.

The perfect clinical laboratory for research into racism did not present itself to me on an Indian reservation. It was in Dresden, Ontario, that I came upon it.

Hitherto the black man in Dresden had felt moderately secure. Unlike the helots of Harlem, he almost became a somebody. As early as 1828, Reverend Josiah Henson got a warm welcome from the devout Christian villagers of Fairport, subsequently renamed Dresden, northern terminus of Michigan's "underground railway." When

Queen Victoria assigned Josiah three hundred acres for an institute to house his runaway brethren, they even contributed additional funds. Only a few miles distant John Brown assembled his "army" for the 1859 raid on Harper's Ferry.

The main street of Dresden displayed a sign directing the considerable tourist flow, chiefly Negroes, to the grave of "Uncle Tom," Josiah Henson himself, who was Harriet Beecher Stowe's model and inspiration. In 1949, the slick chromium-plated offspring of Fairport's receptive Christians converted Uncle Tom's coffin into Jim Crow's cradle – and "Dresden," already German by nomenclature, into "Little Nuremberg"; in a municipal referendum, they upheld five-to-one the refusal of restaurants and snack bars to serve Negroes.

The Toronto clergy was then immersed in a referendum campaign against proposed abrogation of Sunday blue laws and would not be chided by a rabbi about lunchroom legalism in Dresden. I phoned the articulate leader of Dresden's Negro community that I would like to observe the scene at first hand. He invited me to stay at his farm home and preach in the segregated church.

The first symptom I observed in the Dresden clinic was the absence from a restaurant wall of the Uncle Tom prints I had once seen there when speaking to a service club on brotherhood. Tactful probing yielded the logic behind their removal. The snack-bar owner "just got mad" when a descendant of Uncle Tom, an ex-paratrooper, left the counter (and Dresden) after being outwaited by the waitress in a cup-of-coffee transaction. The second symptom was a complaint by the Mayor: "If only the papers would stop writing about this!" Then the day-long interview began; my notes might have been the stenographic memorandum of a pre-lynching bee in Georgia.

"I sorta like the Negroes in our town; they're good, first-rate citizens." Not first-class, I reflected. "We'd gladly lend them capital to set up their own restaurants!" The banker seemed unimpeachably benign.

"Radicals and Reds who just want to sell their damn papers!" This clothing-store expostulation alluded to an anti-bias article in *Maclean's* magazine.

"You Communists can't tell us what to do!" A letter of protest from the Labour Progressive (Communist) Party had annoyed the gas-station attendant.

"We're for free enterprise not socialism see? A businessman has the right to pick his own customers!" The grocery clerk wore a Bible Class pin in his buttonhole.

"Laws ain't the answer. It's the Christ in man. Slow but sure!" I had listened to this argument so often that I fled the antique shop in disgust.

"Look mister! D'ya wanna blackie to marry yer sister?" The rhetorical questioner himself had a smattering of dark pigment in his skin; the later nineteenth century brought considerable blood admixture to Dresden.

"Negroes? They're okay. But I can't ruin my trade!" I suggested to the souvenir salesman that a Negro-tourist boycott of the Uncle Tom grave might hurt him more, although I secretly doubted that Negroes from nearby Detroit would long be inclined, in any case, to visit the Uncle Tom shrine and sip the chalice of his servility.

"Of course Negro vets are welcome to join the Legion; they went overseas with the rest of us. But I can't see one dancing with my wife!" The wounded war veteran did not tell me Negroes had to fight for the right to fight and die by enlisting repeatedly and that his Legion Branch would soon feel impelled to replace dances with stags.

"Them coloured chaps can join the Orange Order. We'd love to have 'em! Of course," the truck-driver added, "it would be a separate Negro lodge!"

"This furor about prejudice is mainly froth. Look at those school children strolling arm in arm – blacks and whites together!" From the parsonage window the pastor's assurance induced mild euphoria, until he confirmed my suspicion that an unscalable automatic barrier arose when they neared the age of work and marriage.

"No one can be blamed for prejudice. It's been here a long time." In addition to this benevolent disclaimer, the coloured preacher intimated that some of his parishioners were halfhearted about the balloting; a victory would bring out the Ku Klux Klan!

"Canada had seventy-five thousand Negroes in John Brown's time. The twentieth century lured many more from the West Indies, and American Negroes migrated here to porter on transcontinental railways. Today there are less than forty thousand. Why? You've seen the reason!" The schoolteacher's face was a pictorial version of guilt conflict.

That night my Negro host and I sat on the edge of the bed. He broke his laconic brooding long enough to say tonelessly that no coloured person had a well-paid non-manual job in office, store, or service club. His vivid, personable young niece, whom I had met at supper, went from the top ten of her sophomore year at college to a canning-machine.

The other tale he told me was bizarre. A Negro high-school athlete had inadvertently touched platinum-blonde hair. Within hours telephone lines simmered with a scheme to disband the co-ed clubs, and mothers glowed with relief that they had squelched a community swimming-pool.

The next morning, Sunday, I spoke my piece at the Queen Street Baptist Church. It was lusty, loud, and long. It demanded to know the difference in spirit between Dresden, Ontario, and Dresden, Germany during the reign of Nazism; it demanded militancy of the Negroes; it demanded an iron-clad Bill of Rights. It was a rousing and sulphuric sermon, and the newsmen chorused "good stuff." The dead-pan reserve of the congregation, nevertheless, did not elude me, and the calloused hands that shook mine afterwards felt slack and boneless.

Sundry Jewish nabobs objected to my Dresden pilgrimage. "Our job is Jews. What have we to do with the Negro problem?" In executive public-relations meetings, I retorted that the struggle is indivisible and the plight of one persecuted group the fight of all. And there was a shabby practical rejoinder too: the appetite for someone to hate grows by what it feeds on; a Negro-hater "graduates" to Jew-baiter.

One must grant, I conceded, polarities of contrast between anti-Semitism and anti-Negroism. The Jew is penalized for commercial acumen and intellectual subtlety; the "poor nigger" for laziness, profligacy, and intellectual primitivism. Jewish pariahship was interwoven with theological mystique at the very birth of organized Christendom; prejudice against pigment began after the American Civil War and despite the favourable climate of Christian concern for saving the heathen. Anti-Jewish venom has little or no sex-motif and modern-day Canadian Gentiles often consider Jews to be excellent candidates for the nuptial vow; the Negro generally is a target of sexual paranoia, and invested with the subconscious aversions, longings, and inhibitions of the white-supremacist who may envy and resent his supposed pristine virility.

Nazism excepted, the Jew's experience of ferocity, although far more extensive in historic time, is a surface lesion compared with the horror that dogs a coloured man every day of his life. The Negro girl who won an essay contest on the postwar punishment of Hitler by writing: "Dress him up in a Negro skin and drop him anywhere in the United States for the remainder of his days," dipped a pen in the tears of her race. Under the enchantment of the era of affluence, the middle-class Jewish teenager has been crowned potentate over his miniature realm. For his Negro age-peers, that era has not begun to emerge over the horizon, and could not in any case alter the verdict of pseudohaematology, which recoiled from transfusing whites with Negro donations to a Red Cross blood bank.

In the Hebrew prophets, ancient Jews heard the echo of God's voice reminding Amos that he loved Ethiopians no less than Israel. Modern Jews have always been inordinately proud of a unique aptitude for *rachmonut*.* The Talmud insists that putting a man to shame before his neighbours is murder. Modern Jewry must embrace the black man in a partnership distilled by the Hindi tongue into three words: "*Tat tvam asi.*" †

The vanguard position of some Jews in the Negro's march to freedom encourages the confidence that middle-class Judaism has

* Compassion. † "I am thou."

not altogether repudiated social action. Unfortunately for them and for the liberals who abhor white racial arrogance, it is the prevalent evil, not their particular fight against it, which defines Americans to Africa and Asia. We are all assumed to be willing, if apologetic, accomplices.

Possibly, at bottom, that is just what we are. What would Toronto boycotters of South African wines do if they were encompassed by a huge black mass on a black continent in a polarized society, instead of being spared even the necessity to notice a tiny black populace so timid it won't venture a protest? What would I do if confronted by miscegenation in my own family? How valid is the Negrophile's title to exemption from the clash of black-white interests? Are claims of detachment from the power conflict a trick of the ego to conceal inadmissible compulsions?

In the meantime the struggle continues, in a vaster arena horizontally and with heightened tension vertically. But the balance of strength has begun to shift, like cargo in a listing vessel. While the white nations pour out resources with spendthrift abandon in a see-saw of nuclear armament, devitalize their moral substance with the decadent cult of individual opportunism, and subject youth to the commercialized allure of sex, soft drinks and the soft life, the emergent virile people of Africa, avid for knowledge, are beginning to march. They have far to go, they will need to travel on foot for years, but a headwind of time moves with them, and the rhythmic beating of drums, the thunderous tread of feet upon the earth, signal to the black ghettos of New York, Chicago, and Washington.

The meaning of Mboya, Nyerere, and Kenyatta cannot long escape even romantic yearners for the halcyon days when a "nigger knew his place." Only wilfully myopic dwellers in a vanished dream world skirt the grim fact that whites are a minority in a world they no longer own. Even those with insight forbear to contemplate the ultimate denouement, the inventory of catastrophe, because of its chilling implications.

The triumph of the coloured races, soon or late, seems inevitable; it is one of the few forecasts I am brash enough to venture about a beclouded tomorrow. Today's American, Canadian, or British children may yet inherit the seats of the mighty; they will not occupy them unshaken by the monsoons of change. The most astringent and exacting chore of Western education is to foster preparation for an era of austerity, so that our young may be hardened to the adjustments it will demand. The fate of power complexes in the past does not permit the careless condescension that marks Western youth's posture toward the African continent. Negroes in Africa and in North America have entered an era of rising expectations; the antithetical white prospect established by racism may constrain us to lower ours.

Must the future contain an era in which one antagonist can advance only by holding back the other? Since whites are doomed to lose the power struggle, a pragmatic strategy of self-preservation would instruct us to curtail the scope and fury, call it quits, and be glad to obtain a settlement on terms of co-existence.

Character, intelligence, capacity for the arts of civilization, have no relation whatever to kinky hair, colour of skin, or shape of skull. What science has asserted with its mind needs now to be assimilated into the viscera. Inferiority of Negro achievement is not in nature, but in schools, machines, food, institutions, means of communication and can, nay will, be erased. As long as one sector remains unintegrated, the clear implications of anthropological truth will have been aborted by stubborn left-overs from the past. Even the marriage bed can claim no immunity. The "mammy" Southern families welcome into their lily-white households will eventually have to be genuine – the mother of a son-in-law. My great-great-grandchildren will not be horrified at all if one of their number marries a person of colour. Unless colour and no colour destroy each other in fratricidal war, that will be the price of peace!

A formidable, frightening job – to tear out root and branch the whole psychic structure reared on centuries of white overlordship and replace it with a constellation of attitudes adapted to equality. But it must be done, and quickly.

If our children are not to drain the cup of sorrow we have

passed to the lips of the coloured races, they must be trained to resist the champagne of white supremacy. Delay might be suicidal.

What will the black people do with power? Will they refrain from the maltreatment and exploitation from which Alabama, Algeria, and South Africa have not refrained or will they build furnaces for Maidaneks and Buchenwalds on the plateaus of Tanganyika? Martin Luther King and Albert Luthuli, a neatly groomed American clergyman and a resplendently robed Zulu chieftain, both believing and practising Christians, would urge non-violence. At the moment of writing, one sits in an Alabama jail cell, the other under South African house arrest. Together with Albert Schweitzer and Father Pire, they pierce the Colour Curtain as the four-pronged spearhead of sacrificial Christianity in an age wherein it is more difficult to be truly Christian, or truly Jewish, than at any time since the Roman catacombs. The men who imprison and gag King and Luthuli will have reason to thank their parochial God if moderates like the American "agitator" and the African "rebel" shape the thinking of tomorrow's liberated Negroes.

Another, far different, formula would be dictated by Elijah Muhammad (born Poole), head of the American Black Muslim movement, "Messenger of Allah to the Lost-Found Nation of Islam in the Wilderness of North America," whom I interviewed in his Phoenix, Arizona, home. His credo is as follows:

The Negro must free himself from every trace of slave psychology and from the "slave-master" Christian faith which has drugged him into self-abasement. Neither education, law, nor the ameliorative intercession of conscience-stricken whites can alter the absolute dichotomy between white (evil) and black (good), and every human being is typed by skin, forever. Allah, God of Islam, the true religion of the black race, destined it for complete and everlasting suzerainty, but an inferior rival deity fashioned a sub-standard race, the whites, and elevated it to a mastery which would endure six thousand years. That period has now drawn to its close, as first revealed through a semi-divine prophet, Farad Muhammad, whose successor Elijah has been entrusted with the mission of redemption.

As prelude to their deliverance, the self-segregated, God-chosen black people of America demand "to go first class, whatever the cost."

To his cohorts, allegedly one hundred thousand, Muhammad has given solidarity with the Afro-Asiatic non-white masses (all regarded as "black") who will inundate their whilom satraps; emancipation from the discredited and onerous Christianity of immediate forbears; rediscovery of roots in the venerable culture of the Afro-Asian continents; transition from the fabricated stereotype of spastic, jovial docility so infuriating that many Negroes will not even look at a slice of watermelon, to one of dynamism and self-discipline; insistence on, rather than resignation to, inflexible white-black separatism – not integration, but voluntary, maximal segregation – and replacement of smouldering resentment at "white supremacy" with starry-eyed pride in "black supremacy."

The Black Muslim brotherhood has been called an example of the "hate that hate breeds." Martin Luther King, whose "flunkeyism" Muhammad condemns, shrinks from yoking himself with its inflammatory mumbo-jumbo. Phoenix friends warned me not to visit Muhammad. "You're jeopardizing your life! He hates all whites! His house abounds with gunmen!" Instead, I enjoyed a safe, solitary, soft-spoken chat in a tastefully furnished living-room.

Later that afternoon, in musing retrospect, his theology seemed only in a negligible degree more chimerical than that of the Christian Holy Rollers I saw baptizing new Blood-of-the-Lamb beneficiaries in the Ohio River several decades ago. And in the evening, on a bench facing the citrus grove that lends a graceful and serene foreground to the Mormon Temple in Phoenix, I pondered the legend on which its overpowering grandeur was built: the miraculous revelation and translation of the Book of Mormon. Is Mormon cosmogony more believable than that of Elijah Muhammad?

Prospects for the Black Muslim movement are not material for glib prediction. One prophecy is safe: its decline or growth will be determined by the sagacity and clairvoyance of the American whites, who are still potent enough to mould the environment that moulds the black man's mood.

It's getting harder for a coloured man anywhere to wait until tomorrow for what everyone has today, especially when the nuclear age may not leave him a tomorrow. A realistic, grown-up, civilized "Western civilization" will give it to him now. The alternative for Negroes will present itself with increasing clarity: not King or continued second-class citizenship, but King or Muhammad. . . .

One day in November 1960, three pig-tailed little girls, two white and one black, left their dolls to light a candle in the darkness. They walked together through a wasteland of clawing vituperation down the *via dolorosa* of a New Orleans street to a classroom emptied by white boycotters who prefer illiteracy to desegregated children. I am not sure they prattled on the way; the menacing mob of embattled Southern motherhood may have constricted their throats with fright. But the patter of their feet echoed round the world.

Long ago, three boys lit a dim candle for me: Skeets, Dude, and Harrison.

Jesus

FROM early years I was drawn to the figure of Jesus: haloed babe of the manger, in his mother's arms, under the enraptured gaze of the Magi, or as a young dreamer from the hills of Galilee, which I supposed were no higher than those around Bellaire. When I beheld his exquisite, gently moulded face with pointed beard and poignant eyes that seemed to pity the whole world, and knowing from Mom that he was born a Jew, I imagined him an older brother with special concern for me. I saw him in stained-glass windows, in frames on the walls of Gentile homes, and always with a sense of fore-knowledge and kinship scarcely less sharp than the pain of participation in the suffering visited on my people by men who said they worshipped him.

During the Christmas season I envied my Gentile friends with secret shame. The bright coloured lights and gleaming tinsel on the trees, the sleds and skates and flaming plum pudding and turkey – in every home except ours; people eager and cheerful jamming the stores to buy goodies and gifts – not for me; an air of friendliness, everyone booming hello with gusto and zest – but cool and hesitant toward the Jews, related in lineage of birth to Jesus and yet outside the circle of his "family." Even the eight days of Hanukkah, with Hanukkah-*gelt,** seemed imitative and only half compensatory.

Every Sunday morning the younger Feinberg boys, a batch of newspapers under their arms, covered the upper residential area of town yelling *Wheeling News and Register*. The most lucrative stop in my itinerary was the curb in front of the Catholic Church, which disgorged Irish worshippers who had known our family for years and gave me warm smiles with their nickels. On the Sunday before Christmas I yelled louder than usual, because I felt like an alien who needed self-affirmation, and I stood straighter and a bit defiant at the church.

Christmas itself was not totally barren ground for me. Bright and brisk that morning I delivered presents in a grocery-store crate on laboriously assembled wheels or on a sled, for a silver-haired maiden lady who lived alone in a big house and thought it vulgar to send them by mail or by the store-wagon. She never failed to give me a box of candy for myself and a cup of hot cocoa as bonus increment to the fifty-cent wage, and to shake her head and say, "You Feinberg boys are such sweet boys. It's too bad you're Jews, and don't know the joy of our Lord. But he loves you just the same."

Being Christian, I visualized, would bring me fairy tales – Mother Goose, goblins, princesses, castles, like the other kids – and lullabies and hymns. My mother did croon "Rosinkes mit Mandlen" † and "Aufn Pripitchok," ‡ especially when we had whooping-cough or a foot infection from stepping on a rusty nail. She couldn't read

* Gift-money. † "Raisins and Almonds." ‡ "On the Little Stove."

Grimm or Hans Christian Andersen or sing "Onward Christian Soldiers," whose melody set my feet to marching, although I substituted "Jewish." Most of all, being Christian would give me a portion in the soft-eyed Saviour on the Cross.

Today the crucified Christ has been allocated in my theological view to the domain of mythology and the mystery rites of the ancient Orient. The fecund imagination of the teeming pre-Christian East abounded with stories of gods who died and returned to life, just as the sun's rays and the earth itself grow pale and wither under winter's lethal frost, to glow again with life in spring. That Christmas is but three days removed from the shortest day on the calendar, when warmth and light are at their lowest ebb, is no coincidence. It marks the beginning of rebirth throughout the vast realm of living nature, and inevitably in the soul of man, who must clothe nature and himself in the garments of divinity.

According to some Christian historians, the synchronization of the Yuletide festival with the midwinter pagan solstice celebrations originated in the desire of the Church Fathers to minimize persecution by reducing its visibility as a separate occasion. The striking similarity of Christmas to the nature-cycle itself, however, provides what is for me a more authentic and profound explanation for the date.

And the cross? It can woefully distort the subconscious mind of a child taught to contemplate it with reverence as the supreme sanctity of parents, church, and people; it can dislodge the positive concept of life, rather than death, as God's loftiest gift. The wondrously dramatic mystique, imprinted deep in fantasy and physical image, of the Lord's sacrificial atonement for an abstract cleansing from sin is not at all easy for a child's mind to conceive. A psychoanalyst might be hard-pressed to seek in that accent on death an educational influence untouched by negativism toward the intrinsic values of life. Even if I could divest myself of the Jewish insistence on individual repentance, and believe that Jesus perished on the cross to save me from sin and rid my soul of Adam's curse – even then I would not recommend the cross to teach the worth of human life, in which I believe with utmost passion.

One day in my Huck Finn period I attended Mass with Tim Fahey, by best Catholic friend. Through every avenue of sense, I breathed in the statues and kneeling silence, the soothing shadows and Latin chant, the smell and sight of tallow candles on the richly laden altar. The following Sabbath, slipping unobtrusively away from my brothers on the way home from *shule*, I ran to the brim of the river and asked its unresponsive depths why we Jews didn't have such calm serenity and splendour.

It was not long before I realized that the word "Jesus" is bound up for Jews with their own blood and tears, rather than with beauty and tranquillity. I brought home a Christmas card Mrs. Diggity had taken from her fireplace mantel, seeing me admire it; there were white-robed angels flying through a crimson-streaked sky bearing an infant on a blue cloud. My father snatched it from my hand, threw it into the grate fire and sat down with quivering nostrils, his fingers interlaced so tight they were bleached of colour, and muttered in Yiddish: *"Doh in mein aigenem hame, meiner a zoon! Der dovor aher!"* (Here in my own home, my own son!) That much I understood, but the last two words: *dovor aher*. What did they mean? Mother was at the sink, with an unwashed cup rigid in her hand. I sidled over to her apron string. "What does *dovor aher* mean, Mom?" I whispered to the cup. Her lips barely moved. "It's Hebrew, and means 'the other thing.' You should know it from *heder*. We never mention . . . that name. Only *dovor aher!* Many many years he has brought Jews very much trouble. Say not the Christian god's name – never!"

That monotone, and the trauma of my father, told me I had struck the rawest nerve of the Jewish people. "Jesus" is incarnadined with the blood of countless generations who died in, or lived in dread of, savage torment. Jews must grip themselves merely to pronounce the two syllables of a name so often the battlecry of hordes that slew and ravished and of mighty ones in church and state who cursed and enslaved.

One of the chief sources of Jewish history during the Crusades is the *selihah** – elegies composed on the death of Rhineland Jews massacred in their synagogues by the Christian knights fulfilling their vow to redeem the Holy Grail. All martyrdoms were sealed by the basic affirmation of Judaism: "Hear, O Israel, the Lord our God, the Lord is One!" The Office of the Inquisition in Spain gave cultured, thoroughly "Spanishized" Jews the freedom to choose between baptismal font and wrack, stake, and exile, proposing thus to push them into paradise for the glory of the Nazarene Jew whose godhead they were ordained by God to reject. Russian pogroms were usually plotted in the church; my parents never quite conquered their fear of the *galach*.†

The Germany that outstripped all its predecessors in the expertise of Jew-murder had an established Christian religion. Although the clearly verbalized intent of the Nazi usurper was the uprooting of Christ and deification of the "Nietzchean superman," the record of Bishop Dibelius does not include strenuous efforts to protect Jews in the front line; Vatican strategy permitted a concordat with Il Duce and temporized with Nazi-Fascism while individual acts of mercy plucked a few far-strewn thousands of its Jewish victims from the burning; and the atavistic barbarism of Teutonic warriors inspired the neutrality of the New Testament's maligned Levite rather than the intervention of a good Samaritan.

After my regular Sunday morning lecture in Holy Blossom Temple in 1944, a solemn-faced, spare young man asked for a private interview. Following me to the study, he identified himself as a Presbyterian Seminary student, took his ease in a lounging-chair, and with quiet aplomb offered to show me the "key" to Jewish anguish under the Nazis. Despite repeated annoyance by cranks with "keys," and suspicion that he was just another neurotic burdened with Jews en route to hell, I nodded and waited.

"Scripture, your own Bible, prophesies that Israel and the world won't be redeemed in the Second Coming until the Jews return to their Lord. Hitler has been divinely ordained to bring you back by the rod of chastisement."

* Penitential prayer. † Priest.

Stunned, I arose without a rustle, gripping the desk. "Are you telling me that God wants infants thrown up in the air and shot because their ancestors didn't accept Jesus as Messiah nineteen centuries ago?"

"Well, they would be alive today if . . ."

The flood gates burst within me. "Get out!"

I glowered with unspeakable rage as he sped by, yet his face and name remain a spectre in my memory. I have often wondered whether the "key" still jangles in his pocket and whether the "Son of God" whose "return" he tried so persistently to expedite would embrace him as a disciple. Would not the Galilean bow his head over the mass grave in Grinkishok and black serfs in Johannesburg locations whose allegedly sacrilegious portrait of a black Christ was banned from their apartheid churches?

I have never doubted the sincerity of men who stake their lives, and the lives of others, on the teachings *about*, rather than the teachings *of*, Jesus. Despite the opposition of Thomas Aquinas and others to enforced baptism, Torquemada had heretics and lapsed converts torn asunder limb from limb for their own good, that they might be persuaded to rank an eternity of heavenly bliss over the shoddy, fleeting tinsel of an hour on earth. It is the implicit insolence and insensitivity that astound me. The Seminarian went beyond the distortion of Jesus into a montrous Moloch devouring children – to the distortion of Jewish scripture for evidence. He appropriated the Hebrew Bible, whose language he cannot, and whose spirit he dare not, comprehend, to prove that a Hebrew man-god appointed an Austrian house-painter turned demigod to slaughter Jewish babies. Given the power, that young acolyte of the Kingdom could become an Inquisitor, earnest, dedicated, even nettled by pity for the Jew's ignorance and pride – but infants would be bashed and countless lives blasted for the King's coronation.

When Moses reached the end of his days, on Mount Nebo, his burial place was a mystery. In fact, the Bible commented that no one knows his sepulchre to this day. The old rabbis explained the secrecy as a precaution taken by God, who feared that the Children of Israel might misshape the grave of Moses into a shrine and turn away from monotheistic rectitude to supplicate their hero, instead of Him alone.

There is another answer to the blank page about Moses' grave. Despite *Kaddish*-Jews who never enter a synagogue save to mourn their dead, Jewish love of life could not condone the rotating of religion around death. It is through the process of abundant living that the Divine Will and tenderness may be experienced and known – not through a derivative, preliminary earth journey enfleshed with meaning solely by the Father's offering of His only-begotten son.

Endless theological debate has stormed around the concept of Messiah. Was Jesus the Redeemer foretold by Hebrew prophecy? Did Jesus deem himself its fulfilment? Why did his own kin and people reject him? What does the Scriptural text really say? How can Biblical exegesis and historical research be marshalled adequately and without bias? Expeditions into philological obscurities and speculation about the supernatural promise less, to me, than certain seminal intuitions with which I was born. My reply to these queries is simple.

The Kingdom of God is of this realm, not the next. It will be established not by a super-terrestrial authority divinely delegated to order the worlds, to destroy sin and the Law which created it, but by the Messianic spirit God transmitted to all men, who must collaborate to enthrone Him by the prior enthronement of love, justice, and peace. The Messiah was not thrust into history from God's throne; the Messianic Era will be thrust forward out of history from man's heart. Our retrogressive world all too grimly testifies that such a time has not arrived. It may never arrive. Perhaps by its very nature redemption is always a state of becoming rather than of being.

Like his contemporaries fevered by the dream of national liberation from Rome, Jesus believed that a time of great trouble would precede and herald deliverance; he shaped Jewish misery into assurance of the Kingdom – near, ripe, ready in the outstretched hand of God. During the period of cataclysmic transition, society can anticipate the new world by dispensing with the ties that bind to the old; therefore, "sell whatsoever thou hast and give to the poor." Classmates at the University of Chicago, where I studied the life of Jesus under Shirley Jackson Case, a noted liberal scholar, insisted that Jesus was the founder of pure communism.

Undoubtedly, Jesus did tender acknowledgement to a Kingdom "not of this world." In the central body of his teachings, however, the Lord's Prayer, the Sermon on the Mount, the parables, Jesus revealed himself to be a lover of this life, of the good things to be found in it, and of the moral principles necessary for their universal attainment. He did not excite himself about heaven.

The furniture of heaven and the temperature of hell are antiquated mediaevalisms, no more relevant to life than their childishly naïve, stratified location on the map of the Middle Ages. Central in my mind lies embedded the peremptory verdict of the noted Orthodox Christian scholar, Nicholas Berdyaev, that the doctrine of endless punishment in hell is sadism. The sadism has proliferated ad infinitum and ad nauseam in the subconscious heritage of Christian civilization, and has polluted the wells of its mercy. If God Himself tortures the unbeliever and evil-doer in the next world, an obstacle is removed from the savage human drive to visit pain on others in this world.

Ancient authors did not trouble themselves with logical, historical, or textual accuracy. Those who contributed to the anthology canonized and compiled in the New Testament bequeathed enough inconsistencies and vagueness to puzzle anyone in search of truth. One conclusion, however, seems unchallengeable. There is nothing to buttress the contention that the man of sorrows my heart called brother on the stained-glass windows in Bellaire wanted any human being to writhe in an everlasting hell because of disbelief in his divinity.

Young Christians on group visits to Holy Blossom often revealed, privately, a cleavage between their idealistic resolve to make Jesus the lodestar of life, on the one hand, and theological indoctrination, on the other. The highway they sought to a Christocentric career was cluttered with supernaturalism and tales of miracles. They could walk more firmly with Jesus if they were not encumbered with undigestible dogmas.

The delicate personal dilemma presented by these earnest young people was sacrosanct. I never allowed myself polemic with Christian clergy or laymen concerning the rational legitimacy of their faith, be they present or absent. Exploitation of youth-group visits encouraged by their ministers would be unforgivable. Such troublings of conscience led me rather to clarify my own view of the Nazarene's teaching.

In bull sessions with a circle of young guests after the larger group had dispersed, I underscored one conviction I could not escape sharing with them: Jesus often felt under his sandalled feet the tremor and travail of the millennial Kingdom in the placenta of time. It was then that he forsook his Hebraic tradition and training, lifted his head into a light that never was on sea or land, and admonished his hearers to turn the other cheek and sell all they had and give it to the poor.

Judaism would not take its feet off the ground and soar into such airy perfectionism – and for the long pull, its pragmatic ethic is irreplaceable. By the test of practicality, universal love seems beyond the clouds. Yet the compassionate aura wherein the Galilean strode among men has become for our H-bomb age the only light which can lure mankind from the valley of self-destruction. "Love thy neighbour. . . ." What Jews articulated twenty-five centuries ago in Leviticus, and the Jew of Nazareth confirmed and emphasized six centuries later, has become in the suicidal age of nuclear weaponry the quintessential formula for the future of humanity.

I am frequently asked to define the Jewish attitude toward Jesus. There *is* none. No individual rabbi's opinion may be used as the norm. Categorical and undeviating denial of the Nazarene's divine status is the one common denominator for "basic Judaism."

Rabbis hypersensitive or oriented in the past recall the compulsory mediaeval court debates on doctrine in which anything said by a Jew about Jesus was turned, with dire consequences premeditated by king and bishop, against the entire community. If the Jewish spokesman praised Jesus, he was expected to shepherd his flock to baptismal waters, whereas disapproval risked the auto-da-fé. Most Orthodox rabbinical leaders avoid the subject, in the belief that nothing is gained by discussing it. On occasion, a militant voice among them bitterly resents public pronouncements on Jesus by a Reform Rabbi, who may be automatically accused of trifling with apostasy. A generation ago, Rabbi Stephen S. Wise of New York brought a hurricane of censure on his head by proposing that Jesus be envisaged as a teacher in the spiritual lineage of the prophets. On the other hand, a Jewish layman's view of Jesus, if privately expressed, can be expected to traverse a wide gamut, from denying even his historical existence to acclaiming him everything but God.

"Jesus of Nazareth is a myth fashioned by the writers of the New Testament," a German scholar concluded in 1835, and a wide-ranging school of thought elaborated the thesis. No unmistakable reference to him can be encountered in Greek, Roman, or Jewish writings of his century or shortly thereafter. Philo, a contemporary Alexandrian Jewish philosopher who wrote profusely on a multitude of themes, denies a word to Jesus; Justus of Tiberias, who dwelt near Capernaum during the Nazarene's activity in that region, evidently caught no rumour of his presence; Josephus, who plunged a prolific pen into the events of the Galilean's day, knew him not, a few casual lines about the death of Jesus being generally discredited as later interpolations.

The Talmud's reliability for source material has been reduced by severe, centuries-long Church censorship; allusions to Jesus may have been deleted. The hostile scrutiny of both sceptre and mitre alarmed Poland's Jews to such a degree that their own Assembly of Elders in 1631 enjoined communities to refrain from publishing any word which might be construed as indicative of interest in Jesus. In the vast rabbinic writings, one finds only sparse, recondite remnants of possible allusions. According to scholars of solid repute, Christian literature surely yields no impartial testimony on the Jewish attitude toward him.

Other students of the problem, among them erudite Jewish intellects like Joseph Klausner of Hebrew University, accepted as authentic the rare references sprinkled throughout the Talmud, and called attention to circumstances which reduce the significance of their paucity. The Talmud – a stupendous compilation – contains not even the name of Judah Maccabee; Judea's rebellion against Rome and the chaotic turmoil terminating in the destruction of Jerusalem and Jewish sovereignty in the first Christian century may have overshadowed the tenebrous emergence of the man from Nazareth; manuscripts relating to him could have been lost among the documents scattered during that storm-tossed and catastrophic period. Finally, the ethical preachment and conduct of Jesus were so obviously in keeping with common Jewish standards that there was nothing unusual to report. And numerous "redeemers of oppressed Israel" went their way, often to Roman crucifixion, in that period of tyranny and terror. In any case, current Hebrew-Aramaic literature offers no unimpeachable witness that Jesus, during his lifetime, made a deep impression on the Jewish people.

The hassle over Jesus' historicity is academic and secondary; I have stopped pondering about it. The wonder and reverential awe he aroused in me years ago, when I went to Mass with Tim Fahey, are not extinguished. Whether as a historical, once-existent person, a symbol, a mere name, or a deity who grants redemptive grace, he sways almost half the world. The rest is important solely for weighty tomes of research.

In threading my own course through the maze of fact and fancy in which the Nazarene is entangled, I have been guided by the interconnection of two words: "Jesus" and "Christ." Only the very liberal Christian separates them; a Jew may not ever link them into one.

"Jesus" is a proper name, the Greek for the Hebrew "Joshua." It denotes a certain personality, living about 1900 years ago in Palestine, whose activity is reported in the first three books of the New Testament, or Synoptic Gospels. If the French writer Renan is to be believed, Jesus strongly resisted the idea that he incarnated God.

"Christ," on the other hand, derives from the Greek word for Saviour. It means essentially the same as the Hebrew word "Messiah." This Christ, for Christians, is God who descended from heaven to take the form of man and die for the sins of man.

Jesus was a human creature who served humanity by his life; Christ has been made into a deity who saved humanity by his death. Jesus attempted to transform his visible world into a kingdom of God; Christ was to win for men a future paradise beyond the skies. Jesus uttered words of wisdom and beauty for all mankind; Christ is the central dogma of a specific group. Jesus was a man who walked and breathed and suffered agony; Christ is an idea fashioned from the adoration of those who followed him. Jesus is human, but in all probability historical; Christ is divine, but his viability is subject to honest disagreement. Dean Inge, whose profound and perceptive intellectual integrity shone forth from St. Paul's and lifted my Seminary years above paradigms and *pilpulism*, intimated, I recall, that the Jesus of the Synoptic Gospels is historical but not God, while the Christ of St. John is divine but not historical.

How did Jesus become Christ? While Jesus lived, ardent followers rejoiced in the lambent aura of the eagerly awaited Messiah of Hebrew prophecy which glowed about his head. Furthermore, some of the Jewish populace fretted under the rule of Torah. They sought a humanized faith that would inflame the heart and release the intellect.

After the crucifixion, disciples criss-crossed Palestine making converts in his name and spreading the gospel. As the years passed, miraculous tales of supernatural deeds and resurrection accumulated around his memory. A growing assortment of marvellous healings, control over demons, raising the dead, was handed on from person to person, from generation to generation. At last literate disciples began to systematize these stories in writing. The New Testament was the final result, compiled, according to scholars, at least a century after the birth of Jesus.

The first Christians were Jews. The fledgling religion drew its traditions from the synagogue. Not until two hundred years after

Jesus were Judaism and Christianity finally sundered.

The mother faith Judaism and the daughter Christianity could not avoid competition for the conquest of the Roman-pagan world. Judaism had been winning converts steadily. In those days Israel welcomed proselytes, and the highest circles of Rome's aristocracy were penetrated by the rational spirituality of the Jewish religion and its freedom from the noxious self-indulgence of heathenism. But under the stimulus of the vision-consumed missionary and preacher, Saul of Tarsus, Christianity gradually swept the field and began to look askance at its progenitor.

The Pauline system of salvation opened a door, hitherto closed, for the pagan Greeks into the Holy of Holies – without the admission-card of circumcision and obedience to burdensome and sternly enforced restrictions. Jews also could unloose themselves from the yoke, simply by baring their breast to the Saviour, who would wash them whiter than atonement on Yom Kippur in the Temple.

Whereas the religion of Jesus was a way of life, it became through Christ a mode of thought. Under the influence of the Greek bent for speculation, the energy of the early church for four centuries spent itself not in serving Jesus, but in defining Christ – although Jesus was neither a Greek philosopher nor a mediaeval metaphysician. I think he would have pilloried many of the abstruse ideological artifacts attributed to him more angrily than he denounced the squabbles of the Scribes and the punctilious pedantry of the Pharisees.

Jesus was a radical; he probed to the roots of the human tragedy with a scalpel wielded by his own hand, at the direction of his own mind. Conservatism has appropriated him, but while he lived conservatism set itself against him. It was the questing and restive who flocked to hear his message.

Paul, however, diverted the iconoclastic social passion of Jesus into a system of belief, a man whose pristine Judaic teachings all could follow into a god whom only theologians could comprehend. Christianity before Paul was a Hebraic endeavour to refashion a crumbling world. After him, it became a sesame to heaven, purporting to winnow the saved from the damned. Discarding the Nazarene's searching out of the meek and the lowly, the organized church sometimes made his name a flag under which to capture the seats of the mighty. What Christ was became litany in every church; what Jesus taught lay smothered under the thick velvet and embroidery of majestic ritual.

The Old Testament was less than two centuries old at the birth of Jesus; its saga was bringing balm and guidance to Jews throughout the Mediterranean basin. Jesus drew deep from its fountain of living waters.

In a little Ontario town a pastor, somewhat patronizingly, introduced me to a Rotary Club audience by emphasizing that Christianity gave "Love thy neighbour as thyself" to the world, thus deviating from Jesus, who quoted it from the Jewish Bible and declared: "On this commandment hangs all the law and the prophets." Jesus did not intend to forsake Judaism. The Book of Matthew states explicitly that he came not to destroy the Law but to fulfil it. Centuries before Jesus, Amos denounced those who grind the poor. Long before the Nazarene stepped forth from the hills of Galilee, Jeremiah warned the Jews that their temple worship and superficial piety would not deliver them. Generations before Jesus dared the stainless to cast the first stone, Hosea discerned God's forgiveness of sin in his own solicitude for a wayward wife. When Jesus scoffed at the unction of the priests, it was in the spirit of Elijah at Ahab's Court. He blessed the peacemakers as postlude to Isaiah, who glorified peace, the greatest of blessings.

Was Jesus in the line of the Hebrew prophets? He spoke in parables, he suffered under the callousness of the mighty, he added a fresh nuance and meter to the swelling cadence of Judaism's plea for man. He did *not* speak in the name of the Lord, or Torah, or even angelic intermediaries (like the late minor prophets, such as Zachariah); he spoke for himself: "But *I* say unto you." His insight may have been humane and wise; it was *not* Torah and the God of Israel, from whom all truth and teaching went forth to man. Even in the throes of inspiration, a Hebrew prophet never forgets whence he derived it!

The attitude of modern Jews? Mine? Jesus we need not accept, he having been born to us; Christ the god we cannot and will not accept. His ethics, meanwhile, are a portion of Israel's writings – valid and mandatory in the measure of their worth for man's well-being.

The Nazarene was a Jew in birth, spirit, and loyalty. He shared the hunger of his subjected people for national independence. To Judaism he gave a supremely gifted and sensitive individual's expression – but it remained Judaism, not the pomp of Rome and her Latinized gods in the south, Germanic epics and festivals in the north, or hypostasized power drives anywhere.

Compassion, grace, courage! Jesus embodied them, but they are the birthright of everyone, since the upward thrust toward self-perfection moves among and through mankind. All of us bear a cross on Calvary, under sentence of pain; some are crucified, not exceptionally by those they love. Jesus epitomized tragedy, and triumph in defeat – a biography, written large, of man.

In a bird's-eye review of history, one may mark a succession of crossroads. At each one, stands a Jew designating a way, resubstantiating or reinvigorating an old faith for the new time. The heritage of the Middle Ages was dissolving; Baruch Spinoza ignited the waning torch of an anaemic Judaism with a spark that heralded the advent of modern science. Industrial convulsion brought the birth pangs of capitalism; Karl Marx, albeit with contempt for the Jewish faith of faithless parents, and with a cenobite's compulsive attention to worldly materialism, lucubrated a proletarian society. When Darwinism shattered precious illusions of human uniqueness, Henri Bergson's genius vitalized the automaton of evolution with a mystic *élan*. The irrationality of supposedly civilized man began to loom dark on the radar screen of tomorrow; Sigmund Freud then charted the jungle growth of the subconscious and a dim outline of the road to sanity. The advancing frontier of knowledge confronted humanity with a robotized, deterministic universe; for such an encounter, Albert Einstein elevated man's poetic vision to an order which may presage purpose. . . . That Jewish way-showing began almost twenty centuries ago; above the rank odour of Rome's decay and the clanking of the chains of the subjugated, Jesus fanned the lamp of Torah with his own breath – by fulfilling himself as man.

The simple-complex child of the Galilean heights brought to his beloved people in the plains, and finally in Jerusalem, a reverence for human life. In my perspective, that was his gospel. He accepted life with a whole heart. Jesus walked among men eating and drinking, with courtesy and cheerfulness, with noble talk and warmth, in a sequence of events pegged by the sacrament of hospitality to wedding-supper and wine and festivals and celebration of a son's return.

The Kingdom of God itself he saw as a great banquet made by guests who must consent to come, built here "on earth as in heaven." Because he had regard for mankind, he spun the central core of his teaching into a road toward life more abundant. The shrewdness of his insight into moral brittleness – illustrated by the chat with the woman of Samaria – grew from a sophistication impossible for one buffered by a tough hide against the elusive subtlety of the human voyager. He did not admire hypocrisy even when it vaunted the conventional garb of a saint, or respectability which preserves itself by shying away from the net of involvement. Perhaps, in displaying protective and defiant tenderness toward Mary of Magdala, he wished to hint that the sin born of broad-bosomed largesse and of the unrelenting river of joy can more easily be forgiven.

Loving life, he loved the source of life. Indeed, his love, and the love he attributed to God, were so immoderately generous that he questioned the patriot's zeal, the impermeable assurance of religious formalists and family imperialism, thus risking the label: a danger to the public weal. It did not astonish or sour him that men rejoiced when he cured their bodies and reviled him when he ministered to their souls. And in the parable of the talents he taught that fear of living cannot ever be fealty to God, who lavishly proffers

His children life to be quaffed in bold, deep draughts from a brimming cup.

Did he promise the earth to the flabby, passionless and submissive? Perhaps the English word "meek" does not adequately convey his meaning. Certainly he himself was not a lamb in meekness, though subsequent Fathers of the Church made him the Lamb of Sacrifice. Instead, he had the tenseness of leashed passion and could become incandescent with choleric wrath at wrong.

Did he perform miracles? I do not know. In any case, he did not need them to shore up his challenge to love God with wanton self-surrender and one's neighbour as one's self.

Did he vouchsafe blessing to the "poor in spirit" or to the "poor"? Both illumine the Synoptic Gospels, one in Matthew, the other in Luke. I prefer to believe he blessed the poor. Had his followers quoted the single word and ignored the rest, the surge of cassock to throne might have been aborted before it got a start, and vastly different terminology would be required for the history of the church.

Did he arise from the sepulchre on the third day? I do not know. Resurrection can be accomplished again and again, through generations too many for counting, by rebirth within men's hearts through his mercy, which halted at no border, and by the transsubstantiation into political reality of his presence, so that a world black with avarice and rapacity and red with the H-bomb harbinger of bloodshed may yet be won back to life.

In my favourite New Testament story, Philip encountered Nathanael, and told him the Messiah had been found, at last, whom Moses and the prophets had ordained: Jesus, of Nazareth, son of Joseph. Nathanael raised his eyebrows. "Can any good thing come out of Nazareth?"

The episode is casually related – and in no need of commentary. Nazareth was a village not well-regarded, clinging to a cleft in the Galilean hills. A Nazarene might have been Palestine's yokel, a hill-billy. Yet, from that unlikely place, there issued a man who gazed out with super-humane eyes in a little town on the Ohio River from a haloed portrait on a wall to the Diggitys of the world, and to a skinny Jewish moppet already saddened by the evidence of human suffering.

The Galilean's homespun wisdom was the standard equipment of moralists in the early childhood of mankind, as it was the standard equipment of Marcus Aurelius, Epictetus, Buddha, Confucius, and of every religion with its own version of the Golden Rule.

Despite these homilies, our civilization hobbles in a wilderness of feral greed. It would be pretentious to claim that all the teachings of Jesus would in themselves establish Utopia.

Can his fowls of the air and lilies of the field solve the problem of unemployment, or the loaves and fishes feed the hordes of undernourished, or the camel and the needle's eye dislodge the rich from the backs of the poor?

I am not deluded about the immediate, pragmatic efficacy of Jesus to change external conditions. He speaks to my heart as one who dared to love life with a great tenderness. It is the spirit manifested in his living that lifts my own. I call him brother, not only because of his Jewish birth, but because I want to share his courage and compassion. The church has transcendentalized, and monopolized, him long enough!

I Am for the Underdog

THIRTY cents an hour, an eleven-hour day, highest rate in history for unskilled labour, was my summer wage at the Wheeling Steel Corporation plant across the river in Benwood. We had entered the World War, Wheeling Steel was supplying army-camp tubes, I needed money for college. A fair exchange, I thought, and patriotic!

The schedule was hard and fast. My mother's whispered "Abeleh" and her face bending over me at 5:15 a.m.; quick-step down to the ferryboat; glum minutes on the deck, measuring through heavy eyelids the parabolic squirts of tobacco juice and feeling my stomach somersault when they plopped on the floor; the labour-gang muster in front of the foreman's shack at 6:15 a.m.; twenty minutes for wolfing jelly-and-peanut-butter sandwiches and an apple; the welcome whistle at 5:50 p.m.; the bone-weary trip home, a scrubbing-bout at the kitchen sink, and repressed anxiety in my mother's glance, since I was far from husky.

Tom Knox, the bandy-legged gang boss, squatted in clouds of smoke on a railroad plank. His job was to keep the gang busy loading pig-iron, barrowing cans of black paint, derusting machinery, unloading grease buckets, digging ditches and filling them up again.

One day we were put to mixing concrete. The 90-degree temperature aggravated the smell of grease and whirr of machines; rivulets of sweat ran down my face to join the hosed water we caught with shovels and dashed on the cement and gravel, thereby adding salt to the powder that billowed from the cement and stung my eyes. I unbent my back, let my pounding chest slump into the shovel handle, and twisted my neck towards Black Mose, who always manoeuvred himself to a post where he could teach me tricks – like going through motions without actually expending energy. Mose threw me a sidelong glance. I spied his anxious white eyeballs through the filmy wet haze of my own.

Then my feet dragged me to the boss. "I guess I'll have to quit, Mr. Knox." After a quizzical flicker of a smile, he resumed his puffing. My fingers loosened their grip, the shovel clattered to the floor, and I groped to the ferry.

It was Friday afternoon. I surprised Mom stuffing the Sabbath fish, but she seemed to know. A faintly visible knot in her jaw suggested the gritting of teeth. "Don't worry, Abeleh, you'll get something else." I said nothing.

The next Monday I went for my pay envelope. The plant superintendent was sitting at his desk. "What's the matter, Jew-boy?" I was a curiosity – the only Jew who ever worked on the labour gang.

"That cement. Too much for me."

"Yeah? Well, Jew-boy, yuh shouldn'ta told me yuh wanted just a summer job. I woulda put yuh on for trainin' operatin' a crane.

But hell, ya gotta get to college. Show up tomorra; yuh kin sweep up waste. How's that?"

I wasn't sure whether his booming voice hid mockery or concern. But I couldn't afford a thin skin. "Thanks, Mr. Johnson, very much. I'll be here."

"Sweeping up waste" meant gathering into piles the steel flakes pared from pipe by the threading-wheels. The broom was also of heavy metal, the parings got soaked with dripping oil and the mounds had to be trundled over railway tracks.

Prior to the grown-up era of regular, salaried employment, I had understudied my brothers in back alleys and drunk hangouts, on trash dumps and the porches of whispered-about ladies, picking up empty beer and whisky bottles for resale at a cent a piece.

That opportunity for profit strained my friendship with Jim Diggity, whose dad was a glass-blower. I once saw Big Jim at work, when I tagged along after Little Jim, delivering a lunch basket and a pail of beer. There he stood at the door of a huge furnace, shirtless, glistening and deep-red, a long thin tube in his mouth, while a blob of something that shimmered like spring water expanded under his steady breath into an iridescent shell, which he caressed with a paddle into the shape of a gas lamp. No sooner was the new-born bowl adroitly placed on a rack for cooling than he fished out another blob from the furnace.

"Now d'ya see how hard my pop has to work? And sometimes his lungs ain't so good, my mom says. The plant makes bottles too! And you go pickin' up and sellin' 'em, so's my pop won't have work." He crooked a finger under my nose. "Abie, you sheeny, I'm gonna smash every bottle I see before ya gits 'em!"

Being put out of work was the daily dread of every dad I knew. And the hollowness of Big Jim's cheeks haunted me; after seeing the school slides about tuberculosis, I was sure he had it. And I liked him, because he always rumpled my hair.

We also scrounged for junk, thus competing with the bearded scholars of Agudas Ahim on their rickety wagons. Benny and Maxie Kolitzky's father had a scrap-iron yard, with a giant crusher that pressed broken engine parts into a thin plate. With their collaboration, and sundry small fry, we would load a plate on a handcart and lug the whole shebang to Jake Schwartz, a rival junk-dealer, who never showed the Kolitzky lads a sign of recognition. At my father's funeral Jake assured me over a reminiscing cup of tea that he didn't want to hurt their feelings. After Bar-Mitzvah, when I, not my dad, would be held responsible for my sins, I felt a spasm of guilt for the hi-jack operation, all the more reprehensible because Jake was old man Kolitzky's competitor, buying pilfered scrap at bargain rates.

On weekdays the Wheeling papers were delivered by boys on a route. Sunday morning offered an open market. The Feinberg boys had lusty voices; our hawking became a Bellaire institution, and neither rain, snow, dogs, frost, sleet, nor the muscular Larabees, who peppered me with mud for intrusion into their bailiwick, was a deterrent, although I often had to wring my stockings dry, and numb fingers lost part of my stock-in-trade to the wintry wind.

There was a miscellany of intermittent commercial projects. We sold pawpaws, bouquets of laboriously picked violets, sweet anise dug from the glens. We carried baggage from the three railroad depots. On an investment of glasses from the kitchen cupboard, and artificial lemon, vanilla, and chocolate flavouring or a jar of Mom's jam, and an empty fruit crate, a cake of ice, and a fifty-cent shaver, I sold iceballs. I "contracted" with tradesmen to supply boy-power for the distribution of sales circulars under every door in town, and suffered occasional deficits when an irate haberdasher found a few hundred thrown into a sewer by one of my "hired hands." On seeing a *Saturday Evening Post* picture of an air-brake bicycle to be won with subscriptions, I knocked at doors until scared off, forever, by housewife scowls and slams.

I took orders from the uptown Reform Jews for their brand of *matzot** at Passover. They would not eat our orthodox kind because it was thick and hard to digest; we would not eat theirs because it was not strictly kosher.

The profit from these enterprises was given to Mom for our

* Unleavened bread.

clothes. When business thrived, we cajoled pennies out of the maternal exchequer for an evening ice-cream party, a genuine big-league baseball, a surreptitious cream puff from the tantalizing non-kosher bake shop, or a pocketknife for a game of mumbledy-peg, where victory depended on the span from the wooden floor to the handle of a blade stuck there by a flip of the forefinger.

My regular employee repertory embraced every job in town: an Adams Express Company pre-Christmas delivery wagon; the enamel factory where I packed tea kettles in throat-tickling straw; the cut-rate grocery store after school and on Saturdays (7 a.m. to 11 p.m. for $1.75); the Fashion Centre, where I fitted belts to beer-inflated middles, levis to hay-chewing farmers, and eight-dollar silk-stripe shirts to coal-miners during the war boom; the Made-to-Order Factory-to-You Men's Suit Store, whose manager taught me how to measure a man for tailoring, at $3.50 a week, while he played poker in the smokeshop; the Carnegie Steel Works, from whose blast-furnace I carried a test bar to the laboratory, so that no ingots would be sent through the blooming-mill until the chemist certified the correct content of manganese and alloys.

After it had been decided I would go to college, Mom insisted that my earnings would be earmarked for tuition. My sister Birdie, who everybody said was the best secretary in town, stood up to my father almost harshly at times, dared to appear quarrelsome in a forlorn effort to change the pattern that strapped my brothers to factory bench and shop counter before they had completed even the primary grades, and vowed that at least one of us would "leave this town and make something of himself."

During the first college years I accepted an initial modest loan from the Reform Temple on the urgent plea of the Marxes, who had visions of me as a great rabbi because of my "fame" as an orator. During Christmas and Easter vacations I had rush-season jobs in retail stores. While at college in Cincinnati I taught Sunday School. Weekday employment was impossible, because I took two full academic courses: the University of Cincinnati every morning and Hebrew Union College in late afternoon. My freshman domicile was a series of four drab attics at twenty-two dollars a month for room and board with sandwich lunch, and my basic wardrobe unmatched second-hand coat and pants, pressed under the mattress.

At the time I left for college the Feinbergs resided on Union Street, only several yards from the stone pier, under the cinders and soot of roaring trains. The filing-cabinet, as I often called it, had no windows on the sides; it started at a door leading from the brick sidewalk to my father's workshop and down a long narrow hall to the kitchen and patchwork chicken coop in the backyard, past an uncarpeted wooden stairway. The second floor had four sleeping rooms: one in the rear overlooking the alley, a front parlour with a day bed, and between them two rooms into which air and light could be admitted only through a rope-drawn skylight. We kids often slept three in a bed, partners shifting by sex and age.

The parlour was distinguished by three proud possessions: a hand-cranked record-player with "Aloha," a Hawaiian disk I never tired of; a stereopticon with slides of foreign lands; a framed scroll certifying that my staunchly Republican father had donated to the Memorial Fund for President McKinley.

An outdoor one-holer was often fouled by drunkards. Heating depended on a kitchen stove and two upstairs coal grates, clothes storage on cupboards and a coat-rack, cleanliness, strictly enforced, on a portable rubber bathtub, and good manners at the kitchen table, where we all ate together, on our own native refinement, in the absence of serviettes, a maid, fancy china, and pleasing individual variations in the menu. Mom met complaints with the simple declaration that all we had to eat was there on the table.

Our Union Street address offered more diversion than the opulent clipped-hedge gardens on Gravel Hill where the rich resided. A livery stable owned by a friendly neighbour provided the pungent smell of urine-soaked straw, manure piles alive with fishing-worms, the chance to hitch up a horse, cast-off horseshoes for pitching-tournaments, and huge rats shaken out of a wire trap into the leaping jaws of Rex, the owner's bulldog. A nearby Italian confectioner who said I looked "Napolitano" filled our kitchen bowl on steamy

August nights with bargain-price ice cream crowned by bananas and walnuts soaked in syrup. The saloon next door gave us the sound of lusty singing, the sight of beribboned little girls fetching dad's daily bucket of foamy beer, and the stink of lousy, bladder-debilitated clients reeling to the gutter, often leaving for salvage shiny silver coins that rolled from their pockets.

Despite these contiguous distractions, only the river and hills and the hope of college lifted me from a growing sense of dead-end futility. One Jewish "greenhorn" after another came to Bellaire, slaved night and day in a cut-throat ragshop or tiny clothing-store and bought a house on Gravel Hill. Somehow, the Feinbergs stayed below the Bridge, glad to get jobs in factories.

My father was chairman of *hahnosas orhim.** Its combined operating and sinking fund consisted of whatever portion of the twenty-five-cents-a-month tax he could collect by personal solicitation of the members of Agudas Ahim and the disdained but gilded *Deitschen.*† Sometimes the entire brood of an enfeebled New York sweatshop worker on his way to Colorado for a tuberculosis cure would drag their bundles off a B. & O. train, penniless and stranded. They might need maintenance for a week; the usual allotment was a meal, a night's lodging and a "good riddance" ticket to Columbus. In the 1907 panic, two or three derelicts cast their shadows on our doorstep every day. Some were hearty, pompous, professional beggars who berated Pop for the lumpy mattress. Most were the footsore refuse of the industry marts in the Eastern ghettos. One of them I never forgot. Wisps of straw announced that he had spent the night in a boxcar, his hand trembled over a can of sardines, the doglike gratitude in his eyes troubled my sleep.

A long coal-mine strike brought chalk-pale Polish, Italian, and Slovak kids to our door. Mom always invited them in to sit at the table. I often followed a motley group from our kitchen, intently watching them store the handouts in a basket.

Although I was born in an alley house farther downtown in the low-lying flood area, it was on Union Street that I got measles,

* Welcome of strangers. † German Jews.

chicken pox, diphtheria, and semi-annual grippe, and skipped sixth grade, and scrawled points for high-school debates and came home from college to work during vacations. Even after we moved a few blocks inland from the river and freightyards to a half-house with porch and bathroom, Union Street remained my immovable, permanent observation point on social issues. To this day it is gadfly to my conscience.

It would be evasive to deny that the accoutrements of a professional career have progressively widened the gap between Union Street and Old Forest Hill Road. A ramshackle outhouse in the alley is some distance removed from three inside bathrooms and a first-floor toilet; I was persuaded that two family cars were not a luxury before the corneal scar dissuaded me from driving; the fondly recalled whisky bottles that added pennies to my college-tuition cache merely enhance the pride I take in Jonathan's medical-school record and Sarah Jane's performance at Smith College.

The psychological displacement, nevertheless, has not kept pace with the material change. I shall never learn to treat any servant anywhere as other than a human being often better than I; an expensive tailor-made suit would be uncongenial to my bones; platters of food destined for the garbage can vitiate my palate's savour; an Italian knife-sharpener's tinkling bell sends me kitchenward for cutlery that will help him scrounge a free man's livelihood; I rejoice in every corner grocery still eluding the supermarket's maw; every little-man crusade I have no time for and every mendicant I turn away for lack of trust or patience harries my conscience.

Thick blankets of eiderdown swathe my senses against the presence and plaint of the deprived. The trouble is, I am unable to sleep – not because I want to hear the voice of human need, but because Union Street won't let me alone.

This stubborn awareness has intruded at incongruous moments. When the Governor General of Canada received me in his Ottawa residence, I remembered that my first vote in an American presidential election went to the Socialist Eugene V. Debs who, in addressing the court which jailed him for incitement against conscription, said: "While there is a lower class, I am in it; while there is a soul in prison, I am not free. . . ." At a dinner for Her Majesty the Queen I mumbled into the royal china: "What is the son of Nissen Nisselewicz doing here?" only to repeat, in a flash, the prayer of memorial I recited in August 1927, a few minutes after the execution of Nicolo Sacco and Bartolomeo Vanzetti: "They were men of true grandeur and nobility. . . ." On the day my secretary phoned that a magazine poll had named me one of Canada's seven greatest preachers, I danced a jig, until a warning to sermonizers by a Hasidic rabbi jogged my memory: "Take care of your own soul and of another man's body, not of your body and another man's soul."

The Talmud tells us: "Before a man eats and drinks, he has two hearts; he feels his own hunger and another's. After he eats and drinks, he has only one, namely his own – and it is concerned with comfort." I eat and drink, and I want comfort. But peace of mind by pap cannot commend itself to me. If I want that, I might obtain better results from the chemical compound lysergic acid diethylamide tartrate, which produces fantasies, than from Norman Vincent Peale's cataleptic headache powders or Father Sheen's syrupy supernaturalism, both guaranteed not to elevate the blood pressure, agitate the colon, or activate the social conscience.

It would be nice to cozy up to "The Man Upstairs" and blare dithyrambs about the revival of religion, as political strategy against "atheistic Communism"; the healing power of God, as a propaganda item in the cold war; and the commercialized repentance of political deviates, as testimonial to the transforming pro-capitalist bias of the Divine. When faith becomes fashionable and church-going patriotic, religion becomes suspect. The leap of faith may be merely a jump on the bandwagon.

For me, the nexus with mankind is not sympathy for, but empathy with, the underdog. I cannot escape. Have I always really manned the barricade of social justice? Past withdrawals from it leave me no illusions. One vivid incident particularly I shall never be able to erase from my mind.

It all began at an ordinary Friday Evening Sabbath Service when I counted a bare dozen in the audience and revolted at wasting a meticulously written sermon and scooped up my notes and took off without a word prepared in advance, on a subject that flashed then and there into my mind. I was astonished by the results. The saving remnant of loyal temple-goers fluttered about me in a cavalcade of congratulations.

On thinking about it, the reason seemed very clear. When I sat down deliberately to write, I was tethered by distinctions in meaning, by niceties of logic, and by the rope of the unknowable. Unwritten spontaneity gave me wings. The prescription was easy: after a massive injection of self-confidence, the ghost of an outline, index cards for appropriate allusions, a smattering of poetry, and some redolent metaphors.

Then the pastor of the Methodist Episcopal Church invited me to preach at a Sunday Service. My congregation was thrilled; I was delighted. The élite Episcopal parish would expect something scholarly, couched in classic mould – and no wandering. Extemporaneity would be dangerous. I must be cautious. I decided to cast about for a subject and write out every word.

On Thanksgiving Day, my musings were interrupted by the steady clomp of many feet on the pavement. Hurrying outdoors, I realized what was in process: a mass assembly of textile-workers who had gone on strike. I started to amble down to the square for a look. From several blocks away I could hear the sound of shouting and, quickening my pace, I reached the square in time to see uniformed men swinging clubs, men and women being scattered, and an ambulance driving up – and to vomit into the gutter.

Still half nauseated, I hastened home and stretched out on the chesterfield in my study, a prey to a chaos of images: newspaper headlines about "Bolshevik agitators," the Chamber of Commerce summons to defend the "American Heritage," businessmen in my congregation gesticulating that conditions at the mill where the spinners worked and in the swampland where they lived were not bad at all. The final fantasy before I dozed off was a fragment from a long-forgotten trauma which floated up out of the depths. It was Tim Fahey's father, a mine-worker, lying prone and broken on a Bellaire street where strike-breakers had left him after they broke up a meeting called to organize a union. Early next day I telephoned the Methodist Episcopal pastor. My subject would be "Textile Profits, Hebrew Prophets, and the Social Duty of Church and Synagogue."

The next afternoon, when Harold Burman wrapped his arm around my shoulder after a committee luncheon and asked me to drop in at his office, I responded with alacrity. He was president of the congregation – affable, progressive, high-minded – and had proved himself a friend, opening doors and smoothing out kinks, with keen perception of a rabbi's special problems. The moment I entered his inner sanctum and felt my heels sink into a thick sky-blue rug, Harold was already setting an armchair down in front of a broad desk. Within a minute I was puffing on a cigar, and luxuriating in the sun-ripened music of Harold's voice.

They were mighty pleased with me–everyone just doted on the new rabbi – his little girl said I'm the grandest man she ever saw and all the Sunday School kids love me and kids can't be fooled – his wife said I sing beautifully; she hears me hum along with the choir – the non-Jews in town say there's never been a better speaker at Rotary Kiwanis Lions and Community Chest – I had made a terrific hit with the best people – the forthcoming appearance on the M. E. pulpit showed what those who really count think and it was the first week in December, the month of Christmas – a chance to make them sit up and see how broadminded a brilliant rabbi can be – he loves and admires me enormously and hopes I'll be happy with the congregation for years and they'll do everything to make and keep me so – how would I like to go to Europe this summer?

I hurtled forward with mouth agape. "What was that?"

He swayed back in the swivel-chair.

"Well, Doctah, a few of your friends have been sayin' a man of your cultural attainments ought to visit abroad." The voice slowed and softened. "We'd like to make you a present as a token of our esteem . . . if you'll permit."

I scarcely sat on the chair. "Great Scott! I've been dreaming of Europe all my life, Mr. Burman . . . Harold. That's wonderful!"

The sun-ripened music betrayed a slight tremolo. "You'll have it, my boy. Shake!" A clasp of his two hands on mine – and I smiled out in a daze.

That night I stood before the full-length mirror. Every syllable of my sermon must be assayed. It would be the opening salvo in my war for Union Street! I lay down in bed and fondled the words intended for the ending, one by one, to get the sound and feel of them:

Church and synagogue only pretend to be concerned about men's souls when they ignore the swamp hovels that degrade them, the working conditions that debilitate them, and the economic injustice that dooms them with violence.

A moral crisis has arisen in our midst – the textile strike. Let us rise to our high-born part, and meet and match it, as Christians, as Jews, dedicated to the will of God!

Suddenly my chin dropped, the lips parted, and I stared into space. What will Harold Burman think? And all those Christians? My temple and I are guests! I have no right to abuse hospitality or forfeit friendship.

At the crack of dawn, I felt my way through a fog to my desk and pulled out a sheaf of notes. I had been considering a sermon in synagogue on Jesus for the Friday night prior to Christmas. Why not transfer it to the church? Maybe, after all, I should test out that new preaching technique. This was my chance. . . . Fortunately, Pastor Chaney had not yet announced the title when I told him of the change.

I took dinner with the Burmans on the big evening. Even the babbling of little Elsie brought only a twisted smile, and I betrayed scarcely a flicker of an eyelash when Mrs. Burman said how dreadful it would be if some of those black Abyssinian Jews she had read about came to town. Tension almost suffocated me.

When we drove up to the church, a reporter of the *Gazette* was leaning against a stone pillar. The city editor had called that afternoon for a copy of the sermon and was flabbergasted to hear that I would speak without one. "Of course," I hastily added, "my message is universal and belongs to all. Send a man out if you like!"

The church was filled. The first rows glistened with bald heads of Carringtons and Cowperthwaites and the back rows with the bald heads of Cohens and Katzes I had almost forgotten, they came to temple so rarely. It was like Yom Kippur!

The choir sang as angels might sing in heaven; the ritual of salvation unfolded in liturgy and symbol; my soul surveyed the centuries. Blue eyes ogling under broad-brimmed hats, whispered chatter behind jewelled hands, the rising tempo of chained expectancy among hundreds who hardly knew what to expect, the resonant amplitude of Dr. Chaney's introduction – all swirled in a mist. No sight, however, could block the thrust into my mind of the vision of Jesus walking among, defending, and suffering for the lowly and oppressed. Nor could any sound mute the tumultuous crescendo of Jewish agony expressed in *Eili, Eili, Lomo Azavtoni*. True, that cry was wrenched from the pain of Jesus on the Cross. It was also a Yiddish song I'd often sung. As I spoke, its words spoke to me.

The Christianity of Jesus gave way to the Christ of Christianity. The church has often turned away from the poor and humble to worship Christ and offer lip-service to Jesus, man of sorrows, and of the people.

Jesus lived a Jew; he died a Jew. In him Israel gave the first Christmas gift to the world! But his path is love for all the sons of man.

When our civilization takes that path, Christianity and Judaism will walk hand in hand. Then the star that gleamed to the shepherds in Bethlehem, and the star that shone into the tents of

Judea, will merge their radiance into love, and the Kingdom of God will be within us.

Next morning even Harold's "Wonderful! Just wonderful!" could not end the all-night churning of my nerve-raw body in a sleepless bed; even his report of the three-column *Gazette* story, and of how glowing phone calls from the best people in town kept him glued to the receiver, scarcely dented the pall of depression drifting in like a fog over my mind. When he chortled that Bob Carrington, the textile-manufacturer, said I would be America's greatest rabbi some day, I stammered thanks into the replaced receiver, pulled the covers over my head and hissed, "Abraham's encyclical to the Gentiles!" A shower braced me to compose myself for a shave and vow that I would never again be seduced into self-emasculation and treason to Union Street by personal friendship for pleasant Hal Burman, or anyone thereafter.

The somewhat callow oath which ended that incident should not present severe obstacles. The caricature of the rich that coloured my boyhood fantasy – a porcine "malefactor of great wealth" with global paunch, lecherous leer and fat cigar – has left an imprint; bifurcation of mankind into parasite and down-trodden began early for me, with Eastern Ohio coal-operators who starved helpless miners and sent them without safety devices into the bowels of the earth.

For years I puffed on the tennis court rather than switch to golf. Why? Now I know it was an outmoded notion that a golfbag meant affluence. On my first trip to Europe in 1925 I writhed seasick in a third-class cubicle, unable to withstand Union Street reproof for the then incredible luxury of a European tour. *A filet mignon* or baked Alaska at a dinner party was becalmed in mid gullet by a brain signal recalling that garbage from my host's table could feed a whole village of hunger-pinched babies in India, until I realized my austerity would not feed them, and a ninety-cent Havana often had a bite more acrid than the cornsilk we rolled in cigarette paper behind the stone pier on Union Street.

The prejudice is attenuating. In the immediate past, close contact with the well-to-do has been routine; to rub shoulders with the poor required effort. I have no doubt, however, that many poor men are hard, greedy, and insanely envious. Poverty is not a crime – nor a virtue. The Bible enjoins me against perverting justice either for the rich or for the poor.

Some of my best friends are millionaires. Percy Gardiner, a Gentile, purchased Israel Bonds in my honour and donated to the building fund of Holy Blossom Temple. He reaches outside the purview of his money and mansion, without fanfare, to aid and encourage the lonely, sick, and deprived of every race and creed. What President befriended the average man more surely and shrewdly than Franklin Delano Roosevelt? Who more than rich, intellectual John F. Kennedy was marked by the common touch– and by uncommon tragedy? An estate on the Hudson River or on Cape Cod does not seal a man's heart. How well I know that the gold-plated are not exempt from heartache and disappointment.

The worldliness in Jewish religion, its earthy respect for the good life, the norm of material consumption endemic in bourgeois synagogue society, precludes threadbare raiment for a rabbi. His emoluments would be termed princely by the church, although Jews, like Christians, are not averse from tying the "mercenary" tag on a clergyman who may not ask anything more than a chance to dissipate debilitating winter doldrums with Florida sunshine.

The central moral hazard, however, cannot be ignored. When the clerical black robe is doffed for the grey flannel of a high-income executive, "big business" mentality blunts and bends the lineaments of "my Father's business." Whoever has more than he needs may the more surely and subtly be convinced to approve, and defend, the world as it is.

My first savings deposit started a war between the status quo and Union Street. At stake was the integrity of my vision. I had always seen the world around me as an amoral jungle that grants power to the strong, unmodified free enterprise as the vestigial domain of cave-man ethics, the whole massive monetary mechanism as a usurious means to maintain the income gap between rich and poor. Only the ever-recurring image of Union Street prevented me from treating it as a ripe, sweet banana which, in my boyhood, I would suck and savour with sybaritic delight.

A skin impenetrable by another's woe and fingers itching for the jugular seem to be a prerequisite for the man who plans to get along. "In business, anything goes – as long as you stay within the law." How often I have heard, and in how many guises, that rationale of ruthless guile. Can a clergyman be beneficiary of such a carnivorous order and at the same time boon-companion of radicals with a mission to alter it? In our North American society, whose obsessive individual ambition seems to be increase of wealth without increase of weight, church and synagogue should aim to be agents of non-violent revolution.

All three branches of Judaism – Orthodox, Conservative, and Reform – are now overwhelmingly middle-class in roster, rationale, and psychological orientation. The dwindling Jewish proletariat does not pursue mystic fulfilment, as a rule, in institutionalized religion, and his children have largely forsaken the Yiddishist-Socialist orientation of the working-class, to join a *shule* and have their children "belong." The Reform rabbinate now recruits its personnel from middle-class homes with native-American parents, whereas my classmates went to Hebrew Union College from first-generation immigrant families alerted by the mass struggle for subsistence. The new crop of rabbis is sound, competent, professional, far more adequately equipped for the demands of organization and inclined not so much to question the logic and ethic of contemporary capitalism as to soften its asperities.

Resolutions on social justice, fiery debate on labour rights, the ancient thunder of Hebrew prophecy unleashed by valiant voices such as Rabbis Samuel Goldenson and Stephen S. Wise against the mighty who would not "let the oppressed go free," to which my nerves tingled as a fledgling at rabbinical conventions, have ceded priority to workshop and study groups on educational techniques, psychiatric guides for pastoral counselling, ritualistic innovations, trends in theology, and the State of Israel's impact on the diaspora.

Not that these practical agenda are illegitimate or trivial. On the contrary, they have an inescapable claim on the modern rabbi. Not that my confrères have renounced idealism. They join freedom rides to Mississippi, hazardous anti-racism movements in Alabama, ban-the-bomb demonstrations, if seldom, and the perennial battle for civil liberties. Towering Abba Hillel Silver of Cleveland planted his feet four-square on the side of co-existence with the Soviet Union. Yet the lightning is gone, and the suspicion grows in me that I am lagging behind the times in an outgrown generation, keeper of a lighthouse from whose rock-bound eminence the waters have receded.

Perhaps religion is an art. At Seminary during an especially supercilious period I fancied myself an aesthete, soliloquizing with Santayana, pursuing the ideal of Pater to "burn with a hard, gem-like flame," looking down like Zeus from Olympia on Babbitts who would make religion a tool for any purpose beyond its own beauty. Music is listened to, sculpture is gazed at, poetry is simply read and enjoyed, even an idea has symmetry to be contemplated with detachment. Why expect more from the communion of man with God, the supreme Artist, whose creation can be crystallized for our aesthetic enjoyment into a prayer, a hymn, a ritual?

In such a context today I would espouse a good-natured tolerance of things as they are, tempered with a begrudging desire that they improve as far as is compatible with vested interests. Such a moderate, passive understanding would satisfy a deep desire I have always felt, but never fully acknowledged, to inhale the serene balance of Grecian sculpture, frozen in immobility, complete in its being – rather than bind myself to the restless dynamism of the Hebraic spirit, forever in movement, enmeshed in the constant process of becoming; to experience the ecstasy of seeing, with the eye, an already-created thing of beauty in space – rather than the agony of hearing, with the ear, the challenge to create a better world in time; to unite myself, in sensuous contentment, with perfect form fashioned by man – rather than lacerate myself, in divine discontent, to follow the Word of God that demands the conquest of imperfection.

The ancient Greek philosopher looked at a statue and asked, "What is justice?" The Hebrew prophet listened to God's command and thundered, "Let justice flow as the waters, and righteousness as a mighty stream." More often than I like to admit, I long for the groves of Academe and for a furlough from the grubbiness and sweat of a mission to help the underdog. But the aesthete's allure never leads me far. I am not master of myself – only the servant of Union Street.

At the opposite end of the socio-religious spectrum is non-ritualistic, social-action liberalism. Does it provide the catalyst?

Years ago, in my teething stage, I thought so – until I began to exchange books, pulpits, and opinions with a "streamlined up-to-the-minute prelate," as he described himself, of the Congregationalist Church. Doctor Dean's belly, phrases, and cheeks were rotund, but his pugnacity in an argument had a slashing edge. He tirelessly argued on the decadence of established orthodox doctrine, and said nothing about slums, lack of medical care, bare-subsistence wages, unemployment, the huge income gap. When I lauded the corrective socialism of Norman Thomas, he turned with a pucker of distaste to the "bigotry" of the Pope and his encyclical on the immaculate conception. When I confessed that I almost wept at the sight of apples and peaches eaten by worms because prices were too low for marketing, while rickety children cried for fresh fruit, he turned aside to belabour Bishop Manning of St. John's Cathedral in New York for "fanatic fundamentalist flummery." When we sniffed around the corrugated tin hovels of migratory workers, he was horror-stricken by the magic amulets of "sinister superstition" around the necks of scrawny babies.

Since then, I have found the Congregationalists, and even more the Unitarian Church, to be a flinty spearhead for justice through protest, peace through disarmament, and truth through freedom of discussion. In the metabolism of social change, that body of freely assembled, conglomerate individuals is a potent enzyme for the transmutation of social conscience into social energy. Second only to the Quakers, Unitarians are pound for pound the bravest shock troops in Christendom – a tribute I pay with rueful discomfiture, in the light of synagogue timidity.

Yet the perception implanted by Dean has not vanished. Liberal religion is an island of rationality in a sea of Christian traditionalism and acutely conscious of the necessity to emphasize that distinction. Discontent with old-fashioned doctrinalism has become its single centre of cohesion. Its social passion, consequently, does not originate so much in an intensely experienced commitment as in a fortuitous meeting together of unconventionally minded people already inclined to protest. Liberal churches do not inspire the quest for social justice; they merely provide a medium of its expression suitable for disparate elements who stand for little else.

Normal, conservative God-centred religion, on the other hand, does offer theological ammunition for the social radical. Fundamentalism and reaction often go hand in hand. That alliance between socio-political rigidity and fundamentalist "churchianity," as I view it, was welded largely by a historical accident: Karl Marx did homework in the British Museum for *Das Kapital* and the proletarian revolution at the same time that Charles Darwin was brooding about the phenomena he later examined on the *Beagle* and explained by biological evolution. While one fuelled the attack on economic lords, the other set on target the Lord of Hosts and the story of Creation. Inevitably, the two objects of attack, synchronized in time, became synonymous in meaning.

Organized religion had scarcely distinguished itself by protecting the poor; its record on child labour, Corn Laws, and callous exploitation stank to the heaven it prayed to. That record, however, was indited not by the established creed per se, but by the troglodytes who appropriated existent pie-in-the-sky theology as a prop to privilege. Actually, there is no more potent agitator of rebellion against social evils than the simple thesis that man was made in the image of God – therefore an end rather than a means, inviolable, decidedly *not* an index-card, a commodity, a concentration-camp number or cannon fodder.

Radicalism's most dedicated gladiators are not Communist

pedlars of material salvation or evangelical purveyors of celestial salvation; they are the prisoners of an absolute assurance that every human being has sanctity by virtue of the indwelling Divine Presence. I am proud to walk beside "pure" Christian pacifists for nuclear disarmament and work beside "pure" Christian socialists for welfare legislation. Theirs is the passion of Jesus, and all theocentric believers, for the common man – for Union Street.

Of course, the more impecunious denizens of that street can be succoured by philanthropy. Well-lubricated United Appeal mechanisms mobilize communal conscience. Charity has become bureaucratic big business, staffed by "on loan" executives in high gear. Despite their sacrificial ardour, I cannot invoke or speak at a United Appeal luncheon undisturbed by doubt; an epidermal poultice will not cure internal lesions. And we cannot use big business without the risk of being used ourselves. The principle that everyone who needs charity should get it, is laudable; to clog the flow of dollars for a tilt at the windmill of superorganized bureaucracy would be frivolous. But the gate to a better world will be pried open by the principle that no one shall ever need charity because he will, instead, have justice.

In a complex, democratic community, implementation of justice devolves upon the men who make and execute law, and the people who elect them. That means practical politics – the pursuit of social values by the pursuit of votes. Is that the way to serve Union Street?

The Devil's Dictionary of Ambrose Bierce declared politics to be "a strife of interests masquerading as a contest of principles" and thus distilled into an epigram universal cynicism toward the public servant and the process which chooses him. A semantics of religion, however, would define politics as the science of government, entrusted with the realization of moral values in the practical processes of collective living. Because I am not content to await the millennium sitting on my hands, I think politics are important enough to engage the attention of clergymen.

Did not the Hebrew prophets presume to advise kings on

foreign affairs such as entangling alliances and war? They were political analysts. It was English evangelicals who abolished slavery in the Empire. Anglican bishops oppose apartheid in South Africa; the Central Conference of American Rabbis nursed collective bargaining through infancy; two Quebec priests goaded the province into political house-cleaning; Ontario pastors push anti-liquor statutes for what they earnestly believe to be the moral, social, and physical health of the community.

Complaint against a preacher mixing in politics may be complaint against his fighting on the wrong side. When I debunk Moscow materialist mythology, no one warns me in nocturnal telephone calls or anonymous letters to "mind your own goddam business you goddam Jew." An attack on the irreligion of uncontrolled free enterprise attracts an avalanche.

In Canada a preacher-politician does not cast the pew into a tizzy; clergymen can be candidates for, and sent to, Parliament. That tradition stems from Britain rather than from the United States and can point to brilliant exponents, particularly in the socialist camp of Woodsworth and Douglas. Therefore, when the New Democratic Party invited me to take to the hustings as a candidate for federal Parliament, I felt singled out for honour, high stewardship, and recognition as a standard-bearer of the welfare state.

I had just announced retirement from an onerous and exhausting ministry. A political imbroglio for election to office would replace the slow simmer of a roasting-oven with a pressure cooker whose heat would overtax a neophyte of my age. Partisan obligation, furthermore, would limit independence. Could I submit holus-bolus to a platform which must effect fusion through compromise – as a good party man? And I was not a Canadian citizen, although that obstacle could and may be removed.

Besides, I must be free to change my mind. Labour unions, for example. From boyhood they have intermediated my feeling for the underdog. In the mounting bitterness of a violent strike in Toronto, I joined two Protestant pastors for a visit of remonstrance to the employer, a beloved friend and highly influential member of my congregation – and he received us with notable understanding and courtesy. Year after year I have addressed annual conventions of the labour congress.

Now I am no longer sure who is the underdog. Unions themselves often seem dominated by the slogan to "get all you can while you can," by the amoral cynicism of capitalist industrial octopi – and by leaders powered with the marauding urge to power. At a labour convention in the late 'fifties, I aroused the purple ire of Hoffa's Canadian satrap by depicting his boss as a "Cleopatra-siren floating into Canada on a barge bedizened with strong-arm benefits." And I am increasingly convinced that social well-being and human dignity will be advanced by co-operation rather than by conflict.

My commitment to the underdog, whoever he is, will, I hope, endure while I endure. Is it a fighting vent for exaggerated memories of boyhood frustrations, sentimentalized sympathy for humble forbears, a wallow in pity projected from self to others, the belligerence of an angry man? I don't know.

Suppose I had been begotten by a Rothschild banker instead of Nissen Nisselewicz? Since I did not choose, and cannot change, my parentage, what-might-be is speculation gone amok. Can any attempt to identify one's roots yield more than superficial, ego-shielding rationalizations? Perhaps not.

In any case, I know where I stand now – on Union Street. It arose in the mud paths of Grinkishok, straggled along the Western bank of the Ohio and has wound through the dust and din – and often the defeat – of many battles.

Flanked by empty, darkened stores, inexorably succumbing to the tooth of time and the economic cycle, the real Union Street now wears the threadbare garb and melancholy mien of a derelict. Yet I still hear it throb with the heartbeat of the poor and beaten in every land. And as long as I remember that sound, I shall return to Union Street again and again and let fantasy build it into a highway toward the Kingdom of God.

Sex, Sanity, and Sin

JIM DIGGITY'S house resembled one of the caves we dug for cowboy-Indian fights; it rested on a ledge cut into a hillside, around which circled a narrow mud road. A dozen shapeless stones, hyperbolically termed a "walk," were scattered helter-skelter down one side of the house, and turned the corner to the kitchen, from whose vantage point truck-gardens, privies, jerry-built frame houses and wire enclosures for chickens and rabbits shambled in a steep descent to the trolley line.

Late summer afternoons after a swim I often went home with Jim for cookies and cool water from the well. Mrs. Diggity exuded an animal warmth which enveloped me. By the criteria of suburbia she would be tagged a frump; only a peasant sturdiness of limb could stand erect under the weight of her brood and burdens and a bosom that quivered with every movement. I liked her very much.

One humid day kept us in the swimming-hole until dusk. When Jim and I reached the kitchen the tangy babble of salt pork frying on the stove made me faint with proscribed hunger, and dense cloudlets of smoke puffed out through cracks in the iron belly. For many years Jim's ma had worn only a housedress at home. That day was the first time I noticed it, and a rumpled nightgown on an unmade bed.

"Come on with me to the store," Jim yelled. His voice came as a faint echo from a far land. My thoughts cleaved, as hotly as the palate on the roof of my mouth, to Mrs. Diggity's loose-jointed hips rising and falling with undulatory twitching at each pad of her slippered feet. The susurrus of her voice launched a steady soft humming and merged with an aroma as of exotic fruit fermenting in the sun. That night I lay rigid while Jack tossed and turned beside me.

I told no one. Anyway, I did not know in what terms to describe the Diggity episode. Nothing had really happened. It was all inside me. And it was wrong – a sin, dirty and slimy – worse than tittering at the tangle of canine mongrels on the street, worse than trying to sneak a peep into the girls' washroom at school.

That single-raimented, inexorable vision, fragrance, thud of slipper – and Jim's dad – were Mr. and Mrs! What did they do which made them so? The elementary ignorance of everyone in our gang was almost total; well-nigh nothing we believed was true, and of the truth we knew nothing. Each of us pretended to be a connoisseur and shivered in fright.

Any four-letter term concerned with alimentation or reproduction was invested with the impact of a musket shot. We challenged each other to bouts of salacious "swear words." We glued our eyes to knotholes underneath the wooden bridge for the passing flounce of a dress or slip, to the tattered pages of a medical book someone had picked up in the City Hall lavatory, and to the bulls trying to mount cows when cattle were driven through the streets to the freightyards.

Once on a berry-picking we held the clothes of damsels bathing in a pond, only to dash away through the bushes when their worried parents came to fetch them. Leo Lucchesi said a cousin of his father told him masturbation and accidental nocturnal losses could use up so many germs you might never have children. On a bright wind-swept day at the top of a hill, we romped practically naked, affecting the aboriginal costume of Indians, but actually bent on fondling and stroking in the short-grass meadow to which we all converged.

There were divers academic researches into the subject of fallen women. Laborious philological study of the word "prostitute" in the library yielded only frustration; we preferred "whore." Mike's big brother told him the cheapest one in town was Trolley-Car Tillie – "anyone could get on for a nickel." For a week we "cased" her inebriated peregrinations in the hope of seeing her engaged.

Occasionally, rumours reached us about a coloured girl from Ram Cat Alley or a hunky in a Neff's Coal Company house having a baby without being married. And we finally tracked down the definition of "bastard." The vital fluids that circulated with heightening velocity in our limbs hinted at the reason why the maidens got into trouble. Every time I saw my father near home with a sheaf of umbrellas harvested in his arm, I ached to ask him just *how* it happened – but I never could.

Our extra-curricular reading matter gave prominent listing to Dead-Eye Dick, Fred Fearnot, Dick Merriwell, and Horatio Alger's gallery of stalwart heroes: Jim the Boot-Black, Tom the Newsboy, Bob the Apprentice – all pure-minded paragons of American athleticism, capitalist thrift and sexless probity to whom a fair virgin appeared solely as an opportunity for advancement by marrying the banker's daughter.

Our comics were Hall-Room Boys, Happy Hooligan, the Katzenjammer Kids, and Gaston and Alphonse, whose elaborate courtesy we gaily mimicked. I had a supplementary source of literature – *Shepherd of the Hills, Girl of the Limberlost,* and *Graustark,* left around the parlour by Birdie – but summarily cast them aside as non-inflammable.

Sweet Caporal cigarettes glutted our eyes. Every package contained a card-photograph of a famous actress clad in tights or a low-cut evening gown, huge feathered hat, and bustle. My favourite was Anna Held until the Harry K. Thaw murder trial diverted the dream orbit to Evelyn Nesbit. How often I salvaged her ample pulchritude from the gutter or the ashtrays in the Globe Hotel lobby!

School did not help. Talks on physiology stopped at the navel. Special health lectures depicted with graphic visual aids the harm done by too little ventilation, too much whisky, too tight corsets, and cigarettes. We memorized the Latin names of the brain sections and bones, even the scientific nomenclature of some flowers; we held alley conferences about our sex organs in one-syllable Anglo-Saxon. Stray dogs were more informative than our teachers, the Misses Smythe, Townsend, and Hawkins.

One thing alone I knew: girls were pure, innocent of any of the fantasies sizzling in my brain. Passionless, blithe, immaculate as the driven snow. All of them – except Pat the breastless tomboy and Becky Bloom the daughter of the synagogue sexton – chirped daintily at the Philathea Bible Class, averted their faces from the crayon pictures and notes thrust at them by the bad boys transferred to our school from a flood-battered building "away down town," and glided through the circumambient air like the angelic choir. Gentile girls seemed especially remote, all alabaster and ethereality – velvety, placid, delicate of skin, unbeaded with perspiration, demure and soft of speech, devoid of gross appetite.

My first love was Dorothy Caldwell. She sat in my row in the eighth grade. After supper, during the warm months, I stole away to the nickelodeon where she sold tickets, and kept watch like a starry-eyed sentinel at the curb, until darkness drove me home to avoid Pop's question about my absence. While my taste in movies gradually shifted from Fatty Arbuckle, the Keystone Cops, and "Two-Gun" William S. Hart, to Theda Bara, a mad impulse would seize me to walk brazenly up some day when my *inamorata* was alone, close my eyes, tell her everything – and run! But Ed Hardesty had been caught pouring out a dammed-up flood of obscenities through the wire fence into the girls' play yard at recess and was taken off to reform school.

High school tantalized me with whispered tales of boys and girls hugging and kissing at parties where they played post office and spin-the-bottle and dimmed the gaslights. Several of my classmates had access to parental automobiles; the grapevine said Gravel Hill's "smart set" organized a stagger-system car pool that transported three couples to a certain back road almost every night.

When would *I* tear away the veil, and penetrate the strata of sensation, layer on layer, of rapture and self-abandon? I would need to be married, and that was as distant as the moon. And I still did not know, as a senior, just how children are born!

The evening before going away to college, I sat with Isabelle Thompson on the swing of her front porch. Isabelle had lived across the road from us on Union Street for a short time. When her father, a brakeman, died under the wheels of a freight train, they used the insurance for a little house on Gravel Hill. I used to dream about her during the day. She had the chiselled features of a Greek goddess, a tragic bereavement, a wistful penchant for poetry, eyes that matched the pale blue sky after a summer rain, and honey-blonde hair whose sheen drew gold from the sun.

My fingers ached to bury themselves in those glowing strands. I asked myself what she would say if I asked permission to hold her hand and rest my harassed head on her immaculate breast. How often, in the school library, did I find myself so deliciously and fearfully close that I could hear the gentle rhythm of her breathing.

Now I had dropped in to say good-bye. The physical tension of her nearness no longer purpurated like a blackberry-bush thorn in my flesh. In a few days I would be in another world and poised on the springboard of a new life. All other beckonings, attractions, allurements, even the shimmering gossamer of Isabelle, were muted. When Isabelle proposed the swing, as the last afterglow of sunset vanished behind the hills, I had no fear. We talked of the rabbinical seminary in Cincinnati – a hard grind – and money, which I must make, somehow, and my luck in remembering the Hebrew I had learned in *heder*. We laughed over Cletus Wells, the history teacher, and the time he forgot to mark our exam papers. We sniffed the night breeze creeping in noiselessly from the river and made breathless, heavily restrained comment on the unusual pallor of the stars. Several times I told her what train I would be taking; I hoped she would answer my letters.

I had brought a volume of Keats, intending to read aloud; it lay beside me on the swing. Nattering all the while, I fidgeted, and tapped a tune on the cover – but my hand could not lift nor my head turn towards it. An inner voice held me back from the edge of a chasm in whose swooning depths I would forget everything – college, career, parents, Hebrew, the brand of Abraham on my body – and fling off ambition and reason and the cramped raiment of my ancient faith and people. But the crystal fountain of beckoning waters was woman, before whose banned paradise the cherubim swung their flaming swords – and Gentile, thrice proscribed since I was to be a rabbi! Our fingers had almost touched when a steel hinge inside me propelled my back upward and my hand forward. "I have to get home to pack. See you Christmas vacation."

At the B. & O. depot, the train that would bear me away to college got three greetings: dour submission from my father, whose Orthodox piety I was betraying by defection to Reform; dewy-eyed benediction from my mother, who welcomed the clanging monster as my liberator; fervent petition from me that the wheels roll to open spaces of freedom, where I would live and labour, learn and love. . . .

Of those four freedoms, labour and learning came quickly, granted by a massive tyranny. Studies for university degree and rabbinical ordination were combined; for four years it would be morning varsity, afternoon seminary, and incarceration every schoolday, with exercise provided by a post-prandial walk from one cell to the other. The full course then was nine years, subject to reduction by

Talmud-trained "refugee" students from Orthodox *yeshivot* and boys with sufficient stamina, assiduity, and absorptive potential to pass additional tests.

The Seminary teaching-staff was laden with individualism, light on pedagogy, and bred on another planet. Admittedly, I had ceded to the pull of Grinkishok – but I also had poled a raft with Huck Finn! To eggheads who had blotted out their youth in the oceanic vastness of European Jewish scholarship Huck was a sprite from Never-Never Land and American horseplay a pinhead phenomenon to be tamed by the rod of wrath.

The head-on collision between two worlds, and the civil war between our smouldering senses and the savage demands of the classroom, would have engendered acute neuroses had we not found an outlet in tormenting our mentors. I still laugh, with a twinge of regret, at the sadism devised to afflict them.

With wanton cruelty, we mimicked the idiosyncrasies of men we loved: Butzie's dervish gestures over the syntax-riddled corpse of Tertio-Isaiah; Lautie's tic-marked inability to finish a sentence because his tongue couldn't keep pace with his mind; Pat carrying an umbrella in imitation of Kant; the meditative beard-stroking and endless anecdotalism of Deutsch; the touching absent-mindedness of the silver-haired President, in whose classes baseball-game absenteeism broke all records because he could never find his attendance record.

Every professor was unique in his own anarchic way. When on speaking terms, they wrangled about their respective classroom theories with gargantuan mutual disdain. That very intransigeance, the example of men who made the arcana of scholarship a life-long battlefield, implanted in me intense respect for the mind. To think of them is to sip excitement from precious vats treasured in the winery of recollection. It was the sheer audacity, the untrammelled bravura of their individualism that won my boundless affection and gave me a star to steer by.

In the welter of sex, however, we wandered chartless and alone. Our teachers might have enlarged the imprisoning monologue with private chimeras into a redemptive dialogue with a trusted friend. Only a space ship, however, could traverse the distance between the chaos of our private reveries and the Cabbalistic computations in mediaeval Hebrew mysticism or the *hapax legomina* in the Book of Job – a word-world even less satisfying than the cold-shower cure lampooned in bumming-room banter.

While professors droned and hormones danced, I gazed across Clifton Avenue to the leafy bowers of Burnet Woods, and paired its riot of autumn russet and red with the riotous fantasy that swirled around the gold-tinted pallor of Isabelle Thompson, diaphragm-fluttering rumours of a varsity telephone list, and bull sessions on monasticism, which we repudiated by unanimous consent.

I fished *Marius the Epicurean* and *Omar Khayyam* from the litter of a second-hand bookshop, and recited, endlessly, in my Hebrew-grammar-class imaginings, "A loaf of bread, a jug of wine and thou," to a flaxen-haired apparition who had once sent me fleeing like a deer by accosting me bare-breasted on a twilight trek home through the woods.

The pedantic word-curtain of our instructors did show a tiny rent, on occasion. Pat particularized the unique face-to-face posture of human sex intercourse as a symbol of the God-man encounter; Butzie sprayed us with spittle in describing the obsessive infidelity of Hosea's wife; Lautie, a widower, reproved my lapses of attention by suddenly shouting, "Feinberg, you got sex trobbles?" thus exposing his own.

The radical clique on whose periphery I hovered had contempt for dirty stories. We were resolved not to leer at wickedness, but to look at it. What *is* good, what *is* evil? It was Fraser's *Golden Bough* that launched our avidity for transvalued values. Then anthropology, surveying the apotheosized moral codes of diverse peoples, well nigh burst the lid that clamped down desire by furnishing us with the conclusion that morality is relative. We pounced on the debunking dynamite of Oscar Wilde, Frank Harris, and George Bernard Shaw, and ignited it under the drab mausoleum of bourgeois convention; we revelled in H. L. Mencken's war whoops against Rotarian pollyannaism, vicariously flaunted the peccadilloes of Baudelaire and Byron, feasted on James Branch Cabell's *Jurgen*, and whistled with brave exuberance that the only sin is ugliness.

Our eyes traversed a prodigious succession of books, cover to cover. They halted long at pages with sexual significance. Epicurus was a first-class architect of abstract thought; my febrile fingers clutched him tight when he counselled me not to avoid pleasures but to select them. Havelock Ellis's *Dance of Life* unlocked vistas before which I stood spellbound, but motionless! Friedrich Nietzsche was the "Big Bertha" of our self-conscious radicalism. "Live dangerously! Goest thou to woman? Forget not thy whip!" I trumpeted with the others, half-expecting the citadel of respectability to tumble like the gates of Jericho. How reckless and strong he made us feel – if not act!

There were scholars among us for whom unwed continence expressed Christian denial rather than Jewish affirmation. Abhorrence of the flesh, they pontificated, purged early Christianity of the guilt-feelings aroused by its merger with Greek paganism, which adored the flesh. To the church, sex became an amiable weakness, a loathsome indulgence, the "Typhoid Mary" of original sin – after priests had devitalized and tamed the fever with the phagocyte of holy matrimony.

To Judaism, we insisted, sex was not scabrous defilement but wondrous fulfilment, a medium for human collaboration in Divine creativity, and an end in itself, which was ecstasy. Scripture's patriarchs had irrepressible lust. And David the adulterer could sing of God with God's consent.

Did not the Talmud assert over and over again that the *yetzer-harah** was among the things God had found "very good," without which man would not build a house, beget children, or engage in trade? Did not an ancient rabbinic parable recount how the whole vast process of life came to a standstill – even hens no longer laying eggs – when the *yetzer-harah* was imprisoned? Does not the *shehinah*† brood over and bless the bed of marital union?

* Carnal desire. † Divine Presence.

My father, being a Litvak, stemmed from a line of schoolmen opposed to the anti-legalistic dancing and singing of the *Hasidim*. Despite his austerity, their joyous acceptance of a God-intoxicated naturalism gave me hope for release from the iron ring of inhibition. A *Hasid* is not commanded to renounce – but to hallow. Under *Hasidism*, I could be a good Jew and yet taste food, walk across the fields, dance the roundelay, excrete, tie a shoelace, certainly embrace my wedded woman – all in holiness! What a contrast with flagellating friars, the succubi-plagued hallucinations of confession-bleating saints, Cotton Mather's hell fire, and the sin-tortured Bellaire Holy Rollers whose shrieks to God for forgiveness still beat against my eardrums.

Over my attic desk, on the wall, I tacked a Hebraic neo-pagan poem of Saul Tchernikovsky, "Before the Statue of Apollo":

I am the Jew; dost thou remember me?
I kneel to life, to beauty and to strength,
I kneel to all the passionate desires
Which they, the dead-in-life, the bloodless ones,
The sick, have stifled in the living God,
The God of wonders of the wilderness,
The God of gods, Who took Canaan with storm
Before they bound Him in phylacteries.

We began to hear about a Viennese Jew named Freud. He clarified everything. It was all so simple. Free your subconscious. Fulfil yourself or find a safety valve. Id, ego, super-ego! Many doors swung open; four-letter words could be garbed in technological terms. And all the quirks in our little campus world were primly, conclusively labelled.

Amos Bayern's insatiable curiosity about sex phenomena was verbal masturbation. Morton Goldstein's research into homosexuality originated in a mincing gait, high-pitched voice, and penchant for caressing my cheeks. Jack Feld's sententious crusade against penny-pitching in the college basement was sublimation. Myron Vester, who bruised us all on the gym floor, was compensating. Harry Kahanovitch, who followed every girl in sight with his eyes and eventually with his feet, boasted about imaginary conquests, and solicited my partnership in adventures that would have frozen us both with fright, was a victim of narcissistic repression.

And I began to worry about my pocket diary. Every night I would spend a quarter-hour setting down an elaborate list of picayune chores for the next day from "send laundry home" to "ask about biology lab mark" to "borrow a quarter for lunch." Was it a compulsion-mechanism, like never putting on the left shoe before the right or stepping on a crack in Bellaire's cement sidewalk?

The Lord provided safety valves. At zany minstrel shows the sex puzzle was diffused into a Hawaiian straw skirt and a shady pun. I sang solos in the varsity glee club and in the Seminary choir under the baton of a German organist who had a Kaiser Wilhelm moustache and gave me free vocal lessons. A dime bought a seat in B. F. Keith's vaudeville peanut-heaven on Saturday nights and a nickel filled a stein of beer. Sloe-eyed Jewish maidens from proletarian downtown joined me for a trolley-ride to a free concert. One could always attain physical exhaustion on the basketball court. And Abner Goldman gave me an apprenticeship in the techniques of romance.

Ab had a built-in brake which protected him from overwork, a purring drawl which massaged my nerves, a way with girls, breezy nonchalance, and an aptitude for lubricating the boy-girl encounter so expert that it left me agape and bug-eyed.

He put grease on my hair, loaned me a sporty tie, and took me along to a Sunday-afternoon tea dance. The next week, while he played five hundred and penny-ante at a frat house, I went to the dance alone. Half-praying she would be deaf, I sidled up to a girl sitting alone in a corner, and sweated and stumbled and shuffled with her for two hours, because no other boy tagged me with a tap on the shoulder.

Soon Ab conducted me through the esoteric logarithms of dating: how to ask, how not to seem anxious, how to order the cheapest refreshments with *savoir faire*, what to say at the door, and never to act as though you *expect* a girl to let you kiss her good night. He persuaded a high-school sorority to put me on its list. For a few months I alternated between mulish caperings and moping on the far end of a sofa. Then the girls began to ask me to sing, and I memorized "Silver Threads Among the Gold" and "Love's Old Sweet Song."

Finally, I reported to Ab that I had completed my first-grade test. It had been an agonizing dawn patrol into No Man's Land, on a davenport. I couldn't stop talking to the girl, I was so nervous! The monologue started with prickly epigrams I had memorized from Oscar Wilde's *The Importance of Being Ernest*, skipped to President Wilson's Fourteen Points, solved the high-cost-of-living-consumer-goods distribution problem and then sailed non-stop through the hemlock speech of Socrates, Beatrice Webb's Fabian Socialism, Ludwig Lewisohn's *Upstream*, George Jean Nathan theatrical reviews in *The Nation*, my steelmill job during the war, what I hoped to achieve as a rabbi, and why I believe in God. She listened – and let me peck her cheek.

Before long I jiggled my toes to "Everybody's Doin' It," hopped for "The Vamp," slithered with "Dardanella," got a Sunday School teaching-job that paid me eight dollars a month, had my trousers pressed at the tailor's instead of under the mattress – and Seminary turned pleasant. My aplomb did not desert me even when the professor of Bible asked why Biblical virginity had to be proved by a blood test.

In the meantime seminarians who had enlisted in the army were drifting back – some with hard-faced resolution to preserve the freedom-fruit of victory, others harassed by doubt of their fitness for, and the value of, a religious vocation. A veteran blinded by shrapnel in the Argonne would carry on his studies with the aid of Braille.

Lionel Weiss had changed the most. Before his enlistment he used to walk away even from thoroughly theoretical talk about girls and we joshed him about his mother's-milk complexion and popularity with the faculty wives, who thought him a "darling boy."

Now the dandy's pants were baggy, his greaseless hair crisscrossed like barbed wire and the kewpie-doll lips had petrified in a snarl. When I noted that the blue in his eyes had shaded to a greenish grey, he muttered something about "the refraction of rotting corpses."

His prime abomination was the new, youngish professor, Jake Mannheim, who lectured with a sibilant lisp. One night Lionel held forth to me at Foucar's. "Hell's fire! That cootie is always shooting off about Judaism and life. What does he know about life sitting there on his fanny? One day in the trenches and the pansy'd faint. That guff is all right for a YMCA laddie prating about virtue and over-charging men on the firing-line for cigarettes and chocolate. The Bible! It has guts, not eyewash. Jake and all the rest touch up a prettified painting and call it life. Like a Paris whore, furbelowed and full of syphilis!" He pitched his voice in a derisive soprano key. "Crap, that's all! Unadulterated crap!"

Flinging that pejorative word into the air like a hand-grenade, he collapsed into a shapeless hulk, as though the skeletal frame had been extracted from his body, and flopped on a stool at the bar.

"The world of five years ago is gone. Y'hear? Gone! And none of the fifteen million who went to their graves along with that world lived longer or agonized less for having refused a woman!"

With that Lionel threw a coin at the bartender and bolted. In dismay, I plunged after him and caught his sleeve. "Lionel, what are you going to do? Think a minute, man!"

His voice dropped to a stage whisper. "Do you remember what Wise-Guy Nietzsche said? Number one: 'Woman is the recreation of the warrior.' Well, I'm a warrior – just back from the blood-spilling, like Ulysses. Number two: 'Goest thou to woman? Forget not thy whip!' Remember, kid?" He cupped his lips into my ear. "Well, Wise-Guy Weiss has a new word for it. Goest thou to woman? Forget not – this!" With a wild flourish, he held up a five-dollar bill, and sped on. Before that week ended, Lionel had left the Seminary. The prewar world, bundled up and embalmed, was in his duffle-bag.

Since Lionel's Walpurgis-Nacht at Foucar's most rabbinical students at the Seminary were released from sex pressure by matrimony. At the time, only one, and soon thereafter a second, had married, thus generating volcanic tremors that almost blew them off the campus. Now a college wife is not only permissible but routine, and the marital canopy supplies a snug harbour. The situation is less exciting – but healthier and more productive of good works and good rabbis.

That night, Lionel probably had less joy from an illicit bed than from the perverted satisfaction of his hate against the world that had lured him into war. He had appointed himself general of the army of demolition, with orders to wipe out the battlements of entrenched respectability. Actually, his was a minor operation. The offensive which cracked open ever-widening fissures in behaviour patterns had already been mounted and was in progress. Today, Lionel might thumb his notebook for phone numbers of "nice girls" whose receptivity would be at least possible, and possibly certain. The masculine protest he voiced for theologians has become the coat-of-arms, and code, of the new woman.

Church of England ecclesiastics, from sundry parish vicars to the "Red Dean," are notorious iconoclasts. When one canon held charity more important than chastity and another denied that Christ confined sexuality to the domain of wedlock, they represented not so much British maverickism as the widely held theory of Western youth, not excepting females.

Many factors are responsible: progressive disintegration of respect for authority symbols such as church and government; popular distortion of psychoanalysis; protest against the "unclean" attitude toward intercourse; peril of nuclear annihilation, which breeds the desire to have a fling before the holocaust; personal anonymity in an urban environment; the peripatetic automobile; press-agent glamourization of Hollywood harlotry; plenitude of contraceptive devices; prurient, sex-saturated entertainment and advertising; an increasingly pornographic press; and paperback incendiary novels.

I do not believe the trend toward sex-orientated hedonism can be reversed by censorious "platitudes in stained-glass attitudes." Clerical exhortation, either in pulpit or private counselling, is scarcely more relevant than the Colorado footprints of a dinosaur. When television commercials and *New York Times* Sunday magazine ads for bras and panties pictorialize the efficacy of a brand product for inveigling the male into lustful chase, a preacher is cast for the role of King Canute.

In the glacial canyons of New York during the boom years before 1929, I observed how affluence expedited the development of libertinism. Whereas upper middle-class stodginess has always concealed depths of female frustration, like geological sub-strata that increase in temperature as they go down, superfluous leisure, the cult of self-expression, and the sensuous cynicism of the emancipated woman were breeding the twentieth century's most open rebellion: feminism against the double standard.

I have not been insensitive to the female psyche. Any alert clergyman knows that its studiously dignified, circumspect, but sophisticated, manipulation can enormously strengthen his control of the internal synagogue or church structure, where woman plays a crucial role. I always remembered, in this connection, the advice of a bachelor colleague, to be intellectual with pretty women, frivolous with intellectual women, and saucy with old ladies.

The urbane manner I cultivated for Manhattan as co-rabbi of Temple Sinai in 1927 could not stifle a deep-rooted Hebraic conscience. Flitting over the surface of life might even be professionally vindicated, as leverage for pleasant social relations with people otherwise inaccessible – but the changing morality was a serious problem for youth which must have a fixed ethic to live by. The code had to be validated by reason, and yet it must be disciplinary. Talk about the hardy pristine virtues of old might be incongruous, but anarchy would lead to nihilism. A rabbi could not evade the challenge of honest grappling with sex as part of a natural, normal life.

"A pragmatic system of sex ethics," all neatly outlined, lay in the "private" file on my desk. I held it at arm's length. Full equality of woman; a single standard; divorce by mutual consent; treatment of sexual abnormality as a disease, not a crime; protection of illegitimate children; parental subsidy for early marriage (an "old Jewish" custom). "Not bad, really," I grunted. "Not bad at all, for a beginning!"

Then the label "private" on the drawer struck me. "Private!" But I was a public servant! If I had truth, I was bound to speak it. If sermons are to be vital, they must distil personal experience, without retreat.

The first step seemed obvious. Repudiate dodges like emotion, erotic urgency, instinctive need, natural impulse, the brand of nature, and liberate sex from its semantic dungeon. Once people became used to the term, they would be led into accepting the fact as natural. It's the refusal to verbalize that starts the sly laugh and prurient sneer! I repeated the word over and over again. "Sex. S-E-X." My squeamishness surprised me.

A title for the following Sabbath sermon had already been announced: "Ask the Rabbi!" I looked over my notes. The psychiatrist, the lawyer, the engineer, and the scientist were outmoding the rabbi as personal advisers, they stated. Why shouldn't people bring their everyday problems to the minister. No other profession was as disinterested. Excellent! I would simply include sex as one of the everyday problems.

Preaching made me tense. Not until I mumbled a silent prayer did an idea possess me, and set me free. That Sabbath, however, I forgot to pray, and was so unmanned that I spread the copious notes upside down on the pulpit. Nevertheless I plunged ahead with disjointed remarks about the Biblical text, with one eye and my hands on the cards, until they were reshuffled.

The zero hour approached. In the back of my mind "s-e-x" began to form a whirlwind. Having memorized the crucial paragraph, I pointed into the storm.

Questions of belief and religious practice are not the only occasions for rabbinical guidance, my dear friends. There are other dilemmas also – some, if you will pardon the admission, more important than matters of belief – in which young folks might speak to a rabbi. Business ethics! Vocational guidance! Family relations and schools and college courses and sex and books to read and plays to see! Why not restore the rabbi to his traditional status as friend and counsellor?

I had strung "sex" in a series, so that it would not be an isolated cynosure of attention. Now I half wished that I had enunciated it too faintly for hearing. On sitting down, I assessed the response. A dozen pairs of raised eyebrows, a few bald-headed men breathing stertorously in their pews, several ferociously waving fans, and a number of decorous ladies whispering into their gloves! And what normally was the funereal hush of a morgue broke into a Greek chorus of pew-creaking so clamorous the soprano almost gave up in the midst of her solo.

At every subsequent dinner party for weeks my President beckoned me into a corner. "I know as well as you do that people's – er – emotions are not handled right. But what can you do about it? Don't be a chump. Why make trouble for yourself? Besides, you're not married."

In any case, the longer I reflected on the sermon, the more firmly I concluded that moralizing can beget meanness. Throughout my ministry I had never met a zealous acolyte of absolute purity who was not essentially false and a threat to the weal of decent people. For one thing, absolute rightness usually harbours the seed of self-importance, unimaginative cruelty, and arrogance that turns my stomach. For another, anyone who lays seige or claim to sexual impeccability deceives others or, worse, himself. Extreme virtue can be more harmful than vice, because its unrestraint is not tempered by conscience.

Jewish folklore, I reminded myself, approaches the sinner gently; on self-righteousness it visits contempt. There is a Yiddish tale about a prig whose spotless probity bound him to every jot and tittle of the Law. One day, however, while poring over the moral maxims of the Fathers, as was his wont, he had squashed a fly buzzing about his head. At the Court of Judgement, the decree went forth that he be confined in a cell for eternity – with the fly. An hour passed, and a sinner stood with hangdog mien before the Almighty. He had been a tavern roisterer, neglectful of holy writ, and without honour save among the scornful and irreverent. But he once pulled a beautiful woman from a soaking in the river, while engaged in ribald song along the shore. What was his fate? To be confined in a cell – with the lady!

Whatever the debunking case against saints, and despite ecclesiastical over-fondness for the word, sin is real. But what is it?

Surveying the past – Union Street, Seminary, the lonely tempestuous years of bachelordom – the obsession of Western society with the physical emerges as the first challenge to honest, uninhibited analysis. Was it conducive to health, or to imbalance and abnormal disproportion, that a patch of membrane could dispatch a man or woman to hell? Does the supreme moral determinant reside in the erogenous zone? Has God centred there not only human desire but His demand? I must observe that an affirmative answer seems to degrade Him into a voyeur and to enthrone an anatomical condition (often accidental) as the master of human destiny here and hereafter.

If the years have convinced me of anything, it is that physical sex must be nudged off its pedestal as *the* sin, secret, and sacrament. The omnipresent erotic malaise in our sex-centric society cries for relaxation of fixation on the pudenda. Granted, the drive for sex-fulfilment is rivalled only, and problematically, by the lust for power as the most explosive and shattering of all human propulsions – and therefore must be controlled. It is the most complex and tangled of all human sensibilities – and must be subjected to research and reason. It is linked with reproduction, the most important of all human responsibilities – and must be subdued to social well-being.

Must the mad, destructive rage of Othello against Desdemona, therefore, become the pattern, in modified degree of violence, for every "wronged" husband or wife? When a family is dragged through the divorce court because of a possibly impulsive, momentary lapse involving no deeper motivation than an epidermal thrill, I wonder whether possessiveness and pride may not be exacting too high a price. Cavalier promiscuity and barnyard concupiscence need not be condoned in order to install common sense! A high-minded, admirable mother of three whom I tried to dissuade from a divorce belaboured me daily, to friends, in the beautician's salon, for encouraging infidelity!

Is physiological chastity an essential prelude to a happy marriage? If so, the success of many unions justifies faith in miracles, and the felicity of many newlyweds faith in their own judgement. Under sagacious questioning, juvenile sex-delinquents show an almost pathetic eagerness for stability, even monotony; they are horrified by infraction of a marriage vow properly sealed and delivered. Shall these be barred from giving themselves a chance? Benignly domesticated ex-prostitutes prove that premarital excess need not always disqualify a candidate for postmarital happiness. And the alarming increase in the divorce rate among immature youngsters who married early poses a bold question: would a discreet safety valve provided by premarital "romance" not prevent a high-pressure marriage of dubious viability – in extreme cases? Sheer sex-hunger is a shaky certificate of fitness for the connubial voyage.

Possibly the prime sex-sin is dehumanization – that pandemic evil which besets every area of our mass-produced robotized world.

To join wings for nuptial flight with an incomparable *one* set apart and differentiated from all others by a quality of tenderness and desire deeply realized is to distinguish human love from that of the beast. When a conjunction of flesh is thirst slaking itself at any available fountain, the human descends into the sub-human. Lionel Weiss's doxie was a bought mechanical instrument for release of tension; even in marriage a loveless bed perverts a voluntary, highly selective act into reflex automatism; a teenager who goes all the way for "kicks" is bartering the postponed substance for the immediate shell; a playboy cruising for pickups may be driving a convertible, but the animal on the prowl is driving him.

The fatal corruption is casualness, which separates the sexual act from love. Reverence for copulation which rejects it save as the fusing of two persons who care for each other beyond all other caring is, for the sensitive, the firmest potential bulwark against dissoluteness and promiscuity – far more sturdily pertinent than the negative phallus-worship which identifies a spiritual ethic with a dermatological technicality. Sin lies in wait, not at orifices of the body, but at the door of the mind. . . .

Ma Diggity's kitchen! I see, smell, sense it as though only yesterday her slippers pattered softly on the floor. There the wordless ache, the sigh of Adam, the pristine quest for beauty in the beast – which begins for everyone somewhere, sometime – began for me.

Now Ruth is at my side. The craggy coast of Cape Cod, where I met her; the Mall restaurant in Central Park with Eddie Duchin at the piano; Fifth Avenue at pre-dawn – empty, bewitching, and exquisite of colour; Michel's speakeasy door slot and checked tablecloth; opening night at the Met; the ceremony in the posh Temple Emanu-El study of Dr. Nathan Krass, and his whispered remonstrance at my marrying a "typist," which he misread for "stylist" – all these milestones and countless more mark the journey from the Diggity kitchen to beloved, beautiful, bountiful Ruth, and Jonathan and Sarah Jane.

No felicity, however, shall anaesthetize me into bovine acceptance of the hypocritical mess our Western world is making of sex. To "know" another human being is to confront and achieve the sublimity that merges the self-annihilating present of the individual with the self-perpetuating future of the species. Next to encounter with God, it can raise man to the loftiest level of giving and loving. The realization of that promise cannot be advanced by endowing sex with the sinful and secretive, whether in the back alleys of Bellaire or the rabbi's study in a synagogue.

Suburbia, Snobs, and Coddled Kids

My high-school buddy after the Huck Finn days had frisked to their end was Chuck Bingham, son of the Mayor. We debated together, set up the *Beljuan* dummy, played basketball. When he walked home with me, my father's umbrella workbench was as though it had never been; on Friday afternoons he sampled Mom's *gefillte-fisch*.

"The Mayor's boy! A fine young man! He said he would come to eat by us on Shabbas. With Abie he's like a brother!" She vaunted my distinction to the Ladies Auxiliary of Agudas Ahim Congregation with unwonted gusto, and even let me stay for supper at the Mayor's – as long as I did not touch meat.

In the "What the Elite Are Doing" column of the *Bellaire Leader* the Bingham name was a credential. Sometimes, while we hunched over plans for the strategy of a debate, his mother would bring me a piece of cake left over from a party, or Chuck would inadvertently exclaim, "Gee! I met a swell girl at Dulcie's!" I would gabble on about "affirmative" and "negative" until the gentlemen's agreement to rope off certain matters was reinstated; we never talked about parties.

I didn't belong – and I didn't blame Chuck. I was a Jew, he a Christian. A hand-me-down coat hung over my puny shoulders. I couldn't even remember to walk on the outside when I met a girl. Anyway, did Chuck's party pals have any noble ideals? No! Did they ever worry about prejudices, poverty, or dig to the bottom of life? Did they pity the blue-lipped children of dirty foreigners in the coal villages or flare up against strike-breaking police or hold argument with God? Just empty-headed, spooning Gentiles! Thus I argued.

Nevertheless, for months I had been letting Virgil lie unopened on the kitchen table. I would not be the bright Jew-boy any longer – lumped with pie-faced girls who studied every evening because the sheiks didn't take them out on mushing parties! Snub-nosed Elaine Milliken or Rosalind Cornish of the peaches-and-cream complexion or Celia King who floated like a fragrant zephyr up the aisle – for just a smile from one of them I'd ecstatically fail in every course!

Then, in senior year, "they" elected me president.

"*Nu!* Of course!" Mom beamed. "Only you could do the work. When it was made the debating team you was the first captain. In the junior-senior contests, who was the leader? Only you!" I blushed, not in modesty, but because several of the Gentile candidates had been eliminated by poor grades. Chuck himself flunked solid geometry.

After I read my name in the paper and everybody stopped to congratulate me and Birdie bought me three ties to make "Presidential addresses in" and several girls asked me to put them on committees, I felt better about being able to rattle off all the conjugations of *amo*. One misgiving could not be downed. It was easy to conduct meetings and make the class-pin contract and choose designs for graduation stationery – but what of the social affairs? When the class voted to have a pre-graduation masquerade ball, a new stiff collar left a welt on my nerve-tensed Adam's apple. The die was cast – and the evening came.

"Don't be a grouch," from Jack; "Abeleh, your hands are shaking!" from Mom; "You'll see! Lots of boys will be dressed in their sister's clothes!" from Birdie; "Also a comic! My son!" in scorn from my father – and supper started. The ruffs of Birdie's shirtwaist chafed my neck; the patent-leather shoes made me feel hobbled for a sack-race. I stared at my untouched plate; every girl in B.H.S. '16 snickered back from it.

After supper I entertained the family in the front room. "Does my petticoat show?" With a twist and a swish and an asinine smirk in exaggerated imitation of Birdie, the sally brought a guffaw from father – and a passing pang to me when I saw her cheeks redden. I jabbed an imaginary hairpin into my bonnet, minced on my toes, dabbed my face with the feather duster. Finally, the clock struck eight.

In the gym, I joked about my calico dress and mesh stockings and garters while the Committee chairman announced a prize waltz, kept the bowl filled with fruit punch and had the juniors sprinkle the floor with wax powder. Suppose a giddy girl pulled me out to the middle of the floor! I recoiled at the thought. Then I blanched. Wasn't it customary to have a grand march led by the class president?

"Suppose I watch the door! Maybe people who don't belong will sneak in," I screamed at the bouncy chairman. "You take my place!" She agreed it was not a bad idea! No siree! She didn't want any juniors crashing the gate....

What a haven bed was! For three hours I had shivered in silence at the gym door. Stretching until my toes touched the bedpost, I took a deep breath. "Maybe people who don't belong will sneak in. Hah! Hah!"

The next day was devoted to a silent debate. In the morning: "They're right. There *is* a difference!" At noon, on the way home: "Pop fixes their umbrellas. But he did not come from plumed-knight barbarians. He came from prophets! And so have I!" After supper the *Leader* society page might have been a blank sheet of paper; I amazed Pop by reading his Yiddish *Tageblatt*.

Aching to be "in," yet ashamed of the ache, and proud to be "out," yet inflating that pride with self-recompense, I floundered between avidity for and aversion from Gentile companionship. Birdie had no such qualms or complications. She deeply wanted to become a member of Eastern Star, and paid my initiation fee into a Masonic Blue Lodge which I joined at college to establish her eligibility. Being timorous about wounding her, I refrained from questions. Long afterwards, by chance, on a visit home, I learned she had been blackballed. It enraged me all the more because my sister was a lovely sensitive human being some notches above the "dumb clucks" who poured at Eastern Star tea-parties. She accepted her humiliation without a murmur; I never forgot it.

Like many small towns in North America, Bellaire orbited around a prim, white-Protestant, often church-centred "togetherness" into which even Catholics and Jewish converts to Christianity could not intrude. The double-plied isolation of a Jew who also lived across the tracks could be total and crippling. A metropolis like Toronto, on the other hand, provides a Jewish social complex large enough to boast its own beaks for the pecking hierarchy, an enclave of arty, churchless mavericks, eccentrics, and beatniks whose indifference to canons of respectability includes unconcern about caste and creed, and vents for gregariousness less prissy than a sewing-circle.

Rabbis enjoy social perquisites; shut doors are pried open for them by that deference to the cloth which is a hallmark of stuffed-shirt protocol. Notwithstanding the picayune size of Canadian Jewry (less than one and a half per cent of the population), it is among the three faiths entitled to representation at official shindigs. Personally,

I would not have minded being missed on the dignitary list; professionally, I was jealous of my rank.

For the general, however, the five-o'clock shutdown on Jew-Gentile male contact is no less a business adjunct than the junior executive's five-o'clock shadow. Thenceforth, mixed social relations escalate upward from the "little woman's" diurnal dabblings in philanthropy. Exceptional zeal in the leg-work echelons of charity, public welfare, and cultural groups, well-endowed expertise in gracious living and plush cocktail parties, can put a ticket of admission within reach of a Jewish hostess. Only in the agitation of *non*-fashionable causes does male Jew-Gentile unease vanish. An Easter Peace March through the streets makes no provision for class barriers.

Some years ago, Eleanor Roosevelt accepted an invitation to address the Toronto University Women's Club. That noble lady having been a guest in my home, I did not deny myself the right to inform her of its subtle exclusivism, and she cancelled the engagement. The Royal Yacht Club rejected the grandson of a distinguished Jewish patrician who had contributed more to developing Canada's consciousness of its history than any other individual in the land. Die-hard Ski, Tennis, and Badminton Clubs show more anxiety for the ritual of sport than for the brotherhood of sportsmanship.

My wife's first brush with social prejudice anywhere was the reply to her inquiry about renting an advertised summer cottage. "It isn't that *I* have any feeling against *you*. We just don't rent to Jews. The *neighbours* in our little colony would be upset!" Long afterwards, I heard the lone Jewish member of a swank Hunt Club describe the gory abracadabra of dissecting a trapped fox and distributing tail and ears to its valiant conquerors. Then I thanked the "neighbours" for administering a decisive blow to our illusions about the refined graces of a "little colony."

Canadian afternoon-tea society is a disintegrating bastion of Anglo-Saxondom engaged in a rearguard battle to preserve some remnants of its moth-eaten ermine. Politically and economically, French separatism challenges the supremacy of the Anglo-Saxon establishment. Culture has surrendered to the *avant-garde* and to bohemian poets of pronounced masculinity. Toronto's second largest ethnic group is the Italian.

Toronto has entered a post-Protestant era. United Church clergymen, for example, lament the demise of the funereal Anglo-Saxon Sabbath, and lay the blame for the garroting on the broad backs of newcomers from the hedonistic rabbit-hutches of Central and Eastern Europe.

When Toronto crackled with fulminations from the pulpit and with letters from the vicarage against a plebiscite to legalize Sunday sport – and give the workingman the right to watch a hired professional wield a hockey stick or baseball bat rather than being literally bored to drink at home – I denied that religious observance has a legitimate place on a ballot. "Besides," I added, "the city fathers are asking Jews to help decide how Christians should keep a Sabbath which isn't Sabbath to begin with!" Be that as it may, the astonishing affirmative vote started Toronto's necrophiliac Sunday on the road to final oblivion.

Anglo-Saxon hegemony over social columns has also toppled, under the weight of a journalistic equalitarianism which decrees that a Polish or Lithuanian bride's veil and entourage are no less titillating than the ramrod attendants at St. Paul's, and that a United Appeal tea by a Negro Ladies' Church Auxiliary at least has the merit of novelty.

The most renowned stronghold for the salvage of Anglo-Saxon apartheid is the Granite Club, a svelte, *Juden-rein* rendezvous into which I once strolled with studied casualness for a panel discussion of family problems, after preparing, for the press, a letter of protest against the impropriety of the location. I subsequently got so angry with myself for that abominable gaucherie that I did not emit a sound when the Canadian Council of Christians and Jews chose the Granite Club for a meeting to bestow an Inter-Faith Award!

Other than the panel, a foreign consuls' ball, and a toast-to-the-bride at the Granite Club wedding reception of a former Gentile secretary, I have never sat, stood, or spoken in that demesne. Direct testimony, therefore, cannot be adduced to reckon the loss I suffer by absence from its membership roster. In the spectrum of my concerns, few are more irrelevant, immaterial, and inconsequential, although I must caution myself about the sour grapes that set my teeth on edge after the High School Masquerade Ball almost five decades ago.

Sociological reformers have marked that commercial contacts are frequently brought to life, if nothing else is, in a racially exclusive social club, thus creating a ripple of unfair discrimination in the pond of big business. Earnest philo-Judaic voices have lambasted Granite Club fastidiousness as a mild infection of, and potential prelude to, Nazi racism. I am unable to whip up indignation. If anyone wishes to impoverish his personality by confining canasta, cocktails, and mildly off-colour jokes to people "of his own kind," he has that right in law and in morality, whether he be Gentile or Jew. If anyone has a temperamental predilection for the monolithic, soporific, anaesthetic administered by snobbery; if anyone likes heavy-jowled inaccessibility to a fresh idea, ceremonious idolatry of blood descent or bank account, the scraping and bowing of flunkies who often despise their masters, he is welcome to his choice, whether the attendant banalities are spoken with "veddy" British reserve or gestured Yiddishisms.

Discriminatory debarment from educational opportunities, however, acts on me like a dose of adrenalin. My brother-in-law delayed and endangered his exceptional creativity at the mediocre University of Mississippi because his "personality-quotient" did not spark a gleam of recognition in the blinkered eyes that survey applications for medical schools of long-established Eastern colleges. Equally brilliant Jewish students have travelled as far as Edinburgh or Switzerland to qualify for healing the sick – despite a shortage of physicians.

A few years ago, under a Dean who claimed that Jews lack manual dexterity, many potentially competent Jewish students were barred from the University of Toronto Dentistry School for failure to pass aptitude tests. During my term as Chairman of the Joint

Public Relations Committee of the Canadian Jewish Congress and B'nai B'rith, I placed on the desk of President Sydney Smith an enrolment list in which every member of a dental laboratory class was identified by the code-letters "P," "C," and "J." Dr. Smith did not inquire how, or through whom, the tell-tale sheet came into my possession. (It was filched by a student whose name I had refused to know.) I assured him I would not divulge the sensational episode to the press, although certain political elements would have been delighted to charge the University with religious bias. The following academic year introduced a new Dean.

Social self-seclusion is not always spurred on by vicious racism. To relax, unwind, unbend among your own people, who share your peculiar and parochial psychology, understand and tolerate your foibles, and won't nudge one another behind your back, is a universal and legitimate item in the good life. Certainly Jews need such a boon as sedative for frayed nerves. Why not Gentiles?

Inescapably, nevertheless, this normal need for kindred bears the seed of its own corruption. The more one dwells within, the more human beings one can do without. Stuffy smugness soon breeds a pouter pigeon whose entire cosmos nestles snug in his craw. The habit of consorting only with one's chosen people because they are more comfortable than strangers leads to the notion that they are *superior* to strangers. The fact of the Granite Club's defence against Jewish incursion fazes me not at all. When that defence is mounted on the dogma that Jews are intrinsically and collectively a lesser breed, I demur. Social anti-Semitism resembles the simple exercise of squatter's rights on a parcel of land hardly worth the fuss – until it dips into Nazi anthropology.

A Lieutenant-Governor of Ontario, J. Keiller Mackay, while on the Supreme Court bench, rendered a decision against restrictive covenants on property deeds which rang a carillon around the world. The issue was not so much one of practice as of principle. The privilege of owning a summer cottage in a close-knit, Jew-allergic Gentile colony is dubious; the principle that no man, woman, or child may be depersonalized under a blanket label, "unfit for association," is crucial.

Beyond and above his worth as an individual a human being has significance in the measure of his symbolic self-identity with a tradition. Her Majesty Elizabeth II ranks with the thirty-second cousin of a coster-monger, at ninety-eight cents worth of chemicals. In her representative capacity she is all that England was and is: Magna Carta, Francis Drake, the dogged valour of men at sea; the halls of Oxford where reason seeks truth and St. Paul's Cathedral where faith seeks God; Parliament and Westminster Abbey; the colonizing will that built an empire and the common sense to perceive and accept its twilight; the King James Bible, into whose storied pages went the earthy vigour of the English tongue, and the Bard who brought its beauty to fruition; undulant hills, and castles of feudal lords, a pub, the bustle of London's slums, and the fortitude of her children under the Nazi blitz; prim tea-and-cake in a parish vicarage and the rebel whoop of sit-down strikers against the H-bomb!

This capsule comment on British royalty, when I first published it in a newspaper article, evoked acclaim from Anglo-Saxons who would have been hard put to find symbolic meaning in a wizened little Whitechapel tailor humming a Yiddish lullaby over a button-hole. Yet thirty-five centuries are written on his face – without the gory Tower of London beheadings and stranglings which spatter the genealogical tree of Plantagenets and Windsors.

In Grinkishok, main-line aristocracy was founded on piety and learning. Jewish Cabots, born Kabotnik, literally "talked only to God." Among the early nineteenth-century Jewish settlers in North America, Sephardic (Spanish-Portuguese) stock considered itself and was considered by others the well-born of Abraham's children; in Montreal, as in New York and Newport, the oldest synagogue still emblazons Iberian names of rabbis and laymen like De Sola, although they have long been superseded by Ashkenazim from Central and Eastern Europe. German Jews, Occidentalized in manner and mores, whose influx began after the political upheavals of 1848, then had their turn at the turned-up nose.

Today, the clans Cleveland Amory designated Jewish "Grand Dukes" – Loeb, Schiff, Guggenheim, Cardozo, and Belmont (who "passed" via the Church) – are a vestigial afterglow of celestial splendour. But the patent of communal prestige, in the rapidly solidifying North American social structure, is money – clinical proof of Jewish acculturation. Whether worship of wealth and consumption of goods be long-standing and low-keyed, as normally among Gentiles, or colourful, cacophonous and conspicuous, as occasionally among Jews, the nub of the idolatry of wealth is invariable – with one deviation: Jewry's élite must not only have, but give, as more than one tight-fisted tribal tycoon has discovered when a niggardly contribution to United Jewish Appeal blocked his request for membership in a Golf Club.

A Jew finds it difficult, however, to accept the superiority of another Jew on any ground. Historically rooted skepticism about human pretensions, centuries-long severance from the protocol and form which grow out of a stable, secure status, and an earthiness that resists white-tied fol-de-rol, inhibit the growth of a Jewish aristocracy, now that the Grinkishok reverence for intellect has abated, and as financial rank is subject to change from generation to generation.

Deference for a customer does not prevent a Jewish waiter from directing his diet; every Israeli taxi-driver imparts advice to the Prime Minister, who wears the open shirt and air of a taxi-driver himself; in Toronto, elegant evening-gowns, bouffant hair-dos, and meticulously planned social functions cannot press Jewish exuberance into stiff *goyyische* formality.

Swank Gentiles loose-tongued at a bar often hint, with suspiciously vociferous approval, at *nouveau-riche* Jewish affluence. "You people have got all the money now! You're smart!" Most wealthy Jews – when they are – are of course *nouveau*! A fat bank balance rarely spans *zaideh's** generation or comes as an emolument

* Grandpa's.

of birth or inheritance. It is not abnormal, or inexcusable, that people who arrived on their own are tempted by a pride which finds initial outlet in mink stoles, lavish tipping, sixty-foot yachts, and well-appointed confirmation and Bar-Mitzvah parties.

Do the Gentile and Jewish *bourgeoisie* resemble each other like two comfortably acquiescent peas in a pod? There are differences, and the hegira of Jewry to suburbia during recent years provides a clinical laboratory for assessing them. Toronto's specimen for study is Forest Hill Village, legendary subject of an honest and exhaustive sociological probe under the title *Crestwood Heights*. The nearly sixty per cent Jewish population now dwelling there doubled from 1944, the year I became a Villager, to 1963.

Forest Hill Jews are nothing if not gregarious. Hospitality to kin and friends may convert even *shiva** into a continuous serving of sympathy-and-tea. Bridal luncheons make every wedding a *ganzer hasunah*.† Proliferation of parties has created a new profession: the social counsellor.

The first striking differentiation in Jewish suburbia is casual, albeit controlled, approach to spirituous beverages. A good Villager's bad dream is to run short of liquor for his guests. A Jewish teetotaller, when one exists, hides his light under a bushel. Rarely, however, does a Jew overestimate his carrying capacity. All five types of drunks – jocose, bellicose, lachrymose, morose, and comatose – are conspicuous by their absence, even on the festival of Purim when a Jew is permitted enough alcoholic leeway to confound the names "Mordecai" and "Haman."

"You Jews never get drunk! Why?" Save the perennial query about our rejection of Christ, that "why" is put to me more than any other. In a letter requesting me to address an annual conference on the theme, the Ontario Association of Family Court Judges stated that none of its members had ever presided over a Jewish case of desertion, non-support, or family disintegration caused by alcoholism.

* Week-long period of home-mourning.
† A real shindig.

Seventy-five per cent of humanity abstains from or cannot afford alcoholic beverages; the remainder dwell under the aegis of Christendom. This concentration of topers in Christianized lands underscores the rambunctiousness of human nature. Whereas Protestantism ranks alcoholic beverages among the wily devices of the devil, Judaism has no objection whatever, as such, to liquor, and wine is an integral property in ritual practice.

The United Church of Canada, with realistic circumspection, makes total abstinence "a request, not a requirement," although, much to the discomfiture of the "harmless cocktail" drinkers, the absolute pledge has been at times recommended with sulphurous severity. Among Jews, a total-abstinence vow would be considered a psychopathic aberration or a whimsical wager. Overtippling, however, is indefensible – not because of divine retribution, but because of the community's wrath.

My father always had a modest bottle of schnapps in the icebox. Since Judaism never inflated a swallow into a mortal sin or a mystery, he did not hide the amber fluid away or apologize for smacking his lips. I was curious about his gusto, but I never bothered to sneak a taste for first-hand information. Wine was a different matter. On Sabbath Eve and festivals we all shared its flushing of cheek and enlivening of the springs of laughter. But our disdain for the town sots was bottomless, and *shikkur vee a goy** offered a safe, sanctimonious verbal vent for spleen at the Gentiles' contumelious scorn for Christ-killers, just as the Gentile folk-idiom "drunk as a lord" compensated the feudal serf for his humiliation at the hands of his master. The Yiddish exclamation can still be heard at a convivial Village gathering.

It was the pride of the Jewish community that strengthened its ramparts against excessive drinking. The Jew deemed himself a member of a moral aristocracy. Drunkenness violated the code, at the same time that it jeopardized the existence of a people on the firing-line. Unlike Shriners in a convention, a Villager's ancestors could not afford the luxury of a permissive or frivolous attitude.

* Drunk as a Gentile.

During recent years hard liquor has grown from an expression of gregariousness and gratitude to God into a centrepiece of the Forest Hill social showcase. Scotch and rye at the ubiquitous basement bar is shunting sacramental wine from the dining-table. Bar-Mitzvah souses provoke less censure. The new drinking pattern is not an improvement, and the increasingly popular ladies' luncheon cocktail, with its possible carryover into solitary cocktails at home, is a clear hazard. Beyond doubt, psychic stresses impinge with special sharpness on a people conditioned by their historic experience of insecurity, and enhance the lure of a mild binge. If alcoholism can originate in alienation from simple trust in God, in thwarted emotions, a nagging spouse, or the centripetal pressures that erupt into the human brain from ever-widening circles, the discrepancy between Jews and Gentiles will be narrowed.

A survey of solids as well as fluids might conclude that the Villager massages his complexes with *gefillte-fisch* rather than a gin fizz, scotch herring and sour cream instead of a scotch-on-rocks. On European boat trips I have noted that Gentile and Jew can be fingered by a simple test: the former haunts the bar, the latter the buffet.

Not that the Cohens are impervious to calorophobia! Like any fashion-minded female, Mrs. Cohen aspires to reduce outspread without reducing intake, and retreats from potato pancakes and boiled beef to cottage cheese and martinis, whose caloric content is underestimated. The retreat is not a rout. No less passionately than Mrs. Pettibone, Mrs. Cohen dreams of the baths, massages, creams, and rollers at Elizabeth Arden's Main Chance near Phoenix, but she strews the beverage table with schmaltzy chopped chicken liver and miniature meatballs.

Why did Jews move into the Village? Adherents of external orthodox piety cluster within walking distance of the synagogue to avoid a breach of the rabbinic law against conveyance on the Sabbath. Holy Blossom, in 1937, had already initiated a suburban trend which finally brought all the principal *shules* to the northern suburbs. Religiocentric motivation, however, did not spark the parade to Forest Hill. The bait was more mundane.

"Crestwood Heights" reputedly had the best public-school system in Ontario (a bright lure for education-oriented Jews) – and it boasted a non-anti-Semitic tradition, compared to other "desirable" sections of Toronto whose Gentile way of life is armoured against foreign infiltration by discriminatory real-estate agreements which, being verbal, do not violate the Mackay ruling against restrictive covenants. Once the trek started, a Village Jew would have neighbours of his own kind, in a homogeneous community – a "gilded ghetto."

Alerted by the assiduous Lord's Day Alliance, Toronto often elevates a Sunday blue-law regulation into a red-hot issue. Jews do not relish the inflation of a Sunday backyard laundry-hanging into a religious *cause célèbre,* and inevitably gravitate to an "island" where they can follow their own calendar without constant fear of annoying touchy Gentiles.

A do-it-yourself ghetto offers tangible dividends: swift access to weekday Hebrew and weekend Religious School and easy recruitment of car pools for staggered transportation; rotating mother baby-sitters – like adoptees, preferably of the same faith; a reservoir of Jewish playmate invitees for Bar-Mitzvah, birthday, and Hanukkah parties; considerate avoidance by teachers of important assignments or outright dismissal of overwhelmingly Jewish classes on Jewish religious holidays; respite from the "why-don't-we-have-Jesus" question after the school religious period, Forest Hill's Board of Education having availed itself of legal permission to reject the Ontario course of instruction.

An autonomous Jewish society within a society, however, cannot be judged an unmixed blessing. Teachers are so frightened at the prospect of arousing ire by alleged interference with their charges' practice of Judaism that they banish from the classroom Jewish pupils who appear on the second day of Rosh Hashanah – although Reform Jews do not observe that additional day.

A public-school class ninety per cent Jewish would not be

devised by a paternal providence as a Jewish child's preparation for life in a world where he belongs to a fragment-minority. Concentration of numbers in the Village has already infected him with *hauteur*, in protean forms: a facetious, albeit symptomatic, proposal that Christmas carols be replaced by Hatikvah ("The Hope" – Israel's national anthem); conspicuous gambolling in the playground on Jewish religious holidays celebrated by absence from class; sneering quips about the "dumb *goy*"; exclusion of Gentiles from home parties; high-school frats that exact a promise from "pledgees" not to take out Gentile girls.

Disclosure of anti-Gentile arrogance in Jewish kids need not alarm, since it will never proliferate beyond a locale matched, in Canada, solely by Westmount, Quebec, and it need not astonish, since the picture merely repeats, in reverse, an ancient design. For the first time in modern Diaspora, a Jewish majority feels normal and secure enough to manifest the power-mindedness and insolence nitherto and historically limited to Gentiles.

Among the many modest-income Jews in suburbia, some strain purse and heart to "keep up with the Cohens." Fathers have borrowed money for Bar-Mitzvah or wedding celebrations. By proletarian norms, even they would be deemed upper-bracket. Inevitably, youth is stripped of the hard, elementary incentives that goaded its parents. The scholarships won by second-generation dads athirst for higher education fall increasingly to the offspring of newly arrived Japanese, Hungarians, and Italians at downtown schools like Jarvis and Harbord, where pop had *his* start. A cashmere-jacketed high-school frat boy may brag about dad's waiting business, in which his acumen will achieve a meteoric rise to vice-president and his pampered narcissism an utter lack of empathy for the less-privileged.

How can a lad develop such empathy when he cannot name a single acquaintance without at least one family car? Suburbia congeals by irreversible stages into a one-class conformist compound isolated from its heterogeneous urban matrix and dominated by status-conscious parents who might give their sons golf lessons with an eye to future "contacts."

Spectres of self-doubt and decadence often glide across the broadloom. A brilliant scion of a "first family" confided to me in a pre-confirmation interview that he goes to a psychiatrist. "Lots of my friends do," he added with a wry smile. "Mine says I'm self-absorbed, don't relate to people. Maybe I just have it easy and don't *have* to relate!" "If my boy would get himself a *Globe and Mail* route and get out mornings to deliver 'em, I'd be the happiest man alive," a doting dad exclaimed to me. I recalled that he gives "my boy" a Christmas-vacation trip to Miami, monthly tax-deductible cheques for a nest egg, and a continuous dinner-conversation apprenticeship in how to succeed in business by really trying, and I wondered whether Ma's sable and hibernating stint at the Fontainebleau might be relinquished to fabricate privation.

In a crisis, coddled kids neck-deep in hair-dos, convertibles, and the twist often reveal hitherto untapped reserves of character. I have seen them mature, visibly, under the challenge of a family bereavement. A widening circle of stiff-necked young eccentrics baffle their respectability-conscious parents, some of whom were themselves radical and Leftist during the depression of the 'thirties, by turning from the rat-race to research or to genteel academic poverty that ranks a creative PH.D. thesis above a Cadillac, by Easter-marching with the Campaign for Nuclear Disarmament, by managing to be seen with coloured companions, and by going off to Ghana or Guatemala as Canadian prototypes of the Peace Corps.

It is in concern for and about religion, most dramatically, that the latter Village mode improves upon the former. The new generation remembers what its immediate forbears forgot or forsook. The importance of the synagogue, socially and intellectually, to Village youngsters links them more closely to granddad than to dad – however wide the gap between their respective forms of ritual observance.

Twenty years ago the remoteness of God, death, human origin, purpose, and destiny from the centre of a confirmand's consciousness was total, astronomical, and unexceptional. The recent vintage crop literally pulled me into lively bull sessions after Friday Evening Service, to debate what they could believe and why.

In the more rigorous climate of preceding generations, wit and wisdom focused on sheer survival; dad and uncle spent themselves for livelihood and liberty – working to aid immigrant parents, pay college fees, keep above water during the depression, save a few dollars for marriage – and sometimes fought with gangs for the right to walk down the block without being punched. Civil rights are now ingested with mother's milk; Dachau and Auschwitz are ugly words, not nightmares; the shackles of timidity and millennial pain have been sundered. Village kids are normal Canadians – in dress, giggle, back-talk, jive, and the bare-legged cavorting of cheerleaders.

In such an atmosphere, a sensitive, introverted élite utilizes its freedom from earthbound cares to search the heavens for faith. I sensed the symptoms of a similar transition in the youth of Moscow, whose concern about man's destiny *beyond* waxes with the mitigation of anxiety about his bread-and-butter *here*.

For the average junior conformist of Forest Hill, however, the world beyond the spheres and the world beyond his own recreation room are equally insubstantial. He knows he can't change the one; he does not try to change the other. Uninterested in world affairs because they are too vast for comprehension and control, uncommitted to causes because they don't succeed, unidealistic because idealism is impractical, unromantic because one must "play it cool," he limits his goals to a life cushioned and curtained from the dread realities that darken the horizon as the high noon of the twentieth century retreats farther into the past.

What a contrast between Forest Hill and Union Street! The Village psyche is turned askew by an unassailable sense of belonging and having; that of Union Street was shunted off kilter by a sense of alienation and disesteem.

Social and economic improvement explains the difference – but its most dramatic illustration is the response of Forest Hill to the State of Israel. When embattled farmers, workers, wives, and children repulsed the seven-pronged Arab raid of extermination in

1948, Ontario's Premier Frost said to me, "Great, Rabbi! You Jews are fighters – as good as the Irish!" thereby honouring the tradition that physical bravery is the noblest badge of merit – a tradition subsequently manifested when dozens of Torontonians who had denounced me for milksop pacifism telephoned effusive congratulations on reading an imaginative newspaper reporter's story that I had "landed a left hook" on a heckler at a disarmament rally. From Israel's martial courage in defence of its life, Forest Hill's newly militant Diaspora youngsters reaped a rich increment of pride and confidence. They too subscribed to the tradition! Now they could "look Gentiles smack in the eye."

In my boyhood, the tiny strip of land on the Eastern Mediterranean then called Palestine lay at the inmost convolution of my brain. I brooded about it from *despair*, as the only hope for Jewish emancipation. I *prayed* for it, because I could do nothing else.

Every night I held prayerful converse with God. It was private; only the soft muffling pillow heard me whisper for His care in sleep, and for whatever I wanted most next day: nickelodeon, sled, roller-skates, the teacher to like my recitation, Pop to forget the whaling he owed me, Mom to be happy. One item – and one only – was never omitted, because I wanted it *all* the time: "Oh God, please give Palestine back to the Jewish people!" There was nothing in my experience to justify the slightest expectation of its fulfilment. The poor junk-pedlars of Bellaire chanted threnodies of Exile and prophecies of Return, saluted the New Year with *L'Shanah Haba b'Yerusholayim,** and nailed over the kitchen sink the little tin *pushke* with its slot for pennies that would help the Jewish people buy precious dunams of land in Palestine – but when speakers from Pittsburgh tried to organize a branch of Zionists, everyone shook his head and mumbled that he had enough troubles without dreaming a dream that can't happen. I never stopped praying for Palestine in those days!

In these days, brash young Jewish Villagers may propose display of Israel's flag on the school platform at assembly exercises,

* Next year in Jerusalem.

the celebration of its anniversary, and a course in spoken Hebrew! When the Collegiate Principal reported his mounting anxiety to me, graphic pictures, one after the other, stalked before my mind's eye of an incident that occurred a half-century ago.

We were *teitching Humesh** in *heder* when Moshe Zlotkin's sweat-lathered horse halted his wild-eyed gallop in front of Moshe's house. The rising hullabaloo swept away the *melammed* like a cyclone; we bolted to the street, and saw the gnome-like greybeard lying prone on the dirty rags in his junk-wagon. A hunk of coal thrown by one of a gang of "sheeny"-jeering mine-settlement kids had struck Moshe's head. Frothing, I wrenched a stave from the wooden fence. "On to coaltown, fellahs! We'll show the damn hunkies!" Then Davey Platt's father curved his bony fingers under the back of my collar.

"*Meshuggener*! † What can you do?"

I wriggled. "We'll show em!"

"*Nu, nu!* What do you expect? We are *Yidden*! No? We are in a strange land! No? Stay home!" His grip tightened around my neck, but I managed to brandish the stick.

"No is right! Come on! We'll show. . . ." A hand clamped down on my mouth; screaming and kicking, I was carried into *heder*.

Throughout the night I lived in the days of Joshua and Saul, Gideon and David and the Maccabees. *They* didn't stay home and cower! "Sheeny" was never heard in the streets of Jerusalem! "Oh God, please give Palestine back. . . ."

Can anyone fancy a Jew-boy being admonished to "stay home" today, in Jewish suburbia's mansions of liberty and light? It is the Jew who might play the bully, although he would hardly vent his lordliness with a fist or a lump of coal. The cycle of history has run its gamut from Union Street to Forest Hill.

Many Village dads – and probably all the granddads – had their Union Street too. Across the interplanetary space between it and his current abode, each writes, in varying degrees of fervour, a resolution: "I don't want my kids to want for the things I didn't have!"

* Translating Pentateuch. † Madman.

The birth of that sentiment is irreproachable; who can denigrate parental solicitude? Its works are inscribed on the caterer's account for a rococo Bar-Mitzvah reception, a twenty-dollar bill presented to the school-cafeteria cashier for a thirty-five-cent lunch – and the thick, spongy broadloom of a teenage newlyweds' apartment. There are many in Jewish suburbia.

Like Topsy, early marriage "just growed" beneath the surface of an affluent society. For Villagers, it was also an "old Jewish custom." The Talmud recommends the nuptial canopy at eighteen. When Will Durant counselled Holy Blossom parents, in a forum lecture, to subsidize marriageable youth, and specified the amount of five thousand dollars, a teenager's quip – "Five thousand a year, or five thousand a month?" – revealed Forest Hill's unreserved espousal of that dictum.

The Jewish psyche illustrates a Hebrew verb form called *pi'el*, meaning intensive action. That extra fillip of passion characterized the Chosen People long before Forest Hill; a Jew was inclined to do everything – both the good deed and the bad – with intensity. Heat formerly concentrated on his practice of religion. Now it boils in the social sphere; a Villager may not *pray*, but he does *play* madly, as four Toronto Jewish golf clubs attest. The *pi'el* stance also makes the Jewish suburbanite a clinical specimen for the study of a social trend like early marriage.

In the Palestinian climate, puberty was not a laggard; the average Bar-Mitzvah boy, at thirteen, really had attained it – and girlhood unaware tarried but a fleeting moment. Today quick Oriental ripening has been revived. Anatomical development of the Western female is being expedited – perhaps as a by-product of enriched diet, psychosomatic stimulation, Hollywood promotion of bosomy movie-queens, and advertisements like that of Spinnaker Scarlet Perfume, which encourages the hope that "his kiss tonight will start a typhoon."

I have often jested that every girl-child is born a woman, while a boy is lucky if he becomes a man during his lifetime. In the Village, the first half of the epigram is well-nigh realized. The sweet, rosy, schoolgirl look quickly follows swaddling-clothes and kiddy-car into the attic of oblivion, erased by hair-waver, mascara, and eyebrow pencil. A twelve-year old may have a movie-date boy-friend on Sunday afternoon and a baby-sitter Sunday evening. To get paired off with a hand-holding hero the first summer in camp, at ten for some girls, is the sole security against eight weeks of leprous isolation; a Saturday-night date, every-night phone pal, with whom one may go steadily, at fourteen, often necessitates a separate directory listing and number; going steady, being pinned, then the ring, complete the venture into the marriage-mart and middle-aged emotional security, which Carol and Linda want most.

On the threshold of her nuptial flight, a Village belle stands under the canopy as one about to write the final triumphant chapter. Usually she is pretty, half educated but not unintelligent, a jumble of innocence and wisdom. Too often she emerges from the honeymoon bewildered – debating which women's organization to join, whom to engage for apartment-décor, how to have her hair styled, whether to sit with one pair of parents at the golf club all summer or the other pair at the cottage, why they go to in-laws for dinner every Friday evening, what to serve while entertaining the few couples who still comprise her circle of friends, if she should take a university course, jog and prod her mind by joining a book-review group, or just be a housewife with a cleaning-woman once a week – until they can afford to have a baby, assisted by a proud parental loan.

Pressured by peers and sometimes pushed by mother, a Village girl is more likely than most to risk a premature, incompatible, and disastrous union because of other-directed compulsion. The growing bevy of independent brides who teach school or take secretarial jobs, running their homes at the same time, while the lord and master finishes business or professional training, may be not only less bored but more successful wives; the future will tell.

Is my representation of young love in the Village a caricature? The general outline coincides with the anatomy of early marriage in every middle-class suburb of North America. In Forest Hill the lines are more heavily drawn by the anxiety of parents to give the couple a start; that often means making sure it starts where they are themselves. Mom and dad have an inoffensive and often touching pride in their conquest of poverty – together; that sharing of hardship and hard work, the interlacing and intermingling of two persons involved in a challenge, is the durable cement and prop of their blessing. Yet they deny it to their sated youngsters.

A double bed and Van der Velde's detailed diagram of marital gymnastics might well be supplemented by a hard-to-meet budget, sex compatibility by income-adaptability. How often my counsel has been sought by long-wed couples estranged after a measure of financial security terminated their common struggle to make a living – and even by kids suffocated in drapes, Florida holidays, and broadloom they didn't want unless they could get it on their own!

Divorce is not unknown to Jewish suburbia. Acids of modernity are corroding the long-vaunted "Jewish family." The divorce rate among Jews has not yet reached that of the Gentile, but the acceleration is in full swing.

To Jewish Forest Hill divorce is not abhorrent. It is not a crime that should be stifled and punished; it is a tragedy to be deplored, but accepted when unavoidable. Judaism does not regard marriage as an unbreakable sacrament – rather as a contract between two persons capable of fragility and error. In such cases human happiness need not be sacrificed to a concept of "holiness."

In weak moments I envy a monolithic ecclesiastical complacency impervious to the barbarism of Canada's primitive divorce laws, but I cannot condone it. Church control over a concern so private and personal should be confined to those who voluntarily submit to its dogma and discipline. Even Jehovah's Witnesses, against whose fanaticism I have often inveighed, do not ask that *everyone* be denied a blood transfusion. If a man or woman deems divorce a contravention of God's will, let him refuse to enter a court for such a purpose. By what prerogative except political compulsion does he make his opinion the law of the land, applicable to Jews and others who do not share it?

I have seen irreconcilably estranged Villagers to whom the divorce court would have been a door to some modicum of dignity. I have seen Village children with tell-tale tics for whom a clean break would have been less damaging than the cockpit of their parents' hate. There are circumstances in which divorce appears to reason and compassion as the lesser of two evils. Statute should follow them – not an ecclesiastical dogma.

Too many Forest Hill early marriages are in trouble; some seem to have withered with the floral decorations of the wedding. As a rule, they flounder on the rock of immaturity. The most lamentable of all cases in my Forest Hill clinic, however, was precipitated by the strangling embrace of a bride's parents who could not endure that their "darling girl want for anything *they* couldn't have when *they* were starting out in life." Atrophy of bourgeois youth's do-it-yourself muscles, of course, does not always lead to the divorce court; it does induce decadence, a disarmed defencelessness inimical to survival in a steadily grimmer, more exacting world. When the West's future is threatened by upheaval and insecurity, the effect of such fibre-softening may be calamitous.

Years ago, in New York before the 1929 bubble burst, I witnessed its tragic consequences for the children in my Religious School.

I love those kids to this day, with nostalgic, undiminished tenderness. When beribboned little girls glanced up at me shyly under long eyelashes or a youngster was sent to my office for misbehaviour and I watched him twist his fingers and wait shamefacedly for the homily he never got; when I touched the head of Jane Steyer who told her teacher she was going to marry me or smiled at Roslyn Offenbach who wanted my snapshot in her memory-book or patted the shoulder of Jimmy Nathanson with whom I often tossed a football in Riverside Park; when Dorothy Kohn fell asleep telling her granny how Dr. Feinberg tipped his hat to her just as though she were a grown-up lady and Lucy Minton called me up one day before traipsing off to Mrs. Wolfe's Dancing School and told me she was worried because I looked so pale – rivers of affection coursed through my heart.

After Black Friday, in October 1929, chauffeured Packards no longer honked for tykes on Sunday mornings; addresses shifted from West End Avenue to Washington Heights; older brothers left university to cool heels in employment agencies; Adirondack summer camps, riding-lessons, birthday dances, Parisian clothes, evanesced; some fathers jumped out of windows; and teachers' conferences reported a mounting toll of juvenile neuroses.

The coddled kids of Forest Hill – will *they* be tested in the fire? A tinder pile is growing: decline of the West under black and yellow pressure, moral and material bankruptcy inflicted by the nuclear-arms race (not to speak of nuclear war), the population explosion and struggle for living space, continued attrition of the springs of religious faith.

I do not envy suburbia's young. Union Street was a deprived world – but withal a microcosm of, a prelude to, the world we would enter. Life was a hard nut to crack, but the tools lay to hand, and strength and skill could use them. Forest Hill Village seems to be a paradise whence the lotus-eaters will be driven with little to cover them, an artificial lagoon wherein spoon-fed fish struggle to the top like aspiring dolphins – far removed from the vast oceanic tides of reality. Today demands less stern stuff than suburbia's kids are made of; I fear tomorrow will demand more.

The Crucifixion

"CHRIST-KILLER Jew bastard!"

The triune obscenity bubbled like a witches' cauldron on the pendulous lips of Bellaire's prize derelict – a scrofulous scarecrow who foraged a doughnut and coffee for physical sustenance, "a cuppla" drinks to feel alive and a shred of ego-satisfaction by cursing every Jew with enough olfactory endurance to venture near him.

The last noun, being a shop-worn epithet of the streets, had long before ceased to denigrate Mom's virtue; the penultimate reference to my faith and people I would not deny; "Christ-killer" stabbed my heart, though I should have been accustomed to it.

Birdie called Bill Cuddicomb an "A-one bum." He had once been "chief cook and bottle-washer," namely, hallway attendant, at the city hall, employed by the Mayor to keep him out of mischief, since he came from one of Bellaire's old families – but mothers complained that he forgot to adjust his clothing after weaving to the men's room.

Though warned to stay away from Bill, I was fascinated by his filth, and had been staring at him for some minutes when his drink-fogged brain finally got around to me as "wunna them Feinberg Jew-boys."

"Come on over here, Bud; somethin' t'tell yuh," he beckoned. Had he hailed me by any other name, I might have skedaddled. "Bud" was in my dictionary a patent of true friendship. No sooner did I stand before him than he placed his hands on my shoulders, bent down to whisper the triad with laborious intensity, and spewed a burning stream of tobacco juice in my eye.

The kitchen sink received my vomit, the parlour couch what was left of my tears, and my mother – silence. She knew when to leave me alone.

That evening I hung around the house, intent on the unturned page of a book and demurring to Mom, with transparent offhandedness, that I wasn't sleepy. Birdie suspected my unusual torpor, but even she finally followed the others upstairs.

With head lowered over the kitchen table, I told my mother what had happened.

A far-distant scene appeared to draw Mom away from me. Was she listening? Then her facial muscles began to tighten and a tiny trickle traced a glistening line down her cheeks. I sat like stone, until a toneless voice spoke to me.

"No, Abeleh *mein zoon*! You did not kill anyone. They say in their Bible the Jews did it, long, long ago. No, no, my son!"

Always, even when she read the New York *Tageblatt* with her five-and-ten-cent-store glasses, her rest had seemed like a spring coiled for release into a chore that needed to be done. That night the coil snapped, and a great weariness was upon her.

I soon realized the far-off scene was Grinkishok. At Easter time, she said, the Jews in Russia were always afraid. The peasants were very religious, but also ignorant, and the priests in the churches made them terribly excited by telling them the Jews had killed their god. Sometimes a Jew would be beaten. After every Easter grandfather thanked God they were all alive.

"That name he called you! Hundreds of years ago – nobody knows what happened. Could you have done it? You wasn't there! Long, long ago!" Her trembling lips drew together into a pencil line, the voice faded and Sarah, daughter of the Rav of Grinkishok, seemed to petrify around an ancient fear. But maternal concern reined in her precipitate retreat. With a quick jerk, as though wrenching herself loose, she leaned forward and touched my cheek. *"Zorg nit, mein kind. Du host kanem nit geharget. Zay, zay hargenen – mit sinoh! Gay shlofen; Gott vet dir heeten. . . ."* *

Before slipping into bed beside Allen, I held up my hands, the better to see them in the darkness. Red? Was my heart black with guilt? My people deicides, befouling their progeny forever? My God – had He condemned me?

These were the questions I asked myself then, in a childish tongue, and for years thereafter. The loathsome calumny of a reeking drunkard merely transferred to Bellaire the apocalyptic infection that terrorized my grandfather in Grinkishok. That night I protested – "Long, long ago! I wasn't even there!" – to the skylight, the bedpost, the empty air, the angels in heaven. Since then, only the physical appurtenances of my apostrophe have shifted; the collision of irreducible fact and irrational fiction remains.

Christmas was birth, life beginning – whether of God, a man, or both; the wide-eyed wonder of a babe in its crêche protruded even through the icy mask of winter. Easter celebrated life everlasting – but its crux was the cross, and on the cross was agony impaled, pierced hands and feet, and death; even burgeoning green spears of springtide could not penetrate the iron shroud.

* "Don't worry, my child. You have killed no one. They, they kill with hate. Go to sleep; God will protect you."

The scalding bitterness of Bill Cuddicomb's tobacco spittle receded mercifully from memory, but the wound deepened. No later than the next Easter a playmate of my sister Sylvia, scrubbed and gleaming in a pink frock and bonnet, assured her she didn't kill Christ – "but your *mother* did!" At the Union Street School my Easter vacation did not really have its official start until Joe Smathers crooked his arms under my armpits, linked palms behind my head and doused it under the fountain to the accompaniment of "Ya Christ-killin' Jew!" A Catholic customer of my dad's to whom I delivered an umbrella showed me a passage from *Bible History* by Bishop Gilmour, which he had studied in the parochial school: "The murdered Abel is a figure of Jesus Christ while Cain is a figure of the traitor Judas and the Jewish people, who put our Saviour to death. . . . As a punishment for their sins in having rejected Him, they [the Jews] are today wanderers on the earth, and will be to the end of time."

"Why doncha get wise to yourself Jew-boy and come back to God?"

The courage to answer failed me – but more desperately than ever I beseeched God that night to give Palestine back to the Jews. Years later, American Protestant missionaries to the Arabs in Beirut vehemently argued against partition and a Jewish State before the United Nations Special Commission on Palestine, and the Catholic hierarchy demanded Jerusalem's internationalization to protect the few already-protected holy places in the Israeli segment. Then I recalled the textbook incident and asked myself whether the hostile intervention of Christian dignitaries had been related to the dogma that Jews may return to the Holy Land only when they return to the Holy Christ.

Billy Sunday, the famous ball-player evangelist, pitched his huge circus tent in Wheeling. I was caught up in mass enthusiasm and my own curiosity, and volunteered for the choir – until we rehearsed a hymn about the "Blood of the Lamb" and a tenor at my side cast a baleful glance at me and mumbled, "That means you, brother." The first day Sylvia taught a class in the Big Run country schoolhouse, a little girl ran from her touch crying, "You're a Jew! You killed God!"

A Passion Play produced in Denver touched a core of hostility in Christian children so intense that their Jewish playmates felt uncomfortable, and a barricade of stony silence rose up between them. I remembered the episode when the clerical collaborators at Oberammergau refused to eliminate the *added* textual dramatization of Jewish "guilt" in their famous portrayal of the Passion, presented so vividly it might have occurred yesterday instead of nineteen centuries ago – or to admit that the principal actors, and the village itself, were a hot-bed of Nazism.

In 1945, I submitted a brief to the Ontario Royal Commission on Education against Christian religious instruction in the public schools, and cited a sampling of sixteen provocative, historically dubious textbook items about the Crucifixion. That same year the Minister of Education stated the manuals were experimental and the Government, during a Parliamentary debate, proclaimed its receptivity to suggested emendations. In 1950, the Commission Report promised careful consideration of my criticisms. Yet a number of reprintings leave the Crucifixion paragraphs virtually untouched.

Bishop James A. Pike, of the California Episcopal Diocese, categorized "Christ-killers" as the most hateful expression used by anti-Semites. Yet, he wrote, Dr. Bernard E. Olson of Yale University finds a number of passages in Protestant textbooks which saddle collective guilt for Christ's death on the Jews. One Sunday School lesson ascribed such intense hatred of Jesus to the Jews on the day of Crucifixion that they shouted themselves hoarse crying "Crucify him!" and thus showed their "thanks" for his coming into the world to save them. A writer of Sunday School material specifically advises teachers to present Pilate as an irresolute judge driven to condemn the innocent by a Jewish mob whose sin was the greater. Another lesson recommends that students give contemporary proof of the curse being suffered by the Jews for their "crime." The Bishop at the same time traced Jesus' death back to the collaboration of

Rome and the Sadducees, a sect which did not in any sense represent the Jewish populace.

In 1942 Dr. Solomon Zeitlin, a noted Professor of Rabbinics, deduced a brilliant theory, from massive evidence, that the Sanhedrin which supposedly sentenced Jesus violated the basic and long-established rules of legal procedure, designed to safeguard the defendant, in a number of vital details. He arrived at a strong belief in two Sanhedrins – the genuine court embodying the rabbinic moral and intellectual leadership of the Jews, and a quisling, rump court, devised by Rome to cloak with legal sanctity her program of cruel repression. It was before the latter, spurious bar of judgement that Jesus was hailed at an irregular hour, on a charge non-indictable by Jewish law, subjected to processes inconsistent with long-entrenched rabbinic jurisprudence, and condemned as a rebel against Roman authority to a non-Jewish type of execution.

Candid penetration into the prejudice and passion beclouding those dim days would require a life span, and would lead nowhere. I might marshal an army of arguments, a phalanx of logical syllogisms, and a galaxy of Christian luminaries. To indulge the hope of changing anyone's opinion on a subject inextricably intertwined with the subterranean roots of the subconscious, is immature and bootless. I have no desire to embroil myself in a polemic whose key lies deeply buried in the underground strata of ancient history – and in the caverns of the human mind.

Freud, Sartre, and others define the murder of God as mankind's most demonic wish – to release itself from moral restraint. In fact, Freud introduced a notion that civilization itself began with a deicide which continues to beset us. The theme of man against God was advanced further by Maurice Samuel, who analysed Nazi hatred for the Jew as a by-product of the amoral superman's great hatred for the Jewish-Christian God of mercy. This "craven Christ Deity" had replaced the heroic gods of Valhalla with a snivelling symbol of weakness and emasculation; now the Teutons would reinstate their divinities – and themselves! In this assault on Christian morality, the Nazis knew they had first to deracinate its roots in Judaism.

The debate about Jewish complicity 1900 years ago leaves me cold. I was not there. In every nerve fibre and brain cell, I protest against being called a "Christ-killer" – not by a scratching, drink-drenched lout who spat tobacco juice into my eye a half-century ago, but by the mood, the aura, and sometimes the very words of religious and secular classrooms. For long generations the sinister Judas-will of "the Jews" to crucify Christ has been annealed on young minds incapable of evaluating its applicability to flesh-and-blood Jews – and it has been reinforced on Good Friday and Easter by wondrous music, overpowering architecture, and ceremonial grandeur. The Crucifixion narrative, after the Gospel of John, has warped the minds of countless youngsters with a fallacy probably historical and most definitely moral, whose viral residue pullulates under the disclaimers of adulthood.

Suppose that history and logic have conspired to deceive us. Suppose Israel *did* crucify Jesus. If God had destined him to be a sacrificial atonement, then the people who brought about his death, whoever they were, acted in accord with God's plan and without them the drama of salvation could never have been enacted. Vengefulness about Calvary is one of the most disheartening examples of illogicality in the annals of human thought.

I cannot share the suspicion that Jesus disappeared into oblivion, like all the other Messianic "agitators" Rome hanged to shield her rule from the revolutionary nationalism of turbulent Jews, although persuasive voices have presented a good case for it. Nor can I accept the Christian estimate of his death as the gift of grace that tips the scale of human destiny toward eternal bliss. I do know, however, that the crucifixion of Jesus is a portent of fear and dismay to the Jews because it colours and transfigures the Christian psyche in a degree unrelated to the validity of the story itself.

Shortly before Easter, in 1961, vandals paid tribute to peace on earth and good will toward men by smearing "Get out, Jew-boy! You killed Christ!" on the walls of Jewish stores in Oakville, Ontario. To hold a collective grudge because Jesus was allegedly slain in Jerusalem appears no less foolish than to persecute Greeks for the execution of Socrates, or Englishmen and Frenchmen because Joan of Arc died at the stake in Rouen, or the descendants of any of the men who built gibbets and pyres for saints and prophets on Calvary hills in every land on earth. But reason has a minor role in this matter! I believe there is no contemporary nation on earth that would *not* crucify Jesus for his teachings although, unlike the ancient Jews, the modern world has had a two-thousand-year opportunity to understand their wisdom.

When did firm belief in the incarnate God and Jewish deicide stamp itself on the Christian mind? Missionary zeal for the "new covenant" of the reconstituted Israel waxed into flame on the Johannine notion that the old, now-expendable Israel had earned God's consuming wrath by rejecting and murdering His Son. And a succession of calamities – conquest by Emperors Vespasian and Titus, oppression under Trajan, final extinction at the hands of Hadrian – seemed to confirm it.

By the time Christianity became the official religion of the Roman Empire, the Jews well knew what would be meted out to them by a merger of religious absolutism and political dictatorship. Through the fiery diatribes of the sub-Apostolic fathers, through Chrysostom, Ignatius, and a host of other tongues of flame, the vindictiveness bred by the Crucifixion story now became civic law. Then the Jews made their choice. Rather than surrender and be absorbed, let us accept the stripes and blows of "God's servant" for all posterity until the coming of the Messiah!

The Church suffered the Jew to exist marginally and miserably, with begrudging assent articulated in 1542 by a Polish Ecclesiastical Synod: "for the sole purpose of reminding us of the Saviour's torments" – not to stand erect with proud awareness of his paternal rank and separate heritage, certainly not to rebuild a theocentric sovereign state in the Holy Land and thus affront a fundamental premise of Christian theology!

From the earliest stages of that theology, Christian domination of Europe synchronized with derision of Israel. First the new faith claimed the Hebrew Scriptures, interpreting them as the harbinger of Jesus; then it pre-empted Israel's place as the recipient of God's promise. Henceforth the Jew's misfortunes were to prove his rejection, and his continued existence the truth of Christian dogma. This accursed people had been an outside, alien sect labouring under pagan dislike; it became a self-excommunicated pariah which had turned its back on the truth and wilfully left God's mansion! In the view of the Church, Judaism was not a different religion; it was a wilful distortion, and in consequence an outcast.

I am stirred by irresistible impulse to stretch forth a hand to the stricken Jesus in Michelangelo's sculptured "Pièta" – but the macabre, blood-dripping, klieg-lighted cross in Hollywood's "Ben Hur" fills me with racial memories of bestialized Crusade mobs bawling hate and slaughter while they stormed behind it into the ghettos of the Rhineland. Can a Jew respond to mediaeval church art that gave him nostrils exhaling foul vapours, and tail and hooves?

Even the steel broom of the Reformation, so relentless in sweeping away images, left the Jewish image intact. The ghost of the Devil wearing phylacteries was untouched by exorcism in Christendom's closet. Luther ascribed Israel's sidestepping of the baptismal font to Satan, who sits "at the Jew's right hand." The astounding longevity enjoyed by "The Protocols of Zion," an incredible farrago of anti-Semitic nonsense, is merely the momentum of the Jew-Satan syndrome.

One ironic twist of history cannot be ignored. The mediaeval elaboration of the cross of Jesus the Jew into a caricature of his people defiling the earth with the faeces of Satan led directly to the lewd cartoons of Jewish diabolism disseminated by Streicher as the spearhead of Nazi propaganda. With profound reluctance and sorrow I must underscore the line of descent between the Jew as alleged crucifier perpetuated by Christian pedagogues and the Jew as actual crucified under Hitler. A comparison of mediaeval documents and *Der Stuermer* will yield a resemblance more than coincidental.

In the numbness and revulsion caused by the evidence at the Eichmann trial, the world glided over one statement which opened up a chink into the dark dungeon of his bookkeeper mind, like the slits through which ss-guards watched the writhing of naked women in the gas chambers. Eichmann's gravelly voice announced that his role in the genocide of Jews was no more culpable than the part Pontius Pilate was forced to play in the Crucifixion, implying that both he and Pilate acted under orders, the latter having been a puppet of Rome and an instrument of the High Priest. There is no evidence that the Roman *gauleiter* of Judea had more deference for the High Priest and Sanhedrin than Himmler had for the pitiful *Judenrat** set up in occupied lands to supply data and machinery for his methodical program of extermination. The pivotal fact is that Eichmann vicariously associated himself with, and found self-defence in, the New Testament account of the Crucifixion!

Adolph Eichmann might even have borne to the gallows the "new-born" assurance of New Testament salvation – had his Teutonic stubbornness not been so impenetrably monolithic. In the Year of Our Lord 1963, the Reverend William Hull, fundamentalist Christian cleric who served as Eichmann's chaplain prior to his execution, declared categorically that the engineer of six million murders would have been "saved" for eternal life by accepting Christ as Lord, although the Jews he helped exterminate would inexorably agonize in hell because they did not accept the Christ. Eichmann and Hull have a profound affinity in that both dehumanized Jews into automatons, one for destruction on earth at Hitler's will, the other for damnation beyond at the will of God. I am not sure that the cumulative long-term martyrdom imposed by the second process in the name of religion can be counted less than the short-term cost of the first in the name of racism.

One of my rabbinical colleagues has noted that the course of Nazism was eased by one convenient auxiliary – a ready-made, built-in villain, corn-fed on the myth of Jewish deicide. Nor did Nazism need to fashion a new hatred; the hatred of Jews and Judaism was as old as the Gospels. Hitler's mouthpieces merely sharpened the knife by supplementing a mediaeval theological legend with a modern

* Jewish Councils.

biological hoax – that Aryan race purity was being sullied by "verminous Jewish scum."

For political persuasiveness, the Nazis did require a magic foe of omnipotent dimension, a scapegoat for the defeat of Germany after the First World War, mighty and demonic enough to sap German virility, honeycomb the Reich with the maggots of defeatism, and gloat in her collapse. Where else could such an adversary be found, if not in the accursed spawn of Satan, the people that had murdered God, spread the Black Plague in the fourteenth century, and drunk the blood of Christian babes on Passover?

The SS-guards at Auschwitz called the camp *anus mundi*, the anus of the world – a term frequently used in mediaeval demonology for the devil's habitat. I do not confront without a spine-chilling tremor the possible link between this curious atavism to Middle Ages semantics, the concept of Israel as excreta, and the irrational delusion that the devil's-brood Jew must be extirpated lest he destroy the non-Jew.

Can the "curse of Cain" be lifted and the chain of hate be broken? Not long ago a redemptive word of hope echoed in the cavernous abutments of Lincoln Cathedral in England. Since 1255 the remains of "Little St. Hugh" have been enshrined there, under a framed notice recounting the "crime." The "crime"? Jews had crucified the lad Hugh in mockery of Jesus Christ.

After seven centuries the Church of England replaced the frame with a new inscription deploring "trumped-up stories of ritual murders of Christian boys by Jewish communities . . . [which] cost many Jews their lives during the Middle Ages and much later. [They] do not redound to the credit of Christendom and we pray, 'Remember not, Lord, our offences nor the offences of our forefathers.' "

Another word kindled a torch of hope – from the Vatican. On Good Friday Roman Catholics generation after generation have prayed "for the perfidious Jews" (*oremus pro perfidis Judaeis*), although *perfidis* originally meant faithless, unbelieving, not treacherous. Pope John XXIII erased it from the liturgy. Later he mulled over a prayer for the last Sunday in October consecrating the entire human race to Jesus, and ordered the omission of a passage concerned with "the children of the chosen people [who] called down upon themselves the Blood of the Saviour." These two demarches were among John's first official acts after accession to the papal throne.

On a visit to Rome, during a personal interview with His Holiness, granted at the request of my good friend, Toronto's Cardinal McGuigan, I conveyed to him Jewry's gratitude for the minor, but immensely significant, rectification.

The opportunity I had to view John XXIII at close range encouraged me in a context far beyond liturgical text-revision. A tall Irish monsignor with a thick brogue told me he had been selected to coach Pope John in English. His Holiness already spoke the language of the heart. Even in the supposedly formal speech from the dais, he greeted everyone – thousands of the faithful massed for audience, resplendent dignitaries, my wife and me – with the eye-twinkling humour, unabashed warmth, and humble kinship of a parish priest chatting with his flock in the family kitchen.

As I watched and listened, my mind sang with the joy of a glad perception. At the most critical chapter in human annals, Providence had performed a miracle through the Church that believes in them! It had brought forth from his late twilight a ruler who combined, for the first time, an iron will and a heart filled with love. Pope John, I felt, is the wisest, kindliest, human being ever invested with such power. If, like history, the Catholic Church is "the lengthened shadow of a man," the crucifixion of the Jew for his alleged crucifixion of a Jew would yet be ended, and the people of Christ taken down at last from the Cross, and cleansing waters of brotherhood channelled from Rome to a parched and fear-ridden world. And I prayed that this avuncular old man might be granted enough time to complete his work. Alas, only a few years later, cancer removed him, and fate had teased mankind with one of its most ironic jokes.

Since that day at Castel Gandolfo I have frequently pondered what the fate of European Jewry would have been had John, instead of Pius, risen to the papacy a generation earlier, during the rise of

Hitler. Remote, abstemious, coldly aristocratic Pius had two polarized "magnificent obsessions": strengthen the church and conquer Communism. By either yardstick, or both, forceful intercession against Hitler's projected anti-Jewish program would not have commended itself as shrewd strategy. Suppose large-hearted, full-bodied John had then been pondering confidential reports from Munich and Berlin in the papal sanctum. . . .

What harvest of good will can be anticipated from interfaith movements? I have diverted countless hours from pressing concerns of a hyperactive ministry into the objectives verbalized by Brotherhood Week. On the fifth anniversary of my Toronto rabbinate, a *Globe and Mail* editorial commended me for a service I would be happy to think I had performed: helping to "break down the prejudices which have long brought sorrow to many people." Anglican Canon W. W. Judd, United Church Reverend David Maclennan, Jesuit Father Noonan, and I launched the Canadian Council of Christians and Jews, after the similarly named Conference in the United States.

After a weaning-period nursed by subsidies from the Jewish Congress, the Council bolstered its status-appeal to corporations with their own "good will" budgets and thus procured funds from non-Jewish sources for a far-ranging program. Brotherhood Week is being promoted with ad-man gimmicks, the Council emblazons important names on the side of the angels, businessmen, communal leaders, schools, and the press espouse it with genuine passion, and educational ventures are efficiently and constructively projected for teachers, welfare workers, and collegians.

Not a shred of doubt, in my mind, is attached to the sincerity of the Council's secretariat or supporters, despite the snide barbs directed occasionally at "conscience money" donated by firms guilty of job-discrimination. But I also am no devotee of mealy-mouthed blandishments. The fact that a rabbi who carps at brotherhood movements might be called an ingrate in itself testifies to their imbalance: the weaker brother is regarded as sole beneficiary, and the stronger as entitled to thanks.

Exchange of pulpits between pastor and rabbi exposes both congregations to the most brotherly thought each can offer, although tainted with a defect: the initiative usually comes from the rabbi. Awards and citations, nearly always by Jews, to politicians, jurists, and industrialists for their contribution to the cause festoon its calendar with prestige occasions – although I wonder why anyone need be banqueted and bouqueted for doing what in all decency he should be expected to do. Jews merit admiration for being gracious to those they need – although they would merit even more by extending help to the black, yellow, and red people of Canada who need *them*.

Exhorting devotees of Protestantism, Catholicism, and Judaism to look at one another with tolerance can be downgraded only by a rasping cynic – but tolerance is essentially a relationship between non-equals, and brotherhood might be better served, not by looking *at* one another, but by labouring *with* one another toward a solution of common problems like race conflict, economic injustice, and nuclear war. A troika of faiths hitched to the star of common brotherhood is refreshing, but reverence for another's creed must not be the derivative virtue of affable extroverts heedless of their own, and togetherness can degenerate into an interpenetration of viscous organisms bereft of vertebrae; inter-faith requires inner faith, and the core of the problem is to combine intensity of religious fervour with the extension of religious understanding.

A joint dinner of Protestants, Catholics, and Jews to learn to love the other fellow, even when you don't like him, has indubitable ritualistic attraction, but platitudes and compliments can reveal logorrhaea rather than love – unless they are condiments for truly substantial fare like a scientific, sociological study of the causes of hate rather than a sweetmeat rally for a "cause." Circuitous mellifluous reiteration of the similarities between Christianity and Judaism and the former's debt to its parent meets every requirement of historic and theological truth – but it can become a convenient anodyne. The differences are deep and unbridgeable. I have been edified beyond measure by the heroically self-disciplined dedication of Christian clergymen to the aims epitomized in brotherhood – but no effort of will, however painstaking and earnest, can convey them beyond the mountainous limits of church dogma and its premise that Judaism has been superseded and is without any claim whatever as an equal, alternative, or viable medium of salvation. A pleasant pact to avoid underground land-mines may lubricate the softly whirring wheels of organized good will – but it leaves intact the seminal tenet of Christianity that neither Jews nor a Jewish problem would exist had not the nation of the incarnate Christ shunned and destroyed him.

"You're too sensitive, Rabbi, believe me. The crucifixion record foment anti-Semitism? Impossible! I never had any feeling about Jews as a result of it – and I don't know any Christian who does!" My friends Canon Judd, David Maclennan, Father Noonan, Archdeacon Frank, Jim Finlay, and Glynn Firth, and many Christian laymen, would probably recoil in horror at any emotion-charged allusion to the "Christ-killer" scurrility. The evidence of history, sociology, and psychology, however, endorses the view that they project their own unspotted innocence into the environment.

We Jews, on target, are surely more authoritative informants about the pain of the arrow's wound. My experience is clear. May I append a footnote – that piety is unavoidably constrained to protect its Holy of Holies? As well expect me to abide an allegation of evil miasma seeping down from Sinai! How can one come to grips with a spiritual condition diagnosed only by its external victim and utterly inadmissable to the sensibilities of the host?

Gordon Allport, in his book *The Nature of Prejudice*, illustrates with a serio-comic tale the durability and elusiveness of attitudes rooted in emotional needs. Here it is:

A paranoid woman had the fixed delusion that she was a dead person. The doctor tried what he thought was a conclusive logical demonstration to her of her error. He asked her, "Do dead people bleed?" "No," she answered. "Well, if I pricked your finger, would you bleed?" "No," answered the woman, "I wouldn't bleed; I'm dead." "Let's see," said the doctor, and pricked her finger. When the patient saw the drop of blood appearing she remarked in surprise, "Oh, so dead people do bleed, don't they?"

Is the "Christ-killer" epithet any more amenable to reason? The open events of history and the hidden processes of psychology both buttress a fatalistic conclusion: we Jews will be linked with the most despicable crime known to or conceived by man as long as weakness keeps us vulnerable and Christian theology makes that crime an essential act in the epic of salvation.

"Christ-killer" saddles on contemporary Jews the guilt of their forbears 1900 years ago. The sin is in the blood! Unlike the Nazis who, being far simpler and more consistent, hewed strictly to the doctrine that haemoglobin is thicker than holy water, the church offered the God-forsaken people an escape-hatch through conversion. Always, the Jews were potentially among the redeemed.

David Pinski, a Yiddish playwright, named three kinds of water that serve no useful purpose: the water that falls in the ocean – it already has enough; the water poured into wine – it spoils the taste; the water sprinkled on a Jew in baptism – he remains a Jew.

Although a plush country club in Scarsdale, New York, excluded from its all-Gentile dance floor a Jewish convert to Episcopalianism, and islanders on Majorca still brand with the name "swine" the descendants of cultured Spanish Jews who fled from the Inquisitors' pyre into the bosom of the church almost five centuries ago, the baptismal cleansing and new identity administered to a Jewish convert can be said to stick, if not for him then for his grandchild.

Some Hebrew Christians submerge themselves utterly and undoubtedly in Christ-Messiah, obliterating every iota of reservation or reluctance. Raissa Maritain brings to the Church spirituality and intelligence. It is well-nigh impossible, however, for the bulk of their former co-religionists to credit the infinitesimal number of proselytes with any motivation other than plain opportunism: an itch to escape millennial hardships – despite the perfervid protestations of radio and television Hebrew-Christian missionaries. The average Jew finds so little appeal to reason in Christian theology that he cannot believe anyone with Jewish discernment would deliberately choose it except for personal gain. He reserves his blackest contempt for the *meshummad*.*

The classic commentary came from Heinrich Heine, who characterized Christian baptism as a Jew's "ticket of admission" to a university career and presumably a status commensurate with his worth. He himself, he later quipped, would not have turned Christian had the law permitted him instead to steal silver spoons.

Does a supposedly loftier morality harden Jewish hearts against the Gospel? In the wake of a gale I stirred up against the tactless announcement by a Toronto church council of a new family-oriented program for Jewish proselytizing, a prominent Christian editor advised Christendom to practise purity and fidelity in the home and sobriety outside it, as Jews do, before presuming to preach the Faith to the household of Israel. Such a challenge is an undeserved compliment to Jewry. The virtues to which the journalist granted Jews a patent are not – even when performed – inherent in, or derived from, Judaism more than Christianity. And the gap between Jewish precept and practice is also too wide to be closed by transmitting the schizoid pattern to others. A good Jew and a good Christian are both hard to find; "home missions" should always begin at home!

Does Israel spurn the church because of resentment against anti-Semitism? I think the identification of the missionary with historic abuse makes a niggardly contribution to Jewish stiff-neckedness. The modern salesman of salvation is no death's-head Inquisitor; the mediaeval wrack has been replaced by exemplary benevolence. Sweet solace emanates from missionaries to Jewish hearts no less lovingly than medicine to African huts – and with the same admixture of altruism and arrogance, since the benighted recipient dwells in darkness.

After the extent of Nazi blood-letting began to filter through the high threshold of Gentile awareness, the beckoning finger of evangelism was coupled with a nod to the martyred dead. The 1950

* Jewish convert.

World Council of Churches Assembly in Amsterdam, reporting on "the Christian approach to the Jews," proceeded from the extermination of six million to a denunciation of anti-Semitism as "absolutely irreconcilable" with the Christian faith. The pronouncement concluded by urging Christians to "meet with our Jewish neighbours" in a spirit calculated to make them share what "God has given us in Christ." This unfortunate sequence stung some Jewish commentators into suspecting that Christianity's sense of guilt and moral failure to appraise and abort Nazism are being energized for a proselytization crusade. One Yiddish columnist even hinted at a "nice" solution of the Jewish problem: the disappearance of Judaism rather than Jews. Another defined "Christian love" as "loving Jews to death"!

A Toronto Anglican Synod, it seems to me, revealed a conflict of conscience between evangelistic commitment and awareness of the contemporary cry for a one-world view when it affirmed the ideal of brotherhood "regardless of race, colour, or nationality" – not "creed," described a pluralistic society as "multi-racial" – not "multi-religious," and suggested by implication that its call to "straight-forward and honest dealing with our Jewish neighbours" forecast a shift in tactic – not in goal. Since then, the appointment of an especially sensitive and open-minded Director to the "Jew-Christian dialogue" may induce a learning process based on the acceptance of their co-existence as equals.

I do not deny well-meaning religionists of any sect the duty to obtain access to Divine Grace for people otherwise "doomed" by the accident of birth. Mark condensed the fate of Jews into a sentence: "He that believeth not shall be damned." St. Cyprian, identifying dogma with organization, devised a slogan nimbly reinterpreted in contemporary Western lands to purge its absolutism – but withal that laconic verdict is the seminal Roman Catholic sesame to Paradise: *extra Ecclesiam nulla salus*, "outside the Church no salvation." Even the undiscourageable worriers about my soul who send me pamphlets, brochures, and Scriptural arguments for Christ-Messiah deserve appreciation more than resentment; it is all for my eternal bliss. If they were not so positive, patronizing, impregnable in rectitude! The recommendation of the Canadian Council of Churches that Jews be treated as "potential" children of God permits no doubt that the potentiality can be actualized only through Christ. And how else, save by absolute, consuming faith in his "truth," can a missionary muster patient, sacrificial concern for the Jew's endless, needless banishment to hell?

Proselytization was not always alien to Judaism. In the time of Jesus, his ancestral faith mounted a far-ranging missionary effort. From the decadent baths of Rome to the slave pens, sensitive spirits in revolt against vice and life-weariness were drawn to Judaism and its austere morality. Does not the Christian scripture scoff at the Scribes and Pharisees who compass sea and land to make one proselyte?

The "Pharisaic" harvest included Queen Helene of Adiabene, Aquila (kinsman of Nero and author of a remarkable Greek translation of the Hebrew Bible), sundry heathen-born sages of the Talmud, and thousands of lesser rank surfeited with the licentiousness and superstition of the Graeco-Roman world in which, according to the famed scholar Adolph Harnack, one-tenth of the population professed the Jewish faith.

In 325, the Council of Nicaea forbade Judaizing on pain of death – and the ban remained throughout the realm of Christendom and the centuries, until the dawn of our "new age." The imperial church-state even proscribed conversation, any intercourse, between Christians and Jews, out of fear that the latter's more intimate knowledge of the Bible and magical cabalistic exegesis might enable him to confound the true believer. But the yellow Jews of Kai-Feng-Foo in China (extinguished during the last century), the Falashas or black Jews of Abyssinia, the brown Bene-Israel Jews of Cochin, India, and the eighth-century Khazar kingdom between the Volga and the Don, were monuments to the infectious fervour of Judaism. The most dramatic modern deviation toward Sinai came, not from Hollywood, despite the publicized pilgrimage of Elizabeth Taylor and Sammy Davis Jr., but from San Nicandro, a remote Italian village whose inhabitants were admitted after considerable hesitancy, holus-bolus, into the State of Israel.

Now that the monolithic church-state has vanished and Jewish missionaries are released from the risk of being drawn and quartered, shall Jews revive their pristine dynamism and compete with Christendom? Some rabbis reply in the affirmative.

I have inducted many Christians into the Torah; almost all the neophytes were affianced to Jews. To paraphrase Winston Churchill, I have no wish to preside at the demise of the Jewish people. Therefore, barring exigent and exceptional circumstances, I do not officiate at an intermarriage without the conversion of the non-Jewish partner (after fulfilling the old rabbinic precept to attempt dissuasion by underscoring the hardships and difficulties of a loyal Jew), or at least a written pledge to rear and educate the children as members of the Jewish community. It seems logical to expect that couples envisaging a Christian family will have the knot tied by a Christian pastor.

On the whole, these mixed-faith matrimonial ventures can boast nearly average success although, as I warn the prospective bride and groom, marriage is a complex gamble at best; difference in religious background magnifies the risk, and the strain on love and mutual forbearance; and childhood indoctrination that sits very lightly under the wedding canopy may loom large at the cradle of one's offspring. But it is noteworthy that former Gentile spouses in Holy Blossom Temple are among its most zealous servitors. The non-Jewish candidate for the heterogeneous nuptial knot, in most cases, was not a pious Christian; rigid intra-mural devotion does not normally lead to an affianced sweetheart out-of-bounds.

Strict orthodox Judaism disparages the second-rate quality of conversion through marriage; after all, a love-convert adopts that status as a means to an end. The logic is unanswerable; only a smidgeon of canopy-proselytes, at most, would join the seed of Abraham unimpelled by an immediate practical objective. Yet I have never accorded myself the right to misprize the motives of any human being; there are too many complications, which God alone knows! If the prospective convert seems mature emotionally and intellectually, I grant the sincerity. After a course of instruction, he or she will probably have a greater store of Judaistic knowledge than many age-peers in the Jewish community.

Pious, or proud, Jewish parents confronted by the dread spectre of a strayed child will often deny the validity of *any* conversion, defining Jewishness as a birthright. I have no traffic with such a notion. To be a Jew, confessedly, is to be part of a peoplehood; nurture in a Jewish home and household communicates, by osmosis, a built-in belongingness no amount of reading about history and belief can duplicate. The out-of-hand reduction of Jewish identity to the bloodstream, nevertheless, is stark Nazism.

I remember a highly cultured young Christian who barely survived an infection resulting from circumcision, which he underwent on his own initiative, as I do not require it. He sweated over Jewish literature so avidly that he far outstripped the rather crude and untutored family of his bride. Yet they denied his certification as a Jew.

That groom had a goal for conversion: to marry the girl he loved. Interviews convinced me, however, that Judaism per se, as well, attracted him. He liked its common-sense morality, irrefrageable confidence in man, and freedom from supernaturalism and dogmas he could no longer accept. Such affinity with Judaism is widespread today among a marginal élite disturbed by disillusion, intellectual misgivings, or vicarious guilt.

Lukewarm, nominal Jews also crowd the periphery of the synagogue. A denominational evangelistic society did well to advise its active workers to seek contact with such wavering, potentially receptive candidates for baptism. Not until this postwar period, however, has the Christian church itself been invaded by vocal indifference, and by outright rebellion of youth groups, who demand a broadening of its commitment: less concern with alcohol, bingo, and creed, more concern with social injustice and war – thus rejuvenating the social gospel of the 'thirties.

The crisis in Christendom is a challenge to Judaism. Never since Constantine has the original bearer of the covenant been tempted by such a tocsin-call to reclaim the estate consigned under duress to his offspring. It is not astonishing that some rabbis are bemused by the prospect.

For me, the basic premises of a missionary Judaism have an appeal far from magnetic. A campaign to spread the truth of my religion would inevitably deteriorate into a crusade to sell the truth. Christianity has founded its evangelism on the claim that Christ is ultimate and final: *nec plus ultra*. A rival Jewish evangelism must begin with the same audacious pretension – or not begin at all.

The official ukase of church fundamentalists that non-Christians are en route to hell is privately shrugged off by thousands of Christians of all stripes who dutifully "decorate" the Home Missions collection plate every Sunday – but to the envoys of Christ in Angola or in the Arctic it breeds a divinely entrusted mandate to serve and save. By its own inner dynamic, a proselytizing movement is spiritual imperialism under the guise of rescue from primal error.

Since the allegedly unique and flawless truth is to be propagated for all men, Judaism's belief in universal unity would not be impaired by its revival as a missionary movement. Because the missionary's thrust is fuelled by the assurance that he is steward of God, delegated to consolidate this errant orb under His rule, the Chosen People can take it in stride. Yet I can think of no world view more incongruous, irrelevant, and anachronistic in the determinedly pluralistic human situation of the twentieth century. When less than a third of the species pities the remainder for being non-Christian, one might cry "naïvete!" Imagine less than one-half of one per cent commiserating with the others for being non-Jewish!

Paul Tillich would fortify both Christianity and Judaism with the Old Testament prophetic spirit. In the "struggle for the Lord of time against the gods of space," he said, the synagogue social-justice tradition will be needed "to the end of history." In evaluating the significance of his assessment, one must emphasize that the Hebrew prophets did not divulge a credal key to individual salvation on which a hermit might take hold in seclusion; they taught rather a way of life which men must take together. The core of Judaism is neither God's cross, nor a symbol for the eye crystallized in space for contemplation, nor yet the total, all-explaining microcosm of human destiny; it is God's word, a summons for the ear, endlessly reverberating in every age, beckoning man toward self-completion. In the twentieth century, that word echoes in a wilderness – and I would rather convert Jews into listening-posts than convert Christians to an absolute Mosaic truth clamantly monopolized by Israel through divine selection and condescendingly relayed to mankind by her compassion.

If the inscrutable Meaning we call God has provided an eternity across the Great Divide for the healing of this world's hurts, I am sure He will not bar admission for lack of a church membership card or certificate of allegiance to any creed. Mankind is weary of people who would let its terrestrial habitat become a hell while they cajole or coerce others into their heaven.

Strident wrangling about the special relationship of Jew, and then Christian, to God, is ghostly creaking in an outworn, outlived house that should come down. I would surrender the self-cosseting image of Israel the Chosen People, in the hope that Christendom might abjure the sanguinary symbolism of the Cross. Since the singular role of Christianity in the Divine scheme has flowered from that of Judaism, their joint abdication could be guaranteed by Jewish initiative.

Although the fire that percolates from Sinai's peak has ignited whatever socio-religious passion I can deploy on the battlefield of truth, I gravely suspect the doctrine of Israel's exclusive high-priest rank at the receiving end of revelation. It must be rationalized in candid recognition of the widespread secularization of Jewish life, or abandoned. Does it justify the resultant perils? I wonder. A subject of angelology easily becomes a subject of demonology. A divine mission can be twisted into an implacable conspiracy for evil, such as that conjured up by the sick, sinister alchemists of the "Protocols of Zion." The penumbra of partnership with God which Sinai flung around Biblical Israel has endowed the modern Jew with a fateful aura of power, ready to hand for the scapegoat-seeking demagogue who needs to pin-point some diabolic "Jewish plot." Was not Lucifer himself a fallen angel?

Would mankind and Divine wisdom be better served if both Jew and Christian repudiate their polarized claims to incomparable familiarity with the Lord of the Universe? I have no doubt the average Jew wants an average man's privilege to live a normal, healthy life as a human being. It is Christianity which freezes us into the mythic role. We are compelled to be the "chosen," whether we like the part or not – to establish a foundation for the consummate chosenness of Christ.

Once the incubus of Divine selection is removed and the halo of the cross dissipated, the Christ atonement gives way to Jesus martyred for truth and freedom, and the adversary reveals itself to be human nature, which opposes the Galilean teacher anywhere, anytime. He is slain today again and again by piety that hoodwinks the faithful into cruelty, by fear that hardens into hate, by a crucifixion-canard which subtly envenoms the Christian conscience and blackens the mirror of life for the Saviour's own kinsmen.

Love has admittedly been the most verbalized jewel in the Christian diadem. It may be germane to recall, as well, the rejection by Judaism of a hell contrived either for unbelievers or enemies. Homiletical and historical tributes to love are scattered profusely throughout Jewish lore – and a measure of delicacy forbids me to gape at tirades against the "vindictive, jealous God of the Hebrews" by evangelists who imprison my children behind a barrier of shame for a crime supposedly perpetrated by their forefathers a hundred generations ago.

In the Greek version of the New Testament, *agapé* (love) is encountered over two hundred and fifty times; sentimentality anchored to the mood of our time might translate that word to signify mutual forbearance. Is anything more quintessential for sheer survival in an atomic era which demands living together on the same planet to avoid dying together on the same day?

In the lexicon of Brotherhood Week, "love" means the self-immolating, consciously undertaken effort to gloss over differences, forgive wrongs, embrace the unlike other, because Judeo-Christian tradition requires it. I do not believe this love can be commanded, taught by precept, or promoted by public relations. On the contrary, the standard it imposes is so far beyond the capacity of mortal flesh that it can bring only frustration, which breeds self-loathing, which vents itself finally in resentment – against whom? Against the poor Jew who started the cycle by murdering God and putting himself in a position to require and test a compassion inevitably inadequate. Thus the garland of "Christian love" which earnest acolytes of interfaith amity press to the brows of their Jewish brethren may become a crown of thorns.

During these late-afternoon years, my thought and energy have rotated less and less around love and more and more around justice. Since the day Plato asked "What is justice?" libraries have been filled with tomes tracing its spoor in a legalistic labyrinth. One characteristic, however, is constant and clear: justice can be concretized through the deed – unlike love, which is an airy creature of emotion.

Mankind's dependence on love is an ultimate fact which history will verify; for that moment of truth, Jews, Negroes, North American Indians, the oppressed and maligned everywhere, must wait. In the meantime, justice waits on man – now!

The Crucifixion story is a tumour in the Christian conscience – benign as glorification of Divine Love, malignant because it multiplies the seeds of collective hatred. Should Jews postpone incision of the archaic guilt until the advent of love's universal reign? I think we should compliment Christianity by asking for justice, in the faith that it will be freely and fully given.

Talleyrand is said to have been accosted by a brash youth who had come upon a "new religion." "How shall I get it started?" the young man declaimed. The answer startled him. "Get yourself crucified!"

I dare not assess Talleyrand's oblique hint that the cross became a contrivance to cradle Christianity. It *did* prepare the loam for anti-Semitism. Bill Cuddicomb gave me warranty for that – fifty years ago!

A Rabbi's Preaching Mission: How It Was Found and Lost

THE first rabbis I ever met were not really rabbis; they were students. Bellaire's Congregation Sons of Israel could not afford a fully ordained rabbi. Rummage sales, card parties, membership dues, a few bequests from old-timers, and the half-rate clergy railroad fare, brought a bi-weekly Senior from the Reform seminary.

Arthur Marx, in Cincinnati, was studying for the rabbinate there. I once heard him preach a sermon in the cameo-like pressed-brick Temple uptown. On the immaculate pulpit, between the two *menorot**, he was so tall and his eyes so brightly black I felt sure he

* Seven-branched candelabra.

beheld God's dwelling-place. How pleasant it must seem to have so many friends and relatives whisper about you in reverential tones and listen with rapt attention to everything you said!

In my last year at high school Mrs. Marx angered Mom by telling a customer in their clothing-store that I had natural refinement and would make an excellent rabbi – even if I did come from a poor family. She bridled like a bantam. "*Nu*, does she think only *Deitschen* can be refined?" But I could see she was pleased. Maybe she had been hiding her disappointment, all these years, that Pop did not continue his rabbinical training in Ponevez Yeshiva long ago.

Also, the Marxes said, I had been raised in an Orthodox home, with Jewish background, and everyone knew I was such a grand speaker. They often talked with me about going to Cincinnati.

Deitschen bought meat from a Gentile butcher shop and served it with butter. In my father's judgement they were worse than *goyyim*; knowing the Law, they flaunted it. But my mother was determined that I must somehow get to college. The Marxes could advise and assist me; they were fine, educated people, despite a *tref* table. After Mrs. Marx had invited me several times to have dinner with them, Mom said I should accept; Pop would not have to know.

There was a daughter, Susan, in the Marx family. Generously endowed and good-looking, she got the highest marks in my high-school class, taught a half-dozen Sunday School kids at the Temple, and intimated that she would consider it a great honour to be a rabbi's wife. The dinner lacked familiar elements: reaching, paternal frowns, heatwaves from the kitchen stove, a cat jumping in your lap, and a dog raising his paws for a chicken-bone. There was a special dining-room, with napkins, real silverware, a servant-girl, sirloin steak (unsalted, with the redness still in it), and Susan to ease my self-consciousness by chatting about votes for women, the subject of our next debate, and Emily Pankhurst the suffragette.

Pop had strenuous objections to the Reform Temple. He could not endure the sight of male Jews sitting in synagogue and reciting the sacred tongue without hats. Even when the District President of

B'nai B'rith came there to speak at a public meeting and the older Feinberg boys put on white shirts to hear him, Pop stayed home. With Mom's timidly whispered encouragement, however, I donned my first long-pants suit (blue serge, bought at a fire sale for graduation) one Friday night, and walked up Belmont Street with the stiffness of a marionette, Susan at my side, some discreet yards in advance of her parents, to Temple. It felt good not to be alone.

The sanctuary exhaled balm and well-being the moment its door opened to me. Not like Agudas Ahim, with its darkness, din, oriental prayer-shawls, separate cramped quarters for women behind a trellissed barrier, and cacophonous crescendos of lamentation! Except when the Service called for the congregation sedately to rise, the men sat with rosy-cheeked wives and grown children, most of the moderately beseeching prayers were in English, and one man led them with august and unchallenged formality, instead of a dozen worshippers shouting at once. This, after all, was America, not Grinkishok!

Most of the student-rabbis were spectacled and shy. Their table manners inclined toward the awkward side, Susan told me, adding, "That is to be expected of unworldly men." Since I could never decide whether to fold my napkin or leave it wrinkled on the tablecloth, I favoured the unworldliness. Whenever I detected a pulpit lisp, a stammer, a swallowing of the final word of a sentence, or a befuddled shift from one foot to the other, I was sure I could speak better. Nevertheless, as I sat in the front row, radiant with the golden light of the candelabra, a snug comforter closed around me and I breathed down to the soles of my feet.

That night, eyes wide open, but unseeing, to the taut skylight rope, I listened as regal words strode majestically through my mind. Man, God, Soul, Values, the Meaning of Life, Eternal Verities! They seemed to have been nestling there since I was born. What if doltish muscle-men called me "sheeny" in the excitement of a gym-class basketball game? Those young rabbis-to-be, not many years older than I, gloried in the compulsion Jewish birth had placed upon them to probe under the multi-coloured surface, and made the urge to know God a thrilling adventure! What if the white vision of femaleness floated down the tide of every waking moment and into sleep? They, too, were men. Yet purity shone from their faces. What if my father was a penniless mender of umbrellas? Those youths groomed for leadership also went forth from humble households. What if *heder* had weighed me down with a sense of apartness? If I schooled myself in Jewish history and teachings, I too would realize and make others feel the beautiful tradition Jews stemmed from. What if coal strikes and cripples and chemistry did almost cause me to doubt there is a God? Had those clear-headed boys not found Him? They believed in God so utterly that they were willing to preach in His name every week of their lives. What if I did feel like a fish out of water at the senior masquerade? My destiny would be fulfilled among my own people. What if an Atlanta mob did march around the courthouse where Leo Frank was on trial for rape, shouting "Hang the Jew," and months later dragged his broken body from prison and strung it up on a tree? As a rabbi, I would have a voice to be heard on behalf of innocent Jews and persecuted people everywhere.

I finally screwed up enough courage to tell one embryonic preacher I liked his sermon. He let me accompany him to the hotel lobby and waved me into the rocker while he told me about Hebrew Union College. What an ideal place it was, to produce men of such saintliness and poise! My imagination sped on wings to a vernal campus, library stacked so high with books that ladders were needed to reach them, patriarchs who taught the Torah, Jewish Ethics, Prophets, Talmud, all things high and sacred. The course of training normally took nine years, which could be reduced by extra work, and after the first year a student with satisfactory grades was entitled to an annual three-hundred-dollars stipend-loan, even if he did not win a free scholarship.

My leap into the rabbinate did not gather momentum until spring 1916. It began with a series of exclamations from my father, on his return from a rally in Wheeling to raise relief funds for Jewish war-refugees.

"The All-Highest, blessed be His Name, has sent a messenger to lead us. The Divine Voice speaks through Rabbi Goldner. The Divine Voice! The Divine Voice!" Instead of going to bed at nine, as was his habit, he walked back and forth from kitchen to workshop, shaking his head and muttering in Hebrew, "The Divine Voice! The Divine Voice! The Divine Voice!" Birdie finally explained Pop's excitement. It was Solomon Goldner, the new Wheeling rabbi, fresh from Cincinnati. He had evidently electrified the vast audience. Everybody was talking about him. Pop chortled that he knew Talmud like the Yeshiva prodigies in the old country – and he was a Litvak!

The next Sabbath Eve I let myself unobtrusively into the back row of the Wheeling Temple just as the eight-voice choir burst into the anthem. The rabbi sat huddled in a high-backed chair on one side of the altar, leonine head sunk into his palm. Bushy brows barely saved his black torchlike eyes from a hairy jungle of the same colour that reached down over the forehead.

The choir finished. Rabbi Goldner uncrossed his legs, placed his hands on the two arms of the chair, and pushed himself up with elaborate slowness – a Lincolnesque giant bestirring himself from repose. Then the voice began, like a soft syllable prying loose an avalanche, its music packed with enormous power and gaining force with each word, until the air quivered with pathos, rumbled with wrath, and glowed with sheer grace of phrase and thought. When he closed his eyes, mine were opened on a realm of harmony and rapture. When he stepped back and lifted his mighty arms, an intellectualized thunder rolled up and out from him, and shook the clustered lights and swept from pew to pew into the choir loft and out through the windows into the night. . . . Before I began to distinguish objects in the Bellaire-bound streetcar, it had borne me home.

At five-thirty the next morning, I required only the faint rustling of Pop's hens to awaken from dreamlit sleep. Taking the shortcut that led across the railroad tracks from our alley, I ran up through the early morning mist past brewery, pesthouse, coal mine, pawpaw patch, until I reached the highest wind-swept spot in the hills, where all the world I knew lay dozing at my feet. I lifted my voice and fancied that I heard it strike the hills across the river miles away. Then I loped down to the City News Store for the *Wheeling Register*. It would surely carry an excerpt of the sermon! I would have time to read it before reporting at Hen Taylor's store for my Saturday job.

"It ain't come down yet. Any minute now," doddering balloon-shaped Mrs. Cosgrave cackled to me across the counter.

The City Building clock allowed me only ten minutes when the orange-and-yellow trolley clattered down the street. I lugged the paper bundle from the gutter where the motorman had flung it, fished a knife from my pocket, and left a nickel absent-mindedly on the cashbox, while my head swung like a pendulum over the swiftly-turned pages.

We Jews have a special mission to perform. The priest-people, the wandering people, has found, at last, a shrine. Ours is the task to be forever protestant and forever conscious of our prophetic heritage. America has given us freedom – we shall give her vision! America has given us a physical home – we shall give her a spiritual home in the great company of Isaiah and Jeremiah, Amos and Hosea. America has bequeathed democracy to man – Israel shall not rest until America has brought peace to the nations and caused justice to flow as a river and righteousness as a mighty stream throughout the world.

I bumped into a telegraph pole, stepped on a dog, knocked over a squad of empty milk bottles. Men with dinner pails stared at me and laughed. Mike Humphreys the cop jabbed me playfully in the ribs with his mace. The Hershman Clothing Store clerk sprinkled my face with water from the window-washing brush. A vegetable wagon grazed me so closely that the horse's tail lashed my eyes. America, tutored by the Jew, would lead men to peace and justice and brotherhood! As a rabbi in Israel, I too would catapult the spoken word against the ramparts of falsehood. Truth would compel men to do justice, and justice would be the harbinger of peace.

Later, sundry scruples flitted like bats through my mind. Had my conduct been the better for the preaching I had heard at the Temple? Maybe it was easier to deliver a good sermon than a sermon which does any good. And I began to notice how one student would summon organ tones from the navel, point a forefinger upward and furrow his brow in deep thought even when he ordered cream and sugar from the waitress at the after-service reception.

"Do as I say, not as I do! There's what preachers tell you!' Al Meyerberg yelled out from a little knot of punch-drinking men at a special Purim party in the Temple schoolrooms. The barb nettled me. Were a rabbi's sermons the beliefs by which he habitually lives – or just a rare vision of his best moments? How did Amos and Isaiah comport themselves between preachments?

Whatever the answer to that question, I knew that when I arose to speak shyness and insecurity dropped away like a cloak and I stood unafraid before the universe. What joy to speak in the name of God! Like Solomon Goldner, I would make the pulpit the hallowed medium of my art and my ideals.

Throughout the years at Hebrew Union College, dark hours of despondency were irradiated, and barren moments redeemed, by the inexpungeable sound of a Voice summoning me to use my own in its service. Many study courses resembled sheer mental gymnastics or endurance tests; in outside reading – Lewisohn, Santayana, Buber – I freed the line of contact with depth of vision and beauty of expression. Despite their detachment, some professors inspired me to keep the core of the Goldner pattern. No loneliness or gloom or disillusionment could quench the lustre of the day when, as a full-fledged rabbi, I too would speak the word of a living God. . . .

My first pulpit was Niagara Falls, New York. It had witnessed the nuptial ecstasy of countless honeymoons; to me it meant a starting-point for my mission.

I often sauntered around the falls, to think. They bewitched me. With the onslaught of cold weather an unimaginably delicate veil of ice began to spread inch by inch from both sides; by mid winter the two invading hosts had met. Near the land's edge the pattern was as fine as hoarfrost, and tiny jungles of almost microscopic ferns and underbrush were etched upon the imprisoned waters. In the centre, thick pillars hung down in ridges or were knotted together like the fallen oaks of a storm-whipped ice forest. At the bottom of the gorge, beneath the long, tapering icicles in which the white coat, like a frayed garment, ended, the water flowed off, dancing a hundred feet before winter again held it fast. The mist flung up in that brief spurt for freedom settled and froze, layer after layer, upon a nearby rock – a huge pyramid rising to the bridge at Prospect Point. It reminded me of a candle I had seen in the Bellaire Catholic Church.

I would thread my way among the bushes and small trees of the islands and along the bank of the rapids. It was a fairyland of feathery whiteness, though I knew what brutal, senseless force nature had leashed and tucked away beneath the lace. The snow crunched under my feet; the lights of the giant power plants, cut into the sides of the gorge, shone hazily through the mist. I peered hard at the power-house lights one day and mused: "More like the eyes of an ogre than the torches of progress!" Then I smiled at myself.

Israel Bettan, my beloved professor of homiletics, had repeatedly sustained my courage at Seminary by telling me I was blessed with a rare gift for preaching. But he also warned me against the "preacher's curse." Yet there it was. After a few weeks in the ministry I was already moralizing life from a pulpit instead of meeting it head-on at full tilt; a jaunt around the falls had become dry grist for a sermon. The smile curved downward into a frown. That tiny red notebook in my vest pocket! Since the day of my arrival I had been stopping to jot down ideas whenever something happened which could be used in a talk. My landlady's husband squealed like a flapper when he got Cuba on the radio; every program had value according to the air-distance it travelled. I had the same kind of disease; I couldn't even read a poem without weighing its usefulness and sound from the pulpit.

Slipping a hand under my woollen muffler, I drew out the notebook and held it a few seconds. Then, making a wide arc, I flung it far out into the air and watched it flutter down over the edge of the falls.

Beth-El's congregants already took brilliance in a rabbi for granted. I didn't need to substantiate the claim. After the first Sabbath I knew that the mere title "rabbi" conferred omniscience. Two sure-fire shortcuts to the hygienic flawlessness of my rabbinical halo were polysyllabic erudition so deep Mrs. Heidingsfeld could not understand it, or saccharine banalities so sentimental she loved them.

As to the alchemy of sermons, I had already learned the basic formula: magazine articles, a Bible concordance, modern English anthologies of Talmudic wisdom, a huge dictionary of illustrations and thousands of apt quotations from my college reading, all alphabetically indexed in a file. Although I preferred the excitement of digging ideas out of my own viscera, these ingredients could make preaching a breeze – with a generous pinch of sweetness and sentiment. Steady *shule* attendants asked nothing more!

The temptation to coast along, however, could not banish the self-image it conjured, of a heavy-lidded pundit, paunchy with Shabbas roast duck and red cabbage, touching his fingertips like a statue of Buddha. I could never be that kind of a clergyman. Instead, I bent over the pulpit week after week, goading my Friday Night contingent with verbal pincers, dramatizing man's agonized climb toward moral perfection, pouring the phials of spiritual conflict and turmoil on the rock of self-righteousness. It was the penitential pilgrimage of a John Donne, the scourging of my own soul, that I bade them witness!

Lethargy was undisturbed; they drowsed in a torpor my bitterness said was porcine. One Friday evening I stung myself out of the post-sermonic stupor induced by the amateur choir's anthem, and untethered my lofty glance to graze over the congregation.

Hugo Strengel, a mother-bound bachelor beyond eligibility, who could not resist the dumpling recipe his mom had brought from Darmstadt, was suppressing a protracted belch; widowed Katy Bravert, after long back-breaking hours over straw shapes and ribbons in her tiny millinery shop, was nodding; Abe Kris, who once warned me against using hotel towels because they carry germs, sat rigid with nameless fears; the chandeliers gave Richard Neuman's skin the yellowish-green tint of a malignant liver ailment; Emily Kantor, who supervised the vestry-room sewing-circle for underprivileged tots, to forget (they said) the cold contempt of her playboy Casanova, was slumped in vacant dejection; the eyes of Kitty Stein, the only youngster present, glistened like arc lights in a drizzle with tears for her mother's death; Adolphe Weill stared fixedly at the floor.

Adolphe was my only outspoken critic. No sooner did I rise to preach than he lowered his head. By that gesture he intended to pictorialize a conviction often expressed vocally: "Why isn't Feinberg like Milt Cohen? That's the kind of rabbi we need. A man interested in us as people!"

Parishioners often mentioned Milt, with a regretful sigh too audible for my comfort – since he was my predecessor. Without temperament or talent for the pulpit, his specialty was pastoral work: a Jew-Gentile Boy Scout Troop whose evenings with Milt were the talk of the town; shut-ins and the aged; orphans sponsored by the Rotary Club; hospitalized sick of all faiths; the families of Beth-El itself, to whose living-rooms, kitchens, and hearts Milt was a bearer of fellowship and cheer.

Adolphe's defiant cranium exasperated me. Even a small-town rabbi need not shrink into a Scout-master, or the call to duty into the duty of calling on his members twice a year like a Baptist elder. The rabbi's role was public leadership and his prime instrument the pulpit. Maybe I was badly adjusted; maybe I was seeking an excuse to avoid pastoral chores that did not feed my ego; maybe I ought to fit my energies into the needs of Temple Beth-El, so that it would outstrip the competitive growth of the new orthodox *shule*. But I'd be a poor specimen indeed if I scuttled the ideas and insights I had been codifying almost from the first day at the rabbinical college. If a small-town congregation could not appreciate and encourage a preacher, a big city would!

Thus did I parry and thrust at the doubt gnawing away my resolve to wield a pulpit like Excalibur for truth. Hugo and Katy and Abe and Richard and Emily and Kitty had needs and problems no more medicable by forensic eloquence than a broken arm. They were my spiritual responsibility. Perhaps the day of great preaching had receded and the personal counsellor's era was peeping over the horizon – and over the broken dreams of the wounded who knocked on my heart that Sabbath evening in Beth-El. But I was an afflicter of the comfortable, not a comforter of the afflicted, and hell-bent on my own map of heaven.

The next morning at the Saturday Service – attended by a minuscule remnant of pietists – I told the organist I would like to chant an old solo remembered from the seminary choir. It was an ode to the Torah: *Etz Hayyim* – "A tree of Life to those who lay hold of it, and all its paths are peace." I did not sing to the glory of God, though that was implicit in its hypnotic joy, nor to prove artistic merit, though the coaching I received from a scholarship at Cincinnati Conservatory had left a residue of mechanical dexterity, nor to edify the congregants, though I sensed an emotional communication with them hitherto unattained on that altar. I sang because there was something in me I could release in no other way.

Those brief moments were dedicated to the Scrolls of the Law, upright and stately in the Ark, with their silver ornaments, gold-embroidered scarlet covers, ivory tips, tinkling bells and crown, and the unblemished manual perfection of the writings – to the beauty of holiness. But they celebrated the holiness of beauty. Every Sabbath morning thereafter, I sang *Etz Hayyim*, and it brought life to my spirit.

I sought balm in another device. On the wall directly over my desk I fastened several index cards; on each was written an apothegm culled from one of the great poets and philosophers who had been my sustenance at Seminary. By sheer visual impact, day after day, as I stared at the wall, I hoped they would sink into and shape my subconscious. Instead of mumbling "Every day, in every way, I am getting better and better," with Coué, I would open the spaces of my mind to seminal truths....

Only a little more than a year later, both cards and song could be forsaken. Dr. Joel Tauber, most famed orator in the American Rabbinate, recommended me to Sinai, one of New York's largest temples, because he had read one of my sermons in the Seminary student journal.

The first dividend of my promotion was a secretary. When she appeared with a shorthand pad that morning in January 1927, my sole greeting was a flustered frown. I had never given orders to a hired person in my life! By the time Miss Pless diffidently said, "Someone phoned; I told him you'd be back at three; shall I call him now?" or "Do you want these clippings filed?" or "Please sign this letter," I hoped a classmate would drop in to see me.

The Temple Community Centre Director intimated that I should never pick up the receiver to take my own calls or permit myself to talk before the other party was screened both by the Temple switchboard operator and Miss Pless. I did not take kindly to the inviolate prerogatives or paraphernalia of a fenced-in mogul. And a worm of unease insinuated itself into my paradise-apple. Was Temple Sinai like a business corporation? If so, it had a competent executive staff, and did not require my managerial services.

I delved more intently into the roots of personal commitment. What did I stand for? The makeshift walk-up room I had rented on the West Side was a vestigial fixation from years of penny-pinching. But musty air and faded drapes provided a backdrop for a regimen of self-exploration no less austere than that of a monk in his cell. I scoured the convolutions of my brain. And well I might! The most promising hour of my career would soon arrive: the official installation!

At twilight, on the auspicious day, I strode in front of the mirror, twitched at a stiff collar and Brooks Brothers tie, shook like dice the gold cuff-links Birdie had sent from the family, sat absent-mindedly on the bed, and folded a silk handkerchief with elaborate care, then closed my eyes in a trance and opened them on the clock.

"Holy Cow! And I haven't had any supper!" Then I riffled swiftly through the pages of my sermon to the final paragraph, which I had memorized.

In a far corner of Schrafft's, over an uncracked soft-boiled egg, I thanked God that I had begged off a dinner-date with the Chairman of the Pulpit Committee on the ground of possible nervous indigestion. The tears could flow without embarrassment or restraint when I reread, for the tenth time, the Yiddish letter from Mom. Abramsons and Nisselewiczes had given rabbis to Israel in every generation. I would be the most renowned. She was very proud.

"An all-star program tonight, Doctor! Tauber and Saraband! Wow!" Mr. Falk the sexton shouted to me from his post near the door.

"All-star program!" I huffed down the aisle. "What does he think this is? A theatre?" I peered sideways at the crowd already milling about in the vast sanctuary. "Have they come to be entertained? The trustees said they were counting on me to draw the crowd! Am I to be a black-gowned prima donna, a sort of buffoon of God?"

The air in the Senior Rabbi's study began to crackle as the door swung open to a flurry of chattering voices, and a black-clad giant entered, tufts of raven hair hanging down almost to his eyes, like stricken trees on a bare cliff. The massive head rose up from regal shoulders and stretched forward like the prow of a Viking galleon. I braced myself against being sucked into Dr. Saraband's magnetic orbit as one digs his feet into the sand against the outgoing tide. Suddenly the spell broke – and a spare, swarthy man, muffled in a huge overcoat, stood before me, grinning and holding out his hand. Joel Tauber!

"Hello, Abe! Big evening! Your big chance, my boy!" I glowed with delight. "Get the crowds be dynamic dynamic Saraband here and I speak a dozen times a week they come in droves move them thrill them be dynamic!" In Tauber's eyes there was an eerie, luminous daemonism that penetrated and possessed everything.

The Saraband thunder billowed out through half-clenched

teeth, the Tauber staccato spat, the organ began a doleful fugue, the distant babble of the congregation was receding to a few murmurs, and I would have been mesmerized by sheer magnitude had not the President stabbed me awake with a frenzied question: "In what order'll we have 'em speak?" "Saraband first," I hissed, shivering from the trickles of perspiration that scurried like serpents down my back.

Ensconced in the plush-backed pulpit chair, I fended off panic by anchoring my gaze to a random succession of things and people: Cantor Weingarten's operatic tremolo; a dazzling diamond brooch in the first row; my brother Jack, who had closed his little grocery store for the weekend to represent the Feinbergs; the fluffy tassel jiggling a tune on the baretta; my first artichoke at a Park Avenue hotel wedding banquet; President Weisfeld, who told me over wiener-schnitzel and beer at Luchow's how much everyone appreciated my refusal to officiate at a socialite's Temple wedding unless my Senior co-rabbi was also invited; Emil Behr, the Treasurer, who trembled with agitation when I read "love" instead of "fear" of God, in the prayers, and shouted that "any change in this here ritchel will be made over my dead body."

Suddenly a voice pierced my reverie. Tauber had just reached the pulpit. Throughout the ritual he had sat as though petrified, fingers interlaced stiffly on his lap, head bent – an image of chained intensity. Now the fingers around either edge of the lectern seemed to liberate a demi-urge; one upon another, like the drummer's rat-a-tat-tat in the Bellaire band, the word-bombs exploded. His overwhelming intellectual and forensic power bound me in a spell as if by cataleptic magic. Not until he turned and faced me, did I arouse myself.

"In the person of this young man, in the person of this fine young man, American Jewish youth consecrates itself anew to its people. I am proud to introduce him!"

Through paralysing seconds of eternity lead-weighted legs pulled me to the pulpit. I touched it with my hand, for companionship, fastened my eyes upon the bronze memorial plaque on the distant rear wall of the sanctuary, eased my mind into a groove traced by a week of *sotto voce* rehearsal – and was soon lost in lone, ecstatic monologue.

Upturned eyes, pillars, balcony, bronze plaque vanished, while pages of the speech turned over in my mental eye. Unconsciously I stepped backward. A filmy haze shrouded the pulpit. As the closing sentence ended, my heels touched the dais of the Ark and severed all contact with things, people, written word; I was free to stretch up my arms and head, close my eyes, loosen all reins from my heart, and beseech the Almighty for guidance and strength.

Thou Great Unknowable, I thirst to know Thy Being! Thou Great Unsearchable, I hunger for Thy secret! Thou Great Alone, I yearn to walk with Thee! Let me but behold the hem of Thy garment, as did Isaiah. Let me but hear Thy still small voice within me, as did Elijah. Speak to me O God that I in turn may speak to man and bring him to Thy truth. Amen!

It was over! Mrs. Matz elbowed through the buzzing throng, puckering her mouth against my ear while she folded both hands over mine and assured me I didn't have to take a back seat for anyone. My President boasted that Sinai knows how to pick a winner and was anxious only about my health. "Don't overwork, Doctor. You were limp as a rag when you finished that prayer." Mr. Falk grinned and gabbled. "We won't have any trouble selling Holyday seats next September, that's sure!" Silver-haired, matronly ladies gently pressed my hand as they filed past the receiving line. I saw the janitor shake his head and mutter, "He'll be at Emanu-El before long!" The Community Centre Director held up thumb and finger to form a circle and winked.

Dr. Tauber took me aside. "Great, really great! You've got what it takes. *It!*" He dropped his voice. "You know what I mean." He turned to leave, reversed his steps and bent toward me with a conspiratorial air. "That prayer! Magnificent! And extemp! And the way you dragged yourself to your seat and slumped into it to dramatize how you spent yourself. Smart!"

"A Campaign for Youth" – my first foray against the "big town's" irreligion – began with widespread advertisement of sermons on topical subjects: "Is Judge Lindsay's Companionate Marriage Feasible?"; "What Are the Seven Deadly Sins of the Jazz Age?"; "Should *Desire Under the Elms* Be Censored?"; "What about *Elmer Gantry*?"; "Is Prohibition a Fiasco?"; "Should Russia Be Recognized?"; "Jimmy Walker – Jimmy Valentine?"; couching them as questions to underline the clash of opinion. There were other stratagems – neon lights on the outdoor bulletin board, arty comic cartoon-sketches in *Temple Tidings*, a young folks' questionnaire on the subjects they preferred.

An international symposium on the Youth Movement by the YMCA chose me for a panel discussion. Instead I made a speech, frenetically appealing for a world-wide consecration of youth to a better world, while huzzahs in a dozen tongues bounced against the ceiling. For months I rode the subject hard at service clubs, ladies' luncheon associations, church junior societies, and even Zion-centred Hadassah.

Suddenly, dithyrambs to the Revolt of Youth rang hollow and I remembered how college cynics had converted Nietzsche into a procurer. I saw youth as anything but modern, with its inability to feel, its tough-minded realism, promiscuity and nomadism. Rather, I saw it as a reversion to type! Save for greater sex freedom, the God of Conformity ruled them undesecrate. When a tow-haired German Socialist on a mission to America laid before me photographs of the *Wander-Voegel* being aroused to a chauvinistic goose-step by followers of a demagogue named Hitler, I felt like regurgitating "Youth Movement" as the Pollyanna projection of a Christian Endeavour pink tea-party.

I refused, however, to let the fear incubate in my mind that sermons could provide nothing more than a flight from reality. "Campaign for Youth" ground forward. To attract attention, I picked quarrels with people in the news – a playwright who asserted that clergymen are thwarted Thespians, a judge who recommended the lash for a young Communist distributor of "seditious" handbills, a free-thinker loudly demanding the taxation of church property, a college professor advising students to be snobs. On every occasion, I hurled the Hebrew prophets at the rich, the arrogant, the oppressive. *I* would not equate faith with creed, religion with church, holiness with Holy Writ!

One Friday evening I flagellated myself into a supreme effort of optimism; the young men and women of Sinai *would* look to its pulpit for light from the peak after which it had been named!

The suffocating black robe seemed to fall away, the bothersome Temple budget Mr. Falk had spread out on my study desk dissipated into air, Mr. Behr's white sock swinging back and forth from his crossed knees no longer semaphored a warning against ritualistic heresy, the tea-and-cake collations of the Ladies' Auxiliary ceased to press upon my brain. And when I flung into the rafters the Masefield call to high emprise:

I must go down to the sea again, to the lonely sea and the sky,
And all I ask is a tall ship, and a star to steer her by,

the salt wind whizzed through my hair, the pulpit was a prow, and Temple Sinai's youth the stout-hearted crew of an armada setting out to save the world.

At the lectern for the closing ritual, the "tall ship" sank with my heart. Not a single candidate for the "priesthood of youth" sat in the sanctuary – except confirmands who had been assigned a special report on the sermon for homework. When mourners stood up to recite *Kaddish* I emasculated the majestic Hebrew-Aramaic cadences into a desultory memorial for a lost cause.

During more mature years, I learned to renounce the arithmetic of results. The pulpit is not a cash register. A businessman can tote up assets, a lawyer his acquittals; an architect watches a blueprint tower into stone and steel, a surgeon the healing of a wound, the teacher an expanding awareness in his pupils. No certain answer comes back to the preacher; he purveys the intangible and may not view results for a generation – if then. Almost two decades after the fruitless call to youth at Sinai, one of the mourners who arose for the *Kaddish* that evening, whom I had not seen, told me he then and there began "bucking the whole family to be an F.D.R. New Dealer." And for every sparse letter of thanks, grateful greeting from a former Sunday School pupil, or casual, heartening word about a long-forgotten speech, there may a hundred minds into which a sermon dropped a mite of ferment. But when I surveyed the wreckage of my Youth Campaign from the pulpit of Sinai that night, I myself was blinded by youth's impatience.

In later years, I lowered my sights and joined the healthy trend away from a hortatory pulpit to the pedagogic, relying less on flights of vision than on facts. At the synagogue's birth more than twenty centuries ago, while the Temple still rose on Jerusalem's height, sermons were just that: a scholarly exposition of the Biblical text. Besides, I sometimes suspected that ordinary human beings are more responsive to a radical message after they have been treated with an amiable massage. A clergyman who wins friends in the pew can say anything from the pulpit.

In those crusading days off Broadway, however, I would have cursed such calculated mellowing as cowardly evasion. I preferred prophetic pugnacity to an Aristotelian philosophy of moderation. Above all creatures, the fawning sycophant repelled me. I winced whenever a chairman introduced me to an audience as one of New York's most popular rabbis "whom we all love." A *Hasidic* sage once exclaimed: "Woe to him whom nobody likes – but beware of the man everybody likes." On reading it, I plumped for the woe. An anonymous letter heaping abuse on me for being a "pinko" rejoiced me more than the syrupy adulation of Mrs. Matz. I admired a dour curmudgeon like Harold Ickes more than a lip-pursing purveyor of sweetness and light. I was an angry young man!

In later years, the hub of the vast circle wherein I strove to do my job moved from the cosmic challenges of the pulpit to the privacy of my desk and troubled individuals of every creed, race, and class who poured out their problems across it. Do parishioners prefer the amateur psychiatry of a clergyman to the professional ministrations of a psychiatrist because it is devoid of shame, or because it is free? When an estranged husband and wife with whom I spend countless hours join forces to throw brickbats at me, I question why they sought my help. Perhaps laymen in search of firm footing still assume that the most likely source is the man steeped in God. Yet serious dangers ensue when the untrained and inexpert pastor ventures beyond his competence. After several blunders costly to the "client," I withdrew from counselling in any complex case and insisted on professional treatment. All I got for honest solicitude was gossip – that "Rabbi Feinberg doesn't deign to be bothered."

As the fiery pulpiteer of Temple Sinai, I *surely* didn't deign! Principles were easier to confront than people. Personal encounter found me as tongue-tied as the kid in Bellaire who could not tell his mother he adored her.

The more I pitied someone caught up by sorrow, the less I could articulate, involved as I was in the numbness of his grief. Only on a public podium did the private "I" emerge. And innate respect for the human situation hobbled me; I found it impossible to apply the glib, glucose placebos of the professional solacer.

Happily, I discovered laughter. Most subversive of conspiracies, and on *our* side, it is the hallmark of a civilized human being. Jewish folklore equips man with two pockets; in one is the humble reminder that he is dust and ashes, in the other the proud affirmation that he is the son of the King of Kings. A sense of humour dips my hand into the pocket of humility, makes me smile with irony at a mirror instead of clamping jaws in rigid Messianic resolution. But when I flung Masefield's clarion summons to brave adventure at the last row of empty seats in Sinai's sanctuary that fateful Sabbath Eve, I was not yet thirty – and the redemptive art of laughter lay sealed in the chamber of tomorrow's experience.

The public accepts a rabbi at his own evaluation, I told myself, and my star had designated me a crusader for social righteousness!

Possibly the potter's wheel faltered and I got around to becoming only a censorious, pretentious prig. But I hewed stubbornly to the line of my fate.

Another test soon faced me, in the outstretched hand of a soldier's torso strapped to roller skates; the papers had termed it a "basket case" shipped home from the Argonne. I hurried to Tenth Avenue and up beside the railroad tracks; the chug of shuttling freight trains did not drown the thud of rubber handpads the torso used to push itself along the pavement. They stomped me into restless sleep and played a dirge in my throbbing head. "You speak of God, of God, of God, you speak of God, you speak of God, of God, of God, you speak of God!"

At university I had lost a semester rather than wear an ROTC uniform. There I was a mere flea. Now I could speak from one of the most prominent Jewish pulpits in America. I would defy militarism. If the Board ousted me, I had no wife or child to support.

For thirty minutes I stood stockstill in the pulpit, my feet rooted in the floor, thus identifying with the torso on roller skates. Only the jaw moved, and the mouth; my unblinking eyes stared into the pit of hell. At the end I lifted my hand.

Religion dare not endorse war! I will not engage in conflict with my fellowmen for territory, trade, glamourized terminology or extravagant hypostasization of national honour. I will engage in unending conflict for the sacredness of life. When the next war comes, I pray to God for the courage to oppose it. Our true loyalty is man, our enemy – war itself!

After the benediction, I stalked down the aisle to wish the congregation good Shabbas at the door, with hands clenched under the robe. Just let anyone call me a traitor! I was tired of a religion that pounces on pornography and prays for "God's side" in war, sick of a synagogue that strums with muted strings on shop-worn platitudes, fed up with being a fashionable friar pandering to somnolence!

Black-garbed mourners filed past. I gaped vacantly at their

retreating backs. Mrs. Matz sidled up. "As usual, Doctor! You did grand!" I muffled thanks behind a handkerchief. Mrs. Geiger asked me to officiate at the unveiling of her husband's tombstone a week from Sunday. "Shall I tell you about my dear one now?" "No, Mrs. Geiger, that Sunday will be time enough." Mrs. Behr reminded me I had overlooked announcing my book review for the mothers. Mrs. Mosessohn waggled her forefinger playfully under my nose. "You have a date tomorrow night." Mr. Kroneberg, who always brought up the rear because, as the conscientious Chairman of the Property Committee, he made a cursory tour of the premises with the caretaker, laughingly shook my hand. "That was a brilliant sermon, Doctor. But you can't get any of *us* upset. Today the stockmarket reached the highest point in history." Before finally falling asleep that night, I read about an Austrian house-painter called Adolph Hitler who had written a war-glorifying book entitled *Mein Kampf*....

At Temple Sinai the rabbis attended meetings of the trustees, whose pivot was the Treasurer, Leopold Tannenbaum. If he said "It can't be done," a retaining-wall in the cemetery or a new basketball for the gym were alike unmentionable. His placidity could withstand anything except a complaint against an overdose of Hebrew in the ritual or an increase in a stenographer's salary. A bourgeois German in family background, he loved a boisterous *Tannhäuser*; American by adoption, he hated life's fundamental, occult enigmas. I found Leopold warmly humane, convivial, and generous of spirit.

Leopold had been growing strangely raucous of late. The Wall Street boom brought no blessing to Sinai! Every month a founding father yielded to spouse and debutante and moved to a fancier apartment – and pew – on the East Side. Replacements came from bargain-hunters flocking to West End Avenue from the Bronx. Competition also worried Leopold. A nearby Conservative *shule* had laid down the cornerstone of a million-dollar structure; the neighbourhood Orthodox congregation accumulated such a huge debt because of overbuilding that even a cantor "second only to Yossele Rosenblatt" could not rent enough Holyday seats to meet the mortgage, and now family pews were being sold at suicidal rates. And Union Synagogue, almost around the corner! It derived such an enormous income from cemetery plots in an old Brooklyn farm, purchased before a new municipal ordinance forbade the further spread of burial property in the area (on an advance Tammany tip-off, they said), that it was able to give weekly dances, with a high-class orchestra, without charge. "Too bad we're Republicans!" Leopold muttered to his cigar.

The fiscal crisis drew a record quorum in January. Even before the previous minutes were read, redoubtable Leopold announced the *leitmotif*: unless additional revenue is found, the budget is doomed. "Why not raise dues? Yessir! Raise 'em! The more you ask the more respect they'll have for you. I'm a real-estate man – and I know."

Faces beamed enthusiasm – except robust Ike Elsasser's; he curled his heavy eyebrows and shot a satirical glance across the table. "If you real-estate-niks held that piece of propaty on Third Avenoo, instead of dumping it for pennies, we wouldn't be in this muddle. Besides, Rosh Hashanah comes near Labour Day this year and people will be stayin' in the country. We won't be able to sell Holyday seats even in Gimbel's basement!"

Saul Levine arose with painstaking deliberation on his beige spats and slowly removed a pince-nez from the bridge of his nose. Conspicuous and immediate boredom was written on all faces. Saul was a corporation lawyer; his wife repeatedly said that he would have made a fine rabbi.

"Young people are athirst for the living God. We have the finest community centre in the land. That's a truism! Fill it with classes in French and parliamentary law, Boy Scouts, Girl Scouts, rhythmic dance. No effort is too much if we can bring back our young to the House of Jacob!"

A growl burst from Ike's abdomen. "Dammit, we already have French conversation and fat-reducin' on Mondays and Wednesdays, and Yogay lessons or whatever you call 'em. Humbug! Do the people who come ever join the Temple?" He sputtered in scarlet spleen, slapping the air with his hand. "My granddaughter or your son would never come near the place anyhow – and you know it, Saul!"

Ike stopped chomping his cigar and leaned across the President's lap to grimace. "That'll hold Levine for a while. He makes the same damn speech every meeting. Once ran for Attorney General and he ain't forgot it. *Shlemiel!*"

Before adjournment followed approval of a special finance committee, Leopold's protean mood shifted to engaging affability. He had been authorized to select the committee. All benevolence, he raised his hand. "Don't forget one valuable asset, gentlemen – our new rabbi! A star attraction!" I felt a hand on my shoulder. "His work is a business too." I blushed. "And he'll deliver the goods." I shrank. "This is his Temple!" I raised quizzical eyebrows.

All the way through Central Park (I had refused a ride home in order to think), the valedictory salute nagged me. *Was* the rabbinate a business? It would undoubtedly be smart and simple to treat it as such! I knew just the kind of businessman I would be. I would explore and exploit my resources with cool detachment, engineer self-promotion schemes, camouflaged as ideas, through the Board, grease my path with unction, manipulate people by careful measure of their usefulness, scrutinize every impulse, gesture or word that might retard the popularity chart, keep my eyes fixed on becoming the biggest rabbi in New York, put a price tag on every moment of time and every foot-pound of energy to maximize its dividend, and eliminate every role on life's stage save that of supersalesman with a marketable commodity: myself.

For the first time in my life, I soliloquized aloud. It was startling: "Be a Babbitt! So what? Trustees run the Temple and trustees have a business mentality. Maybe they're right! An institution can't perform any service without earnest men of financial experience who are willing to sacrifice their time. If I can end this self-mortifying tripe about being true to myself and develop a business viewpoint, they'll feel more comfortable with me, and love me for it! Besides, what *is* my true self?"

I had already learned the sagacity of the lacquered dispassionate mood at funerals. In the beginning I tried desperately to penetrate the grey gulf around a grief-stricken family which, in most instances, I had never seen before and would never see again, except possibly at Sabbath Service for the thirty-day period of mourning. With driving urgency and haste, since I'd met the bereaved only once prior to the obsequies, I probed for the most responsive spots in the sub-surface terrain of family relationships. I achieved nothing – except awkwardness, discomfort, and exhaustion. How much easier it was to act the dramatic routine of comfort, extract a eulogy clue from the index file, after tactful inquiries of the immediate kin, and be an emotional neuter. Such an investment would yield profit – maximum display of wares with minimum expenditure of self!

The "business" formula offered another advantage. It dissolved a contradiction that was vexing me with merciless insistence: a professional rabbi's status as employee. He is enmeshed by a paradox – hired and handsomely paid to fight the dominant values of the very people who supply his emolument, committed to making them think, feel, and act by rules that deny their worldly self-interest and nature, and to making them reward him for it.

Until the fifteenth century, the rabbinate had not yet been professionalized; livelihood was sought elsewhere. As a result, the rabbi bowed to none save God. How can a vaunted spiritual leader lead people where they don't want to go, and also accept a hireling's wage? But the word "business" dissipated confusion like a magic capsule. Swallow that premise and demand nothing from my congregants except gratitude for not disturbing their complacency about this world or the next – and from myself nothing except to be a lovable lapdog!

That night, by habit, I took the paved, well-worn route through Central Park which had been my brooding-ground for months. A path through the mazes of my mind was not so clearly marked; it had to be hewn. I glanced at the stars, so near I almost reached up to snatch one and warm my cold gloom with its lambent flame. Instead, I cursed the stars which had made me so worrisome and perplexed. Why? New York was my oyster! Pry it open, and eat!

Even Harry Emerson Fosdick, my favourite preacher, could not escape the squirrel cage. One afternoon, while taking a brisk walk up the Drive, I had passed the steel skeleton of Riverside Church. Hundreds of feet in the air workmen were hammering the final red-hot rivets to the tower. Over the doorway carved figures gave tantalizing promise of interior splendours. The structure was a precious jewel of workmanship, a cathedral on a hilltop overlooking the Palisades!

How proud Dr. Fosdick must be, I had speculated. To see a shrine rise up under one's hands, to build a House for God and cause His word to go therefrom! I stopped and held my hat that day against the wind blowing up from the Hudson and imagined a great hill-crowning diadem, with a vast solar dome symbolic of the unity and harmony of the universe, and a golden Ark of the Covenant – Feinberg's Temple!

My mind had turned the last socket in the gigantic candelabra which would flank the Ark when I sauntered over to a bench and sat down. Within a few minutes a camera-laden couple plodded wearily up the path and sat beside me.

"That's Rockefeller's church, isn't it?" the woman said.

"Well," replied her companion, "he's paying for it!"

"Not bad looking!"

"Not at all."

Then – silence.

Leopold had dubbed Sinai "the new rabbi's" temple. I heard not only my imaginary synagogue topple, but "my" Sinai as well. "Rockefeller's Church"! The minister of a large metropolitan congregation owned neither it nor himself. The physical edifice belonged to the rich who contributed a tax-exempt dollop from their superfluous hoard; the clergyman was a slave of the organization fashioned for its justification and maintenance.

Could I find the mustard-seed of faith under tons of brick and brass and brocade? A gaunt, leafless tree trembling in the night breeze reflected my vacillation. I wasn't sure.

Home, hunched over a desk, palms in eyes, I turned to next day's appointment pad. There, between the close-packed lines, I sniffed the scent of my dilemma. The rabbinate *had* to be a prosaic, pragmatic business; it was a full-time job! Amos tended sycamore trees, the rabbis of the Talmud earned daily bread as sandal-makers, carpenters, wine-growers, tradesmen. Today, all twenty-four hours are scarcely adequate for rabbinical chores! The prophets spoke because there was a raging fire in their bosoms, because they had something to say, and not because they had to say something. The professional pseudo-prophets, the profit-seeking propheteers whom the real ones held up to contempt are all forgotten. But a rabbi in 1930 has a full-time job. If he is to live and beget a family, he *must* be a professional.

Surveyed for the first time with analytic intent, my engagement-list left me in a daze. A nine o'clock class at Columbia in the Philosophy of Religion where I would dissect the concept of holiness. At ten-thirty a wedding ceremony for a couple who had run their fingers down the Yellow Pages to find a geographically convenient minister. The Social Hall Committee meeting at eleven, to decide whether underprivileged dental-clinic children should be given hot chocolate or milk while they waited for examination, how much to charge the B'nai B'rith for the use of our auditorium, what was responsible for the diminution of attendance at the ladies' class in Modern Drama, and whether the Committee had the moral right to include the Sunday School when it presented its annual report on the number of persons who had entered the Hall during the season. A twelve-thirty luncheon invocation for a society being formed to foster cultural relations with the Soviets. At two a funeral – or rather one-forty-five, to glean material for the eulogy and confirm pronunciation of the name. At two-thirty, if the deceased had left no request for a Masonic service and the taxi was not delayed by traffic or rain, in my office, to dictate a cajoling membership proposal to "outside" parents of a boy who had just been Bar-Mitzvah. I had told Mrs. Goldberg, the lady with the diamond earrings, that if she called at three I might arrange to chat with her about the novel I had mentioned in a talk for Hadassah. At three-thirty an hour-long confirmation-class lecture on the ethics of Judaism. A perusal of the Jewish Encyclopaedia at four-thirty, to collate data on the Jewish home for a speech to the Ladies Auxiliary of Christ Church. At five termagant Mrs. Bergamon was holding me to a promise of a chat with her about Monroe, who did not like his Sunday School teacher. By five-thirty, home and a half-hour with Tito Schipa records and another with *If Winter Comes*, which I was to review for the Sisterhood. A Mrs. Dachman, whom I couldn't recall for the life of me, expected me at seven. I had warned her of a Mothers' Association meeting; she would permit me to leave early on condition that I return. Unless there were interesting guests under forty or a pretty, single girl, I would plead fatigue, a Rotary Club address next week (speeches to Gentiles always had priority) or my ignorance of bridge, and reach my hotel long before midnight. Then I would hopefully phrase and rephrase a spontaneous, impassioned press release on the Saturday sermon for the Sunday *Times* rabbinical round-up.

"A damn auto-mechanic shifting gears all day!" With a sweep of my arm, I brushed the datebook to the floor, walked over to the window, and mused into the night. Maybe I could make the search for God a hobby, like Leopold's brother-in-law, who had once led me into a storeroom hideaway where he searched out the goddess of art during his leisure time. Why not throw in the sponge, take off the hair shirt, let myself be melted by the warmth of Leopold and Ike and others for whom I had a hitherto-reluctant fondness – and stop being pursued by Francis Thompson's "Hound of Heaven" down the labyrinthine years? People with a nose for insoluble enigmas don't help the world along. They stumble over broken hearts to reach the clouds – like my father, who wrestled with sterile Talmudic dialectic about his soul, while unmended umbrellas rusted in the corner and the rent bill lay crumpled in the cracked sugar bowl.

I loved to sing, and was taking lessons from one of the best voice teachers in town. Did not the *Hasidim* hear a melody in every blade of grass? "Il mio tesoro," from Mozart's *Don Giovanni*, "Se 'il mio nome," that paean to love from *The Barber of Seville*, "Una furtiva lagrima," from *L'Elisir d'Amore*, Schubert's "Staendchen," "Fear Not Ye, O Israel" – God, what they did for me! Reprieve to a man on the gallows! I hummed them all, one after the other, into the windowpane over Fifth Avenue. But the gloom settled back, like the mist that condensed on the rocks at the base of Niagara Falls and lifted them into a pyramid of ice. I was not an honest singer of songs, to make men happy. I was a courtly popinjay warbling inanities and pretending to be a preacher intoxicated with God.

"Popinjay!" I jerked my head upward and squinted. A Protestant minister had set down for his own ironic amusement, with deadly accuracy, a list of clerical chores, all beginning with the letter "p." I had seen it by chance in a church paper. Maybe I could try *my* hand at such a list! Before I could laugh at the zany impulse, I grabbed a pen.

"Pew-filler, preacher, prophet, priest, poet, patriot, pietist, propagandist, philosopher, purifier of morals, patron of art, public-relations expert, pamphleteer, psychoanalyst, philanthropy campaigner, political prognosticator, personality kid, pacifier (not pacifist), punster, panel-pilot, protocol-specialist, professor of geriatrics (and pediatrics), property overseer, photogenic publicity parson, post-prandial rib-tickler, piscatorial prize-winner, peripatetic encyclopaedia."

I read them over – ponderously, punctuating each in turn – in a masochistic spree of self-laceration, finally mumbling, "A combination of Lord Chesterfield, Savonarola, Dale Carnegie, Moses, Ignatius Loyola, Isaiah, Einstein, and Maimonides – with Fred Astaire for good measure!"

That was not enough to purge my spleen. I had to open some cloacal vent for the acid bilge that overflowed the dam of self-deception and now rose up to stifle me. So I wrote down ten occupational hazards of the clergy:

Pomposity	*inflationary balloon for the phony and insecure.*
Sentimentality	*a clowning caricature of emotion.*
Saccharinity	*the peddling of treacle.*
Insularity	*strut and storm in a narrow sheepfold.*
Sycophancy	*substitution of flattery for faith.*
Egocentricity	*progress from God's lieutenant to tin god.*
Timidity	*the coward's version of meekness.*
Triviality	*an escape from conscience into detail.*
Obesity	*fatty degeneration of the spiritual arteries.*
Ambidexterity	*expertise in water-carrying on both shoulders.*

These perils did not threaten the integrity of all ministers. I had met many who were really men of God, humble, self-consecrated, inwardly aflame. There could be no doubt, however, that a big city aggravated clerical malaise. Super-organization–that was the disease! It builds empires, not a sense of God's presence! Maybe the shamans of the church and synagogue must stop blocking the highway every individual must walk alone. A soapbox might be a more productive medium than the soft soap of a fat pulpit! I was a "success" as rabbi, and on the road to failure as a human being. The ministry must espouse and apply ideas in direct and unavoidable collision with the dominant interests of contemporary civilization. Was I strong enough?

My mother had visited me in New York not long before. All the pride and intuition and grace that had been strangled so long burgeoned in her eyes, walk, tinkling laughter, the carriage of her head. The President's wife gave her an initialled marcasite pin as a souvenir of affection and respect. It was at her bedside when she died.

My perfectionist love of the rabbinate had lured me into disappointment, decadence, or half-demented, compulsive disapproval of myself. No artful dodging could rewind the tangled, once-hypnotic skein of illusions. My profound love for Mom gave me, during her visit, a vicarious happiness beyond any exhilaration I had known in New York. But that love could not halt my headlong flight into crisis.

Was it possible for me to incise the tumour bred by one love without betraying the trust of the other? To resolve that dilemma, I went to Bellaire, and returned with the assurance that my mother understood.

Anthony Frome, Poet Prince: To Broadway Razzle-Dazzle and Return

In December 1929 Sinai's Board received my resignation; it was impelled, I wrote, by "an inescapable inner necessity to cultivate the art of vocal music." I had a scholarship at the Juilliard School of Music and was studying voice with a renowned teacher who bade me lie on the floor and grunt, for abdominal breathing, at fifteen dollars a lesson. But my letter to the trustees contained more syllables than truth, and I was troubled.

The President had announced "deep regret" at my imminent departure; I knew it was no less genuine than our close friendship, which lasted until his death. Though we inhabited different intellectual worlds, many of the trustees and members of Sinai were linked with me in mutual affection. The Sunday School children trusted and loved their rabbi.

For weeks I fought on both sides in a conflict of loyalties which ended with an advertisement of a farewell sermon: "Why I Am Leaving the Professional Ministry," to be delivered Sabbath Eve February 28, 1930. Vocal music had only a minor part in my resolve to forsake the pulpit. A critical crossroads in my life was no time for deviousness. The debacle of organized religion cried out for exposure.

The Temple was electric that evening, with the massed expectancy of a huge congregation. I stepped to the pulpit.

Before the war, the power of religion was something to be reckoned with. What now? The mummy of Tutankhamen, loaded with material glory and bereft of life.

Clutching the lectern with blanched and clammy fingers, in a low-pitched monotone lest emotion undo me, I closed my eyes and plunged.

Sigmund Freud moulds more lives than the saints, Amos n' Andy reach more hearts than the most brilliant preacher, Clara Bow has more influence on morals than Bishop Manning, Wall Street's recent bust gave rise to more prayer than the liturgies of church and synagogue. The mood of America has descended from the imaginative introversion of Woodrow Wilson to the commerce-saturated traffic in things that marks Herbert Hoover. . . . Organized religion is a deserted lighthouse; the tides of human energy beat on other shores.

The requiem had to be recited! I could not halt midstream.

Once an ideal becomes a cult, creed, or church, it begins to die. We hear about the religion of business; a more realistic phrase is the business of religion.

But I was not an unbeliever.

I do not repudiate faith. It is not absolute belief in spite of reason, but sincere living in spite of consequences.

And I did not fear the future.

Victory is not achieved in a hothouse but on the sweltering battlefield against evil. There my life will be spent, with faith in God's work, in life, in man!

Halfway around from pulpit towards altar chair, I raised two hands to the clasp at my throat, automatically, and like a sleep-walker, unfastened it – and the robe slipped to the floor.

This has stood between us long enough. Now I belong with you.

Scooping up the robe, I draped it over my arm and descended from the altar to the first seat I could find.

Saturday morning launched a journalistic bacchanale. From New York to California newspapers illustrated excerpts of my sermon with cheek-by-jowl photographs of the personages it had mentioned. The Sunday *Times* published two tight-packed columns: the blast against organized religion in its entirety, and one sentence from the equally long latter section which emphasized my positive personal faith. Wires streamed in from outraged Bible Belt Pentecostals who would gag or jail me and battle-scarred Bob Ingersoll atheists who hailed me as a redeemer from the tyranny of clericalism. Pulpits and editorial columns crackled. In Moscow *Pravda* recounted my swan song as the obituary of religion; capitalist youth at last had seen the light of godlessness.

The President of the Freethinkers of America, Joseph Lewis, invited me to help him lead a campaign for truth; one Manhattan rabbi dubbed me an "underdone idealist"; another, in San Francisco, after conceding that my diatribe was "factually true," attributed its "recklessness" to my prospective nuptial union with a Park Avenue heiress; with delighted gusto, Heywood Broun, Charles Francis Potter, and Harry Elmer Barnes leaped to my defence.

The following week, Dr. Saraband made me the subject of his Sunday lecture in Carnegie Hall. He agreed that religious over-organization had become a fetish, and even proposed to "liberate religion from the churches." But my farewell address was a "futile valedictory" which "should have been spoken earlier." And also, he thundered, I "had never been active in Zionism."

In the summer of 1928, long before Jewish Holy Land pilgrimages became fashionable and comfortable, I had travelled the length and breadth of Palestine by burro, camel, foot, and horse, on a weather-beaten, bruising saddle, in shorts and hatless, under the sizzling sun of the Valley of Jezreel; I had dug the soil with bare hands as a kibbutznik in a new-born malarial settlement. On my return I had driven myself to the brink of exhaustion pleading for support of beleaguered Jewish pioneers – in synagogues and community centres, at bowel-curdling banquets, from Far Rockaway to Washington Heights to the warrens of the Bronx – and, as I sulphurously fumed to Ruth, Saraband must have known it! Yet his pointless accusation supplied a prop to my ego, by diverting me from a charge which had more than a grain of truth, namely, that I was a deserter who should have stayed to fight.

In June of that year, I forsook argument, a series of women's club philosophical lectures illustrated with songs, a book, and my daily chat with Ruth, to study opera on a scholarship at the Conservatoire Americain in Fontainebleau, France, with Salignac, famous tenor of the Opera Comique.

Four months of rejuvenation, freedom, release from inter-pulpit caterwauling and the merchandise-mart of religion! Fontainebleau was a heady anodyne: riding a bicycle down cobbled streets and in the fabled forest; chilly stone corridors that smelled of royalty, intrigue, and Napoleon; solo-singing La Marseillaise on Bastille Day from a balcony over the courtyard; Salignac railing at my Anglo-Saxon *mise en scène* heavy-handedness in *Manon, Faust, Carmen, Romeo and Juliet*; the shrilly screaming train to Paris.

Paris – and heart-ache memories of a lost world: midget-restaurant landmarks of my first trip abroad in 1925, like Le Cul Blanc near the Madeleine, destroyed by the Nazis in 1943, a gendarme told me, for harbouring *maquis*; the gargoyles of Notre Dame; bookstalls;

the ebullient chaos of the Flea Market; *jambon* sandwich and hot chocolate in predawn bistros, onion soup in Les Halles, and long-haired Left Bank café-dwellers excoriating American materialism while waiting for a chance to sponge off its beneficiaries; arty parties at the home of Nadya Wanger; Heinrich Heine's grave; truffles and paté de foie gras with Ike Elsasser and his wife at the Crillon; lamp-light on the Place de la Concorde where I pined over Ruth's letters; above all, freedom – freedom to feel, sing, love, be eccentric, anarchic, heroic, quixotic, erotic, in an atmosphere that often stank with urinals, unwashed linen, the cumulative dust of centuries, and yet was the breath of the European spirit.

Manhattan's asphalt desert flung me back to bread-and-butter reality. My new maestro, Ernesto Cosentino, swore he would put me on the stage of the Met by brow-beating me into the arcana of Italian *bel canto*, but the abrasive criticism by Salignac had purged me of illusions. Opera stars drank *Aïda* with their mother's milk. I was too old for decades of apprenticeship. Then I read an ad – and shifted my dream from the garret of a Neapolitan zealot to the Liebling School for Radio, which offered a miniature broadcasting studio, intensive check on needle vibrations and "blast," opportunity to get the feel of a mike, and shrewd advice from Estelle Liebling, best-connected coach on Broadway, for "that crazy young man who gave up a wonderful rabbi career to starve," as she described me to Ruth.

Mrs. Connor, the school's piano accompanist, had a Sunday-afternoon half-hour program on local station WMCA and invited me to be a guest star. Turning over the selected song scores on her lap, she snapped out a comment for each one. For the "M'Appari" aria from *Martha* – "That classy bit of tripe"; "Rose of Tralee" – "You, a Jewish priest, sing like McCormack"; "My Little Grey Home in the West" – "Corny ballads, the older the better"; "Ay-Ay-Ay" – "Hang on to that high note till the gals faint"; "Parlez Moi d'Amour" – "Your French don't sound like a cold in the nose." The wisecracks gave me qualms about the new life I was beginning. She said nothing, fortunately, when I insisted on ending the radio recital with "Serenade" from *The Student Prince* – my special song since the night I crooned it to Ruth on a moonlit beach at Cape Cod.

The next comment I heard was a "Damn!" from Miss Liebling. "You on the air with that name? Who ever heard of a romantic lover called Abraham?" I had just reread Edith Wharton's *Ethan Frome*. "Anthony" would complete the "A.F." initials. Anthony Frome it was! Mrs. Connor chuckled. My reincarnation as "Tony" would put my "phiz on the dresser of every drooling moron in America."

It was the engineer on duty that Sunday who really brought my new-born image to birth. "That there needle didn't budge! The boy's a natural! Smooth as silk!" The program director sent me a note: a ten-minute sustaining (no pay) slot, Saturday, 4:45 p.m. "Not prime time, Doctor!" Miss Liebling gesticulated, "but you're on!"

I was. Every week, after a Liebling pep talk and a keyboard sitting with Mrs. Connor, I manfully transmuted the rectangular honeycomb of steel standing so cold on a metal rod in front of my face into Mom, Ruth, someone I loved – and tried to communicate, as with a living person. Every week I cast a swift glance at the autocrat in the control-room, ground my feet into the floor, got a firm grip of the mike, took a deep breath to squelch queasy intestinal rumblings, and nodded to the yawning pianist.

The break I prayed for came when Ed Wolfe, an agent whose very name tingled the spine of would-be radio stars, began to seek a replacement for Arthur Tracy, "Street Singer," the sensational "find" with whom he was embroiled in a lawsuit. One Saturday at 4:45, he tuned in, to quote Ed himself, "on a guy with a tear in his voice, a song in his heart, and a socko in his style." On Monday, he told the boys he had signed up a new star.

Thin, sharp-nosed, ferret-like Ed penetrated the secretarial wall around a network president and the cigar-chewing snarl of a talent scout with undiscriminating aplomb. He praised me in curt monosyllables that left me floundering in self-doubt; he rebuked me with outcries that might have shattered my morale in the bewildering razzle-dazzle of Broadway – but he dedicated himself to the metamorphosis of a moody rabbi into a toothpaste-ad radio god.

First, Ed took me in to Manny Goldstein, who could squeeze shmaltz out of a cadenza exercise. "That class stuff," Manny said, "is okay – but you ain't gonna get nowhere unless you give 'em the hits, like these here on my piano. Not hot rhythm! Ballads! Tons of 'em."

Broadway between 42nd Street and 59th was a printing-press for songsheets. Every bootblack dreamed of writing a hit tune or lyric. The prize was fabulous – a zillion copies, ANSCAP radio royalties, a penthouse, and Japanese silk pyjamas – and one never knew on what spawn of corn and drivel the lightning would strike.

A song must be heard, however, before it can click. Every music house had a plugger. His job was to sell the firm's tunes to the singer, and then show him how to put them over. Soon Ed dragooned every good plugger on Broadway into nursing my "style."

I talked vocal technique with Jan Peerce, a knowledgeable, devout Jew and good friend, whose phenomenal voice, under Roxy's tutelage, was changing Pinky Pearl, once an obscure violinist, into an operatic celebrity. In my Riverside Drive kitchenette, I sat, listened, and analysed before a radio box. The top-notch crooners themselves would teach me how to master radio!

Bing Crosby croaked in his thorax, Rudy Vallee twanged with his nose, Morton Downey shrilled from the roof of his mouth. One quality, however, they all evinced: simple, direct contact. The message might be banal, an apotheosis of trivia, dedicated to the ineffable revelation that "moon" rhymes with "soon" or "June," "heart" with "part," "shine" with "mine," and "love" with "above," but it was addressed to *me*. Surely *I* could do that! What maestro Cosentino called *voce parlata* – the spoken, communicating word – was my life-long vocation!

Ed's second step lifted me from WMCA to WOR, a station with more kilowatts and coverage. Then he got his brain wave. Casting about for a peg on which to hang a series, he came up with the "Poet Prince," wandering over the earth in quest of perfect love.

While the script was being read, improvised organ music would supply a background aura and cue the hero into his songs, which would emerge unannounced from the story. The WJZ coast-to-coast network of The National Broadcasting Company had agreed not only to spot the "Prince" five nights a week; it would proceed at once to give Anthony Frome a stellar build-up: Radio City's Dick Liebert at the organ, Milton Cross, Frances Langford, and other royalty at the script!

The NBC star-makers took me in tow. They were precision-tooling an original product: a mellow romance-symbol, a scholar-lover rather than the brashly high-pitched troubador of prodigious escapades, and with unprecedented material – a rabbi!

Radio Guide spread my portrait across the cover, highlighting the unique antecedents and rabbinical attainments of a newly risen "radio idealist." *Radio Stars* unveiled my boyhood dreams and struggles on the climb "From Pauper to Poet Prince."

"The approach is stupid! What female in Omaha or Patchogue would weave her fantasy sex-fulfilment around a rabbi? They can't even think of one without a long beard!" a junior promotion-executive despairingly confided to me while I stroked my beardless chin. "One thing we can do – let them see you!"

Soon a photo streamed from the publicity mill: wavy-haired, dark, serenely poetic, in dressing-gown, smoking a pipe, and reading in the library, for distribution upon request. Word circulated among columnists that I resembled, in appearance, voice, and repertoire, Nino Martini, the rising young Met luminary, and was often accosted on Broadway by his admirers. Since the Poet Prince spot followed immediately after the eleven o'clock Fireside Chats of President Roosevelt on the same network, someone whispered that F.D.R. relaxed by tuning in on me.

Meanwhile, Tony Frome crooned, coaxed, crashed, pianissimo and fortissimo. My repertoire ran the gamut from flash-in-the-pan tunesters pounding out romance for Bing and Rudy to Victor Herbert and Stephen Foster, from Richard Rodgers, Jerome Kern, Cole Porter, and Noel Coward to Schubert, Puccini, and Verdi, from "Valentina,"

"Siboney," "La Cucaracha," and "The Night Was Made for Love" to "The Rosary" and "Kol Nidrei," from tender lullabies to sombre lyrics of passion in every tongue – but always from heart to heart!

Ed hired a press agent – not a Madison Avenue manipulator of mass tropism at the top of the pyramid and beyond our means, but a procurer of palate-tickling tidbits, artificed secrets, planted pellets of keyhole peeking for radio columnists. Ed Wolfe had never compromised my dignity by vulgar exploitation. Therefore I did not veto Bill Hoffman, even when a squib that I was augmenting my multilingual versatility with Chinese brought a dozen slant-eyed tutors to my door, and nonsense about a pet alligator flooded me with complaints from the SPCA and animal-lovers – although I began to fidget when Bill congratulated the Ringling Brothers press agent who popped a circus midget on J. P. Morgan's lap.

Three of the piquant items in the ever-thickening scrapbook were genuine. I invented a strikingly effective fade-out for a croony ballad. On reaching the final note, often raised an octave, I slowly retreated from the mike, holding the note until it slipped gently away into the night. Bill sent in a true story to Ben Gross, radio columnist on the *New York News* tabloid, that my shoes squeaked so noisily one night the control-room panicked, and I thenceforth sang in my socks!

The second morsel of truth involved Dick Liebert. Dick's daily stint in Radio City had extended his repertoire to vast proportions. While improvising behind the serialized story of the Poet Prince's peregrinations, he would close his eyes, lose all contact with the Prince, and forget to lead me into the correct key of my next number. Fortunately, the Lord, through the intermediation of my father, had granted me the knack of recording a pitch tenaciously on my inner ear. One night, however, I glared at Dick so fiercely that the tender good-night theme sounded like the "Anvil Chorus."

The third incident had to do with Judge Daniel Direnzo, who sent adulatory telegrams to my studio night after night. He proclaimed me the finest lyric tenor in the world, made plans which I never quite endorsed to put Anthony Frome ("the personality and artist, not that Poet guff") into a big-name night club, and even had me audition at the Riviera, across the George Washington Bridge in New Jersey. One night I got word of a terminal heart attack, and after the broadcast sped to his bedside on Staten Island. From the balcony of a little Greenwich Village Roman Catholic Church, before the priest intoned High Mass, I did what Judge Dan had requested before closing his eyes; I sang "Ave Maria."

A fan club, "The Anthony Frome Fellowship," had been born in the hieratic adoration of Mrs. Lorna Palmer, of Arlington, Virginia. Years later, when the club and the songs that tied it together with strands of sentiment had become a memory, she died of cancer, and I spoke in tribute at her grave – although, like the overwhelming majority of Fellowship members, she was Gentile. Then I learned with something like abashed awe that the club sprang not only from compensatory love for the Poet Prince and pleasurable identification with his romantic quest, but from active concern for interreligious brotherhood.

When Lorna Palmer used a list of names compiled from fan mail to circulate a letter proposing an Anthony Frome Club, she envisaged it not only as a fellowship for me but as a model for the fellowship that must bind together the religions of mankind. Whenever the Poet Prince was on the air they were all listening at once, people of every race and creed, each in his own home, but united heart to heart. They would inundate NBC and Pepto-Mangan, my sponsor, with "raves" about Tony – but they would also try to achieve a better understanding of each other's faiths.

At the Fellowship's birth, however, I blushed with discomfort. Ritzy membership cards adorned with my photo, a beautifully mimeographed six-page publication, "Court of the Poet Prince," a roster of branches, and the summons never to forget that Anthony Frome is "Prince" of ethereal space! "Ed Wolfe, what have you got me into?" I expostulated. He squinted. "You'll be damn glad some day, Tony."

"Some day" arrived; the Poet Prince was booked into movie theatres for top billing as a radio star. My only stage service stripes had been garnered in 1925. One stint was a Little Theatre piece, Rostand's *The Romancers.* Wearing zephyr-weight swim-shoes to facilitate levitation, I had jumped over a wall, fought a duel, and supplemented the love tryst with a serenade. The other bit, a month later, on board ship to Europe, was a group of songs in a seamen's-hostel benefit concert arranged by Anna Pavlova.

With a wooden sword – two amateurish stunts – tucked under my black-velvet, ruffled-sleeve costume jacket, I was to compete with seasoned moguls of the entertainment world four times a day, five on Saturday, singing to a mike under the blinding glare of spotlights with a case-hardened orchestra of strangers, a tough manager scowling and pacing in the wings, cobwebbed dressing-rooms that offended my nostrils, and a nervous system which barely repressed vomiting even in an empty broadcast studio. I didn't even know how to walk on!

The weekend try-out, in Paterson, New Jersey, was a baptismal nightmare. Ed's burly field-assistant, Nate Levin, who never failed to cheer me with a roistering joke before I approached a mike, forgot to initiate me into the mysteries of makeup. After a frenzied tour of neighbourhood cosmetic counters, Molasses 'n January, Ed's comedians on the same bill, loaned me tubes of grease paint. The dingy theatre engendered the romantic atmosphere of my father's hen coop and was far less picturesque. Had Ruth not gone with me, I would have wept. But I caught Ed nodding to Nate as I bowed off stage – with a ramrod spine – and later he said I was a "money-singer with guts."

The psychological distance between the Paterson crackerbox and the glittering vastness of the Earle Theatre in Washington would have been non-negotiable without the Fellowship. Under Lorna Palmer's shepherding, a contingent gathered in a body at every performance during the entire week to applaud. It was almost a torch-light parade! They huddled around my dressing-room for an autograph and handshake: middle-aged matrons, entranced teenagers and, always, a sprinkling of men who admired Anthony Frome emphatically because he was a "real artist, not a crooner." I never quite conquered a disquieting and humbling sense of shame, that human beings could live in a vacuum from which such vicarious, artificial sensation provided an escape.

While Atlantic seaboard theatres marked a terrestrial circuit for the Poet Prince, he continued to pursue his lady-love on the air-waves. In Baltimore, the WJZ network had no outlet. Every night after my final performance I leaped into a car and reached Washington just in time to rattle off a song-sequence for the pianist and press a script into the hands of the announcer, Arthur Godfrey,

In Buffalo, old Beth-El friends drove from the Falls to catch the Shea's show. At Brooklyn Fox, Grace Moore, in "One Night of Love," stretched my run to three weeks, the stage presentation synchronizing with the movie. I arose out of the pit on an elevator-contraption singing "Torn'a Sorriento," then "Love in Bloom," "Eili, Eili," and "When Irish Eyes Are Smiling," into which, according to Ed, I always "packed a Jewish *kvetch* at the Al Jolson finale."

The final bastion fell when the words "Anthony Frome, Poet Prince" appeared in the heartland of Broadway – on the Paramount Theatre, together with Lillian Roth and Pat O'Brien. The setting suggested a high-school lad's version of Wagnerian opera: white-robed Brunnhildes topped by mounds of blonde curly locks lolling about on ledges in moon-struck adoration of Lohengrin. I might have been understudy for Gilbert and Sullivan's Wandering Minstrel, strumming a fake guitar and singing "Amapola," "Play Fiddle Play," Toselli's "Serenade," "Night and Day," and "Did You Ever See a Dream Walking?" Boris Morros, Paramount's five-by-five Director, evidently liked it, Fellowship females fluttered at the stage door, Ed didn't bark, Ike Elsasser wrote me an effervescent note, and Joel Tauber waited backstage to pat my back after a matinée.

During the early period of personal appearances, I hugged the dressing-room in sheer fright – scared of draughts that might cripple me with a cold, of disreputable rear alleys, of stage-hands who could ruin my act, of the dancing-teams, magicians, animal-trainers, orchestra-leaders, talking violinists, trapeze-flyers, Gallagher and Sheen – Potash and Perlmutter comics to whom I was, beyond doubt, an upstart interloper, and of all that I had heard about the uncontained libertinism of stage people.

After some weeks, I began to mingle freely between shows; small talk assuaged tension. It was not long before I realized that stage people live under a more honest morality than many respectable bourgeois burghers outside. For one thing, the performers I chatted with in dimly lit wings were hanging on by their fingertips to a crumbling ledge over a precipice; vaudeville had almost completely vanished; they were obsessed with livelihood, not lubricity. During my college days the B. F. Keith peanut-heaven in Cincinnati belonged to a cross-country chain that collated a highly popular mixed menu of entertainment for the American masses. By the time the Poet Prince trod the boards, it was as a creature of *radio*, headlined over acts which had been touring the vaudeville circuit for years and now depended on *his* name to carry the show – while down-at-heel rooming-houses swarmed with veteran variety troupers waiting in vain for a call to work for coffee-and-doughnuts.

Before my Anthony Frome period, the son of a Temple Sinai real-estate tycoon lured me to his plush bachelor apartment in midtown on the pretext of an urgent "personal problem." The "problem" was a peignoir-clad, bedded red-head who merrily regaled me with nonchalant chatter about her descent from Back Bay Episcopal clergymen. A few days later, over Corona-Corona cigars at his mother's birthday dinner, he apologized for the "quirk" which had led him deliberately to shock me. "I just wanted to see your reaction. And you didn't bat an eyelash!"

In the murky haze of a chain-smoking, edgy, man-and-wife vaudeville team's dressing-room, I often cursed that puerile playboy under my breath – and also the smug, sniggering fancy which proclaimed starveling show people to be sleazy and promiscuous. And when the couple jigged and gyrated on stage like two kids prancing on the green, to warm up the customers with hilarity so that they wouldn't sit on their hands and to conceal their own Pagliacci heartbreak, I thanked God for real human beings.

The gruelling severities of the theatre did not leave me untouched. Often a late-morning train brought me into town emotionally drained, bone-weary, nervous enough to scream – and with barely sufficient time for a fast runover of my routine with a low-calibre orchestra no less grumpy, and far less interested, than I. I never quite became a naturalized citizen of the theatrical world. Even during my backstage *causeries* on religion, with fellow-performers who invariably got to me about God before the week passed, phantom fears stalked through my mind of all the terrible things that could happen in the next show.

Early in June 1934, Birdie phoned that Mom was ill; "complications from a stroke," she said. I hurried home and sat at the bedside, as corruption besieged the citadels of her vitality. Day after day, I watched the shades of twilight deepen, and blood-weariness bleach her cheeks, and threshing twists of pain give way to coma. Toxic infection beset her with fantasies that slithered through the farthest catacombs of her mind. She would see no one but "Abeleh"; my presence could exorcise the outriders of her night. So I sat – until the day came when I sensed that I would not sit through another.

The cry of Bellaire's fire-whistle stung me out of melancholy contemplation. I remembered that the same whistle, mournful and somewhat shorter, had sounded the curfew in my boyhood days, hastening my laggard footsteps home, sharpening my eyes for the cops. Sylvia slipped away to ask the location of the fire. "It's the Eastern Ohio (Milling Company) on Union Street. You know! The old mill! You can see the red glow," she whispered through the door. I walked over to the window. Towards the river only three blocks away, black cumulus clouds incarnadined with flame were billowing upward so thick I could already sniff the acrid smoke. "To think that it should go now, after all these years! Any day cinders from the B. & O. engines could have set it ablaze!" I murmured to Sylvia, who had entered the room. For a moment eloquent of thoughts unspoken and unspeakable, we stood together. Horse-and-buggy, pirate hunts in the hay, the boxcars with tiny corners of wheat we scraped clean for Pop's chickens! Death throes of an era – and of our mother!

A stir of the bedclothes snapped back our heads. Mom had folded her hands beneath the stark promontory of a shrunken chin, above which white lips trembled in an effort to speak. First the *Sh'ma,* preternaturally loud and clear, knifed through the silence: *Sh'ma Yisroel Adonoy Elohenu Adonoy Ehod* – affirmation of God's unity, the last words of every pious Jew. Then a Yiddish prayer, so gently spoken I had to bend close to hear it, led my mother across the threshold of eternity whereon she stood: "*Oy Gott, nemm tzu mein n'shamah. . . .*"* A few moments more of rhythmic death rattle, and Mom had left the love of this life for greater love.

Shiva, the seven-day period of home mourning, ended only a few days before I was to begin a week's booking into the Steel Pier, at Atlantic City. Mom would want me to avoid jeopardizing my career, for my own well-being and for Pop, whose financial support I had undertaken. She always scoffed at burial taboos, and I had forcefully persuaded the incumbent "Reverend" of Agudas Ahim to respect her absolute prohibition of a eulogy. And tradition ruled that the show must go on. Ed, Nate, and a pair of Jewish comedians on the bill that week clustered in my dressing-room at evening intermission to make a half-*minyan* for *Kaddish.* On cue in the wings, the song in my heart dissolved into a threnody, my legs seemed to buckle, I fought a frenetic impulse to rip the buttons off my Captain Pinkerton naval uniform every time the orchestral fanfare brought me smiling and waving my hand to the proscenium mike – and one of my numbers was "Mother Machree."

By a prearranged stagger plan, the Anthony Frome Fellowship sent a condolence committee to my dressing-room after each show; radio had reported Mom's death. Nate said they were rhapsodic about my songs, which had waxed "more soulful than ever!" It had always been my feeling that a song could unlock the gates of faith as much as a sermon. I was simply playing a single composition with two successive instruments, first the pulpit, then the foot-

* "O God, take my soul unto Thee."

lights – different sonic vibrations, but one meaning. That week in Atlantic City confirmed it.

Movie shorts for Paramount diverted me from grief. The make-up men thinned down my eyebrows to pencil marks with a tweezer because overhanging thickness blacked out the eyes, a contrived camera angle lengthened my legs, the sound track was excellent. Bellaire saw the shorts at the Capital cinema on Belmont Street and greeted them with ecstatic pride. Yet a freshet spring was drying up. Mom's death had jarred loose an impacted mass of misgiving and released it into the stream of song.

From the nadir of the hitherto-suppressed trauma which spiralled to the surface during her delirium, my mother's parched lips had murmured again and again, "*Abeleh mein zoon a rov, a rov! Yetzt gevoren a zinger, a gornit! Ich tor em nit fregen!*"* To escape beyond earshot I once went for a walk to the river. Then, and subsequently, the physical hearing was replaced by a hearing in the mind – insistent, accusatory, and relentless. In my own sight I had decidedly *not* become a "nothing." But in my mother's I had denuded myself of dignity and worth. How many others I loved might point a finger at me if they were not restrained by timidity or concern for my feelings? It was *I* who dared not ask!

The demise of the past directed me toward the future. Only one grandchild, a brother's daughter, comprised the generation to come. My mother had borne and loved ten babies, with a self-effacing tenderness that became pattern and prelude of her boundless love for mankind. After the Steel Pier, Ruth and I, in spirit, joined the Planned Parenthood movement.

Should the son we planned have for father a rabbi or a Broadway vocalist? Singing was decidedly not a matter for apologetics; people who made deprecatory gestures simply exposed their Babbitism. The niggling equivocation in my own mind, nevertheless, could not be deflected by peevishly upbraiding others. A singer's hectic egocentrism pitted against the egocentrism of a thousand competi-

* "Abe my son a rabbi, a rabbi! Now become a singer, a nothing! I dare not ask him!"

tors, each yammering for the limelight, in the up-and-down phantasmagoria of the entertainment world, where one hovers between vertiginous heights of phony fame and the tatters of obscurity – was that a proper model and milieu for one's children?

Estelle Liebling had circulated fulsome praise of my climb to fame among the "trade." In her studio, however, she clucked commiseratingly. "You don't belong to this madhouse, Doctor! A ding-dong life – and it's just no place for a man like you!" At the time, I blamed her conservative upbringing; she stemmed from a long-established old Cincinnati family. Now, with steadily accelerated momentum, the brake applied by a mentor and friend who had herself thrown Broadway to the mat ground on against my self-content.

In February 1930 I had visualized a non-professional, soapbox ministry. For Amos and Jeremiah a corner in the marketplace might well have served as podium. In the twentieth century a soapbox could support only the IWW agitator, free-love advocate, or anti-vivisectionist, I now ruefully observed. Lacking organization, a religious leader is less than a voice crying in the wilderness. Even a hermit populates his mystic community with saints from whom he draws contagion and support.

At Temple Sinai I believed in God but could not draw His diagram. Such a tentative, elastic grip on faith might have evanesced altogether after my resignation, especially when I no longer verbalized Him or moved in a theocentric universe of discourse. And the stupid or purposeful misunderstanding, cheap innuendos, and sneering gossip heaped on me by some colleagues could have driven me into atheism. Yet I told the Freethinkers Society so bluntly about my continuing belief that they heckled me.

I now felt God's companionship not as a professional desideratum but as a personal encounter, not from books hitherto unread but from life itself. I had explored realms fabulously rewarding; radio and stage were a mine of wisdom. Where had I seen courage and cheerfulness in the teeth of a gale such as threadbare vaudevillians were revealing to me every day in theatre? And I had married Ruth, and bowed into Mom's burial shroud. Maybe the suffering from economic depression had given our entire society a character-lift, and an opening for church and synagogue to replace discredited captains of industry.

From my radio eminence, I began to re-examine another, perhaps more basic, illogicality which had finally amended "Abraham Feinberg" to "Anthony Frome": a rabbi's pay cheque for spiritual, and therefore servile, leadership. How might *that* be hurdled? Not by the histrionics of a dramatic resignation which was in effect surrender, but by separating the pulpit from its monetary reward. With the surplus harvested by the "Poet Prince," I could be independent of a rabbinical salary and the people who paid it. The Court of St. James swung open to Joe Kennedy because his wealth could absorb the difference between emolument and expense. Curates of the Established Church in England often arm themselves for radicalism with a private income. Why not I?

Saraband's Carnegie Hall riposte to my farewell sermon, that I should have remained in the rabbinate to combat its evils rather than flee from them, contained a truth whose bitter taste still puckered my mouth. Yet during the hiatus I had proved to the world, and to myself, that the pulpit need not be a crutch or the rabbi a *shlemiel*. Tony had done well; I did not *have* to be a rabbi to make a living.

Several times I solemnized a marriage for the child of an old Sinai parishioner, a song-writer, or a courtier of the Poet Prince. Invariably someone would exclaim, "How can you officiate as a rabbi? You resigned!" As though years of study and the charisma of ordination were validated only by a professional job! Obviously, public acceptance of a marketable ministry could not be argued with or cured; it was inherent in a social structure which reduced everything to a buy-and-sell transaction. Of one simple fact I was dead certain, however: paid position or no paid position, once a rabbi always a rabbi! The pulpit might yet be a calling instead of a profession.

I once defined religion as an awareness of the *whole* universe –

confident, continuous, exalted, and so unshakably rooted in faith that the *details* of the universe no longer bother us. Maybe I could approach the rabbinate by that path. Then the Jacob-Esau personalities wrestling within me might be merged, and the tenor's pagan love of life yoked to the preacher's love of God.

The autobiographical novel I had finally dug out of my memories now lay on the shelf, behind a row of Schipa and McCormack records. It took me to the night I removed my Sinai robe and stalked down to a pew. How fervently I thanked the second thoughts that led me to withdraw the heavily iconoclastic manuscript!

Scribbling, erasing, amending words, phrases, chapters – I had spent months on it. True, they were a purgative. Like the crucible of molten metal at the Carnegie Steel mill I worked in as a boy, the writing had poured the hot chaos of experience into a mould which cooled off for analysis. Yet the sheaf of almost five hundred pages represented arduous, obsessive struggle; the ink was my life's blood. Why did I ask the publisher to return it?

The answer to that question was inscribed in the newspapers, magazines, and marginal-noted volumes flung around my dressing-room at theatres and the den at home. It lay in the articles of Vincent Sheean, Dorothy Thompson, Stanley High, William Shirer, in *New York Times* cable reports and radio speeches, in books by authors like Nora Waln and Gregor Ziemer – about the intention and achievement of Benito Mussolini, initially, and then Adolph Hitler. The burden of my novel was the dismal vacuity of all organized religion, but its centre and circumference were a synagogue and a rabbi. For the personal gratification of debunking, was I to furnish the jackbooted foes of Jewry with a propaganda weapon?

Nazi-Fascism was the ultimate, lethal enemy, for whose conquest all other skirmishes must be forgotten. Its ingredients were intoxicating affirmation of the beauty of war; sublimation of egomania through the hypostasized and hypnotized group; evasion of moral choice in favour of an absolute Yes loyalty; substitution of an elementary functional test for the sensitive assessment of human personality; repression of intelligence the more easily to manipulate feelings; adulation of the hero-leader; replacement of individual worth with barbaric herd values; exaltation of death as the fecundator of life and the will to death as the apogee of human fulfilment; idolatry of the armed, faceless cypher; dehumanization and degradation of the common man. It was the antithesis of all the values and ideals that had been fed to my spirit all my life, by Union Street. As long as Nazi-Fascism was abroad, my world was a polarity: it and I!

Almost the very day Anthony Frome began his engagement at the Paramount, Adolph Hitler began his Thousand-Year Reich fantasy as gang-boss of the "master race." That night I was frozen to the marrow by a half-page résumé in the *Times* of a speech vowing "to exterminate Jewish vermin." The next morning I remarked to Ruth that a Jew *could* not live, and an honourable human being *would* not, in a Nazi-Fascist world.

A Reform Jewish pulpit had just been vacated. Its top-heavy mortgage relegated the rabbi to picayune rank in the budget. The annual stipend did not attract a swarm of candidates; in Ed's lingo, it was peanuts – approximating the three weeks with which "One Night of Love" and Grace Moore had fattened my exchequer at the Brooklyn Fox. But the location was strategic, in mid Manhattan, with immediate access to the public. I told the two most venerated Reform rabbis in New York, whose warm friendship had withstood even the disrobing night at Sinai, that I would welcome their sponsorship.

In May 1935 the press blared that Anthony Frome was to be reconstituted, with fitting ceremonies of installation, as Rabbi Abraham L. Feinberg of Beth Sholom.

The swan-song of the Fellowship paper, "Court of the Poet Prince," gave me more than a moment of poignancy, despite its extravagance. On the first page under the rubric "Minister, Minstrel, Prophet," I read: "His hand touched a star and the magic of it is in his soul and in his song. . . . The sincerity of our affection for him will continue to bind us together. . . . Every member desires to see the crusader succeed as the singer did. . . . We shall miss, more than he will ever know, the God-given voice which, like the soft murmur of wind in the trees, filled our hearts with an indefinable something for which we yearn." There followed a score of tributes: "Though the Poet Prince is dead, long live the King, the Mind and the Voice live on"; "He appealed strongly to masculine as well as feminine listeners"; "His song has been a prayer" – and a poem:

Oh minstrel, yet a prophet, seer –
Whose message reaches out, afar,
You glorify the songs we hear –
And shed a radiance like a star!

That same month I began a series of radio talks on WNEW, almost next door to the WMCA studios where two years before I had quailed under the steel-clad stare of a microphone. I made no apology for having tried to give people joy by singing; religion, too, is ecstasy. But mankind needs faith as never before in our time; I would do my best to give it.

On reaching the spacious Fifty-Seventh street apartment we would soon sacrifice to economy, Ruth drew my eyes to a rumour of counter-revolutionary rumblings in republican Spain and the cloak-and-dagger peregrinations of a Colonel Franco.

My work was cut out for me!

My War Against War, Fascism, and Nazism

Two months after the sinking of the *Lusitania* replaced the Wilsonian slogan "Too proud to fight" with a declaration of war, and the song "I Didn't Raise My Boy to Be a Soldier" with "Over There," I delivered a solemnly patriotic address at high-school graduation. Its title was "America First."

Just as the Mississippi River, Father of Waters, drops effluvial sediment at the end of its journey and joins the broad sunlit expanse of the Gulf of Mexico, so must all the streams of immigration from the Old World of our fathers doff the residue of past loyalties and become merged into a great, onward-flowing, unified nation. America first – in peace and in war!

By the next autumn the bloom on that slogan had withered under Mom's brooding anxiety for her sons, and I began to doubt the logic of a doctrine which would "make the world safe for democracy" by embracing the totalitarian robotism of an army squad. The doubt was not allayed when the University of Cincinnati, which I had just entered, became a barracks, enlistment in the Reserve Officers' Training Corps a requirement, and the Seminary's noted history professor, Gotthard Deutsch, a victim of mob-emotionalism.

Doctor Deutsch would have flunked in pedagogy. His classroom distinctions were a long white beard that left a wake of Gentile kids whispering "Santa Claus" at Christmastime, a lovingly hoarded treasurer of Jewish folklore and anecdotes, and a habit of smiling absent-mindedly at a joke he had just told himself.

He made no secret of his war views. To his hulking gentleness, any destroyer of life was an abomination. And, like most of the Seminary faculty, his academic studies had taken him to German institutions of higher learning. With unalloyed distaste, he alluded to scholars who "spit into wells from which they had drunk" and to "110 per cent Americans" of German extraction. It was not long before the old giant began to wander off lost from the middle of a story and mutter into his now-unkempt beard, while the hand that used to "milk" it trembled.

On a trip home I noted the white in Mom's hair and Pop weeping over his workbench. When Gotthard Deutsch died – of a broken heart, I was sure – following an appearance in court for subversive statements, his head dangled in my dreams with Mose and Jake on a barbed-wire fence in No-Man's Land.

"Ueber Allen Gipfeln Ist Ruh' " ("Above all the peaks there is rest") was the solo I sang at his memorial. During the organ prelude I stood on the choir-balcony with moist eyes glued to the music-sheet, but my mind was a mélange of images: the New York rabbi who went from a pacifist society to the much-photographed overalls of a naval shipyard riveter, Dr. Goldner's sermon about the peace mission of Jews, "American First."

The ink had barely dried on the Armistice of November 11, 1918, when the politico-economic struggle in the United States became a bare-knuckle affair. The House of Representatives in Washington unseated a Socialist found guilty under the wartime Espionage Act, alleged Bolsheviks were hauled to prison for conspiracy, the New York State Assembly expelled a number of Socialist members even in the face of their re-election, the conviction of Big Bill Haywood and seventy-five other members of the International Workers of the World was sustained, Oklahoma race riots flared into thirty deaths, and a Connecticut salesman was jailed for lauding Lenin's intelligence. Emma Goldman and 248 fellow anarchists were piled into a "Soviet Ark" and shipped to Russia, then engaged in the liquidation of anarchists; United States Steel refused to confer with strikers because of their "radical" leadership; more than a score of United Mine Workers of America officials were charged with treason; a Committee of Forty-Eight announced its intention to agitate for public ownership, unrestricted civil rights, and the interests of labour; Attorney General Palmer, under the partial supervision of a subordinate named J. Edgar Hoover, rounded up four thousand Red-suspect aliens and deported six hundred, pulling some out of homes without warrant; the United States Senate rejected Wilson's peace treaty and the League of Nations; Calvin Coolidge denied recognition to Russia – and it was not until February 1920 that counter-revolutionary American troops were withdrawn from Siberia.

Could I bury my nose, eyes, and mind in syntactical exegesis of the Book of Job or recondite Talmudic argument about the geographical extent of a village area subject to the Sabbath ban on carrying? I did bury them – but not my heart, and not without lifting one eye to take a hard look at the world through the editorial lens of the *avant-garde* magazines *Freeman, The Nation,* and *New Republic*; the committee for the defence of Tom Mooney, which successfully solicited a student-body resolution of support; maverick speakers at Literary Society sessions like Roger Baldwin, John Haynes Holmes, and William Z. Foster; and the undismayed courage of Socialist Eugene V. Debs.

The trial of Bartolomeo Vanzetti and Nicolo Sacco brought ferment to a boil. Headlines and world-wide picketing turned a global spotlight on the fish-pedlar and shoemaker who revealed astonishing depths of untutored moral dignity – and on the meanness of spirit of a judge and governor. Had the two theoretical anarchists been sacrificed to anti-radical paranoia or cynically enhaloed by the Leftist apparatus for its own ends? Souls stymied in a bog of Greek moderation might oscillate between the alternatives. For us firebrands, the issue was settled by the undeniable ambiguities of evidence and Harvard President Lowell's self-protective pride in the suspect integrity of Massachusetts' justice, Sacco and Vanzetti were innocent – and their trial by the Dedham New Englanders a travesty! We radical seminarians palavered at meetings, pushed protest resolutions, paraded, and praised Emma Goldman for her fight against any custom, creed, or compulsion that cabined the human spirit.

One day at varsity I collided with a girl in the corridor. Stooping to retrieve her scattered books and papers, I noted a text used in Political Science I, a course I also was taking. Holding out the volume and a fistful of closely written foolscap, and painfully aware of the abysmal silence, I spluttered, "Do you think Dr. Taylor is right about the Constitution being the most perfect document ever drawn by man?" Her blue eyes narrowed to slits and her lips curled. "You're just one of those rabbi Bolsheviks!"

Bolshevik-hysteria puzzled me. Why were the ruling powers so overwrought and frightened? In the radical clique at Seminary, a negligible few gave voluble allegiance to philosophical Communism. Not until the faculty cracked down on them and two students summarily departed, did we take a serious view of their pilpulistic ideological abstractions.

I propped up a pamphlet by Engels behind a fellow student's back as much to register deliberate choice of the frowned-upon and forbidden as to read what the author had to say. The collapse of Czarism afforded me such immense joy that I was astounded by the pathological hostility for its conqueror evinced first by Winston Churchill and subsequently by every backwoods Congressman in Washington. But the incorporation of atheism into the Communist creed disheartened and wounded me. In my thinking, the dynamic of social protest started from the belief that every human being bears the divine imprint and therefore may not be handled, herded, and harassed like an inanimate commodity subservient to the state or system.

A Communist dictatorship transmuting personality into a mechanized cog with solely material needs would have been anathema to Isaiah and Jeremiah – and to me, had Western capitalism safeguarded workers instead of hiring strike-breakers to beat them, and dared the Muscovite to competition in the advancement of mass welfare instead of exploiting popular fears to divert attention from its own catatonic worship of private gain. Also, the Seminary authorities might have invited young idealists to implement prophetic Messianism through advocacy of social change, thus providing a healthful outlet for ferment. In lieu of that, they periodically fumigated minds, in elephantine pursuit of the gnat of sedition, and resolved to get rid of queer ducks and malcontents and build an efficient, well-oiled rabbi-factory.

Mussolini had already strutted on the march to Rome when I was ordained in 1924, but the political pundits of the Seminary bumming-room did not realize that his Black Shirts were thrusting a counter-revolution into the heartland of Europe. The threat from the Left born in the First World War was begetting a monster which would generate the Second World War. The Axis lay dormant in the chrysalis of the future, however, and the ultimate bifurcation of radicalism into Left and Right was still on the planning-board of destiny. In the early 'twenties, we merely mimicked Il Duce's chin and sneered ironically that his masterful will had got Italian trains running on time.

My early pulpits raised no barricades beyond those in my own breast. Temple Sinai of New York spanned the velvety years of the boom, when North America yawned like a fat cat in front of a cozy fire under the blanket of full employment. Before the cyclone whipped up by Wall Street's débâcle reached maximum velocity, I had set sail on the moonstruck maunderings of the Poet Prince.

On January 30, 1933, while I seduced the wondrously interlaced wires, bolts, and fuses of radio into the worship of Eros, Adolph Hitler proved how effectively *he* had used them to seduce the Germans into worshipping *him*, by ascending to the Chancellorship of the German Republic. Could I douse with romantic fol-de-rol an instrument being used to spew forth the venom of a psychopath fraternally embraced by the most influential circles in the West as the hired assassin of Bolshevism?

In Berlin, a mechanism for destruction beyond anything ever known moved toward control of Europe, enslavement of mankind, extinction of Jewry, and the dethronement of the God of mercy. The Nazi juggernaut rumbled and quivered with demonic force, crushing trade unions, stomping faces with jackboots, churning up from anti-intellectual slime a primitive farrago of fantasies about Aryanism, braying with electronic perfection its resolve to substitute the masterfolk for faith in the Master – all in the name of a bulwark against the Red horde from the East. That brazen claim had no more cogency than the assumption that fair play for two Italo-American anarchists branded one a Bolshevik, but millions of avid acolytes of free enterprise and Christian civilization believed it.

Within a few months after my change of costume from the ruffled jacket of the Poet Prince to Beth Sholom's rabbinical gown, Mussolini's bombing-planes swooped for the napalm kill in Ethiopia – and I joined the American League Against War and Fascism.

My first bullets were buckshot; they splattered out toward every skulking shape of illiberalism within range. I inveighed against moneyed interests who sabotage low-cost housing projects, ecclesiastics whom God had empowered to ban contraceptive information and the heinous idea that wedded sex can be fun, manufacturers who would rather see ablebodied men polishing apples on a street corner than abjure exploitation of their need for a job in a buyer's labour market, and bigots so zealous for petty parochial creeds that they resist inter-faith co-operation even to prevent war.

The next arena was Spain. Together with other rabbis alerted for the Jew's historic perch on the signal station, I descried Italo-German planes and tanks, slowly pulverizing Loyalists disarmed by the farce of non-intervention, as rehearsal and testing-ground for later Axis onslaught against the Western democracies. Guernica would be a preview of Armaggeddon.

Jewish laymen did not always agree with the rabbis. Harold Sofer, a distinguished jurist, phoned me. "None of your colleagues have come out for the right side in Spain. The Loyalists are Communists! Cardinal Hayes has heard about you and admires you. He would be most pleased to read that you had put in a word for Franco."

I hesitated a moment. "Be sure I don't like Communism either, Harold. But the Loyalist government is not bad just because Communists prefer it to Hitler and Mussolini. Any rabbi would find it hard to think of Franco as a friend of Jews or of peace. I'll think over what His Eminence said. Hm-m-m! Well! It's a lot to ask!"

"Beth Sholom" means "House of Peace" – but doves did not fly over its pulpit. Avery Brundage and his committee chose Hitler's germinal period as the proper time to stage the Olympic Games in Berlin. General Sherrill warned that cancellation would turn 500,000 American athletes into anti-Semites. I labelled his gratuitous warning an insult to the youth of the United States.

Mayor La Guardia chose a pre-election date and a public meeting as the proper occasion to call Adolph Hitler a fanatic. The German consulate led the howl for his political blood; German news dispatches, radio pronouncements, and official expressions of anger at violation of protocol penetrated the inner council of the Fusion (civic reform) Party, which began to compute the risk of defeat under Little Flower's banner. I joined my tenor to the deep, rolling organ tones of Rabbi Saraband. "The Nazi barrage against the Mayor makes his assault on Hitler sound like a drawing-room compliment.

For years the vile Nazi propaganda mills have flooded the world with lies about a whole people and mocking ridicule of Christianity and Jesus. Now they roil up a furore about one remark concerning their *ersatz* god."

The Duke and Duchess of Windsor announced their intention to visit America. Behind-the-scenes chit-chat linked them with the international Fascist set. The young romantic who doffed a royal crown for love outraptured Charles Lindbergh in his romance with the purveyors of hate. In a Sabbath sermon I urged the welcoming committee to roll back the red carpet. When the Windsor trip was diverted to other shores, a friend congratulated me. "One thing you've accomplished! David and his Bathsheba won't sip cocktails and simper about Ribbentrop – here!"

Sam Rosenman, intimate confidant of President Roosevelt, wrote my role in the next episode. America Forward, a vocally anti-Communist, subtly pro-Fascist movement, was anxious to scotch any allegation of anti-Semitism. Its church contact-man asked me to deliver an address at a nation-wide conference scheduled for August 1936 in Asheville, North Carolina. Was the invitation a trick to entangle me in compromise? Like Roosevelt, I sought the guidance of a brilliant tactician. From Temple Sinai days I had conferred occasionally with Sam Rosenman and Belle Moskowitz, Al Smith's alter ego.

"Accept it, Abe! You can keep an eye on them! Besides, refusal might furnish excuse for open attack on Jewry! The American Jewish Committee would be grateful to you."

With considerable repugnance and trepidation, I disembarked from the train in Asheville to find that a number of America Forward delegates, incensed by a "Jew-rabbi's" name on the program, had broken ranks to set up a rump convention a few blocks away. A brawny deputy-sheriff introduced himself as my bodyguard. At the station for the return journey, I found comfort in his holster; a tipsy dissident delegate had proposed tar and feathers for the "Jew-rabbi," after I insisted in my speech that "neither a brown shirt nor a black shirt can be an alternative to the red flag." The Yiddish press did not lag behind in vehemence; it subsequently pelted me with a choice compendium of derisive nouns for permitting myself to be "used" by anti-Semites.

Munich took twenty days – between September 10 and 30, 1938. I listened with numb despair to the staccato of Trout, Shirer, Kaltenborn, Murrow, King-Hall, Sheean, each adding its decibels to the shrill wail of the doomed. Their lines were composed with an idiot's delight by Hitler, initialled by Mussolini, parroted by Daladier and Chamberlain, and interspersed with prayers by Pope Pius XI and the Archbishop of Canterbury. Frozen by premonitions of disaster, I could find nothing to say except a somewhat extraneous footnote in an article written for *The Christian Evangelist*: "If Fascism is the price for the destruction of Communism, I am not sure the cure is better than the affliction."

Two months later, Reich synagogues were burned and bombed in a national orgy of martial valour. The United Jewish Appeal, created for the succour of Europe's Jews, was called upon to punch an escape-hatch into the wall closing around them. Rabbi Jonah Wise, its leader, was nailed down in New York by the emergency. He phoned me. "Tony, I'm supposed to speak for UJA in Denver! Will you go?"

Before the Denver mission was completed, the President of the Reform Temple inquired about my availability. It was the largest congregation between Chicago and Los Angeles, and I liked Sam Kohn. I told him I could be available. My installation at Temple Emanu-El preceded by only a few months Hitler's sweep into Poland, which superimposed the phosphorescent colours of rotting cadavres and cities on the pencilled sketch he had flaunted with transparent fustian in the pages of *Mein Kampf*.

In the mid West, farmers love twilight serenity after dawn-to-dusk drudging, and soft slippers on tired feet, and the quiet harvest of steady middle-age and sturdy middle-class independence. Besides, effete and condescending Britain didn't pay its debts! And Europeans are "dirty furriners," and what you don't want to know won't hurt you. The retort of this chemical ferment was America First – a crusade for good old introverted isolationism. Warsaw's rubble was still smouldering when the Denver branch of America First let it be known that "the war in Europe is not our business," while I reflected on the quirks of history. The theme of my high-school graduation speech had risen up to smite me!

When France capitulated, I joined Bundles for Britain, a solitary island-fortress in a sea of compromise – Uncle Joe and Adolph having drunk a marathon toast to their friendship – and met William W. Grant, a High-Church Episcopalian whose aristocratic scruples, tyrannical logic, and book-fed literacy barred him from election to a Senatorship. Will's forefathers had roared at feudal fiefs in England and the Deep South while mine ruminated over the Talmud in a Lithuanian ghetto – but I grappled him to my heart.

The magnitude and heat of America First rallies were a microcosm of Nuremberg. I helped Will set up a mild counter-irritant: a Committee to Defend America by Aiding the Allies. The clutch of valiant spirits it attracted could only in self-mockery call it a mass movement, what with speeches in auditoriums so empty my voice echoed as in a Rocky Mountain canyon, mimeographed pamphlets waved aside by scornful passers-by, occasional radio interviews wrung from program-managers by refusing to be insulted. The reward? Hostile glares and phone calls, patronizing editorial admonitions in the press, friendly hints to stay off the streets when Senator Wheeler came to town, and pulpit fulminations from notorious anti-Semitic evangelists like Cowboy Springer and Gerald Winrod, who doubly envenomed the words "Jew war-mongers" by uttering them in a stage whisper.

I did not need the demagoguery of hate pedlars to dramatize the epithet. I had forsworn war! Did not aid to the Allies portend armed intervention? Were the anxieties of a Jew betraying me into betrayal of conscience? Jewish tradition conceded the possibility of a just war – but was I an impartial judge?

It was the Dean of the Denver Episcopal Cathedral who compelled me to grasp the nettle of the moral dilemma. He and I had laboured together in many vineyards related to social welfare; the grain of his compact, ideal-directed spirit ran to the common man. On the issue of the European War, we walked in opposite directions. He put his position before me with lacerating bluntness at a Community Chest inter-faith luncheon.

"Rabbi, that Aiding the Allies Committee bothers me. Let Hitler come to these shores. Christian love will win in the end. It always has! As a brave thinker you surely are a pacifist!"

I clamped my jaws hard. "Dean, you would live to be a priest, if Hitler comes. I – and my wife and children and people – would be corpses, or refugees with no place left to go!"

The blithe reliance of Christians on the omnipotence of Christian love always confounded me – especially when coupled with the dogma of original sin. In recommending love as the prescription for Nazism, the eminently humane priest of a relatively sophisticated church had pronounced a death sentence on the Jewish people. I muttered a Yiddish proverb under my breath: "A boil on the other fellow's neck never hurts," bottled up the purple gorge seething within me, and wheeled abruptly away.

Many times in succeeding years the remembrance of my brief bout with the Dean underscored the realization that a consuming virtue can become a callous vice. And many times I asked myself whether the bland assertion of love's eventual triumph might not have aggravated Christendom's failure of empathy with the Jewish plight.

With mounting pain, then and later, I marked how the moral graph of people who worship Jesus dipped close to total unconcern with the people who bore him. Refugee conferences at Evian and Bermuda, where statesmen hemmed and hawed while refugee-packed, unseaworthy cattleboats capsized and passenger ships returned their cargo to charnel-house Europe after cruising the Eastern length of North America in futile quest of port! Pastor Niemoeller, "hero" of Hitler's prisons, who deemed it non-essential to challenge the Nazi regime until it challenged the jurisdictional domain of the Lutheran Church – and after he had applied for a post as U-boat commander! German Catholics, a majority of whom, according to

Gordon C. Zahn of Loyola University, limited their resistance "to those issues involving direct assault upon church rights and property" and supported Hitler in obedience to the formal commitment of the Catholic press and clergy, although sundry individuals, church institutions, and the Pope himself rescued some thousands of Jewish lives. Bevin's Socialism for the common man, which dispatched the British Mediterranean fleet to intercept Palestine-bound "illegal immigrant" boats and barred myriads from the only people which would receive them – their own!

"Christian love is bound to win; it always does!" Did the Dean of St. Paul's in Denver light a taper for me? In any case, I saw a light. Christendom turned aside from the Jew, and from Czech and German liberals, not like the Levite, because of spiritual sloth, but out of positive morality – because it *dare not* lose faith in Christian love! Of all the possible explanations of its Oriental lethargy, that was the most flattering; in the context of the good Dean's earnestness and virtue, it was also plausible.

When Pilate remanded Jesus for crucifixion, he washed his hands with an ironic, but humble, quip: "What is truth?" The Dean would hand the Jews over to Hitler with a genuflection to love. Did he permit himself to be troubled about its meaning? In any case, unlimited commitment to love led him to deny that man could hate on the grand Hitlerian scale and thus made him hate's instrument for conquest.

The Dean paid me the compliment of assuming that I was a pacifist, as indeed I had been. But the Nazis vowed to encompass first my degradation and then my death. And Jews were distinguished merely by priority listing; others would follow. The Nazi régime placed the alternative of death by its hand, or life by resistance, before every civilized human being. That was its crime: it made pacifism certain suicide, and thraldom to diabolic depravity the price of peace.

The preciousness of life which made me abhor its defilement by war made Nazism the most abhorrent of all creeds. Fired by dreams disinterred from the reeking sepulchre of the First World

War, millions of Germans permitted themselves to be welded into a sword of genocide – not as an act of passion or punishment visited by savage tribes on a captive city in the pre-dawn of civilization, but as the scientifically elaborated, legally formalized, sacred canon of an ultra-modern state. Under its sway, our planet would be populated by an élite corps of sadistic tyrants ranged in a dehumanized power-hierarchy of salute and goosestep and by a substratum of slaves spiralling downward to unimaginable depths, and the Galilean's ethic would be driven underground to catacombs of silence – without his people around to create problems.

Turning the other cheek had never been a Jewish ideal. Hitlerism was madness with a knife in its teeth; sheer survival could not wait for psychiatric treatment – or the rule of love. Yes, I needed to be honest with myself. The Dean's intuitive thrust had found its target. Revulsion from war was the first casualty in my vendetta with Hitlerism. I *did* hope the United States would fight the Nazis!

Sunday afternoon, December 7, 1941, I was dozing on a couch at home when the telephone rang. A friend had just heard a radio bulletin. Pearl Harbor! It changed the world irreversibly. The first Japanese bomb led to the bomb over Hiroshima, the death of an American illusion to the birth of the nuclear age, a day in which nations might be overrun and survive to a day in which even nations that conquer will perish. For me Pearl Harbor immediately transmuted hesitant, half-embarrassed word-pounding into auxiliary-service to the armed forces.

Ruth opened the doors of our home to trainees in nearby camps, taught a Grey Lady course in camouflage at a base hospital, and helped me initiate a Sunday dance-canteen-worship project. I circulated among military installations too small for a Jewish chaplain, shared prayer services for Texas combat units in battledress with a Catholic bishop and a Protestant parson and conducted a Passover Seder at an icebound ski-troop training-centre high in the Rockies.

Hankering for close-range involvement, I applied for a full-time naval chaplaincy. No sea-going vessel boarded enough Jews to warrant a chaplain. Therefore a fixed base immune to sea-sickness, not the open waters, would be my operational area. The navy physical was easy sailing, but Uncle Sam's far-flung naval installations had no opening for a Jewish padre. The army test, normally more lenient, preceded a three-week routine interval of waiting, which I employed to amuse Sarah Jane with salutes and drills, and explain my enlistment to Jonathan, Ruth having given her full assent. At last, the War Department seal lay on my desk. I had been rejected! The medical x-ray showed "recurrent pulmonary tuberculosis!"

In 1917, on entering university, I had been stunned by the same diagnosis – until a recheck traced apparent lung lesions to accumulated soot from Bellaire's soft-coal chimneys. Several years later, a long tussle with pleurisy had left a thickness in the pleural membrane. But tuberculosis now? Ruth and I rushed the Washington letter to a radiologist whose skill and status had helped make Denver the cynosure of consumptives. After one glance at the chest x-ray, he almost literally hit the ceiling. "Some gold-braid kid on a swivel-chair in Washington! This is only a muscle shadow!"

Despite a telegram that skewered the "kid," War Department pride, underpinned by the bureaucratic tradition of an index file's infallibility, could not be budged. The army did not want me.

When Maurice Eisendrath, Rabbi of Holy Blossom Temple in Toronto and an old Seminary chum, asked me by phone a short time thereafter, to undertake a trial-marriage with his pulpit so that he might accept the Directorship of the Union of American Hebrew Congregations, my frustrated military excursion was forgotten in plans for a new rabbinical foray. On November 2, 1943, I set foot in Canada.

My first public meeting in Toronto was a baptism of fellowship. Aid-to-Russia, Canadian-Soviet Friendship, Stalingrad, sent tremors through a huge rally in Maple Leaf Gardens. Bands played, banners waved, grown men wept with gratitude for the vainglorious folly that inveigled Hitler to the steppes of Russia and placed her agonized but unconquerable people at our side! United States, Britain, Canada, the Soviet Union all stood together with the thousands who stood in prayer and song that night, and hearts beat in unison with beleaguered allies throughout the world. And Archbishop Derwyn T. Owen, my neighbour on the platform, distilled his saintly simplicity of spirit into a smile of welcome I would often summon with special joy from the treasured memories of that evening.

The dawn of my career in Canada was midnight in the fortunes of war. Only the stout heart and stirring words of Winston Churchill stood between England and despair. Less than two years later, however, Ruth and I were motoring back to Toronto from a brief jaunt in the north country and had reached a town called Churchill when a sequence of radio reports finally announced V-E Day – to be followed soon by V-J Day. The Axis sun had set; the Fascist sword was broken.

At dinner, I gleefully iced and brought to the table a bottle of champagne earmarked and cached for "the day the war ends." We sipped it like tea-tasters – but the toasts were hearty: "Ruth, Jonathan, Sarah Jane – all together, with me – to the Allied Forces, to Canada, to those who died, to each other – to a better tomorrow!"

"A better tomorrow." This final salute stalled in my throat.

"Tomorrow!" It was a mushroom cloud that brought Japan to heel. But the celestial sons of Nippon had already begun to totter. Did the A-bomb, then, save American lives? Certainly it cancelled sanguinary invasion of the Japanese islands by men, like by own brother-in-law, poised on Okinawa. The total number of beneficiaries will always be a subject of conjecture. There was no doubt, however, that the genie unleashed by Harry Truman would spread a radioactive umbrella of dread around the earth and push mankind across a new threshold of depravity – the totally annihilating, totally dehumanized automation of war.

"Tomorrow!" The toast was still-born for a more immediate reason. Two cognate strands of hate were forming a double-lane road on which an apocalyptic menace would stream into the postwar world. One was the residual deposit of Nazi-Fascism, inflammable tinder subject to ignition by economic collapse, national resentment, failure of current institutions, the availability of "foreigners," like the Jews, as scapegoat, and the shrewdly manipulated threat of Communism.

The other strand was the cumulative antagonism between the Soviets and Western capitalism. The clenched fists of defecting sailors raised in fealty to Lenin and the October Revolution launched it in 1918; ill-conceived Allied intervention at Archangel confirmed its fecundity for evil. A deep-rooted Ivan the Terrible syndrome – monstrous, unfathomable, Asiatic, re-enforced by Trotzky's international Comintern – plagued the Western mind. Its lines were sharpened by Marshal Zhukov's appropriation of Berlin, early stirrings of McCarthyism, sardonic jibes at the Yalta "sell-out," chest-thumping Moscow boasts of military prowess, Washington's unilateral course in bomb research, the death of Roosevelt, and the penetration into the West, behind the victorious Muscovite armies, of the mystique of the proletarian revolt, to subdue, subvert, annex, and frighten.

One sedulous beneficiary of the East-West confrontation was Germany, again stretching her limbs to don the armour of an anti-Communist Teutonic knight, as Stalingrad slowly settled into the stagnant backwaters of memory, and comradeship with the fortress-city became for many Canadians a regrettable lapse from respectability, while veterans of the occupation forces quoted American colonels: "By God, the Russians are next!"

"Tomorrow!" There was yet another reason for its hollow sound. How acclaim the future when the horrors of the past were not yet past? Could Admiral Doenitz's white flag of surrender exorcise ambivalence from brutish-romantic Germany? Hitlerism was bred by the myopia of the military alliance which had conquered its birthland, but it stabbed deep into a culture responsive to the promise of martial glory. Nazism's continuing hypnosis proved to have excellent credentials, even in Canada, when an order-in-council granted asylum in Quebec to a French Nazi collaborator, an illegal immigrant, and simultaneously presented a deportation order to seven Jewish DP's.

A close look at Germany clinched my unease. Near summer's

end in 1949, on the way home from Israel, I steeled myself enough to desert Paris and spend a week in Munich and Dachau.

The Bavarian capital still bore scars – American army scrip instead of marks, bomb-pocked buildings, a thriving black market in American chocolate bars and cigarettes. But reverential young muscle-men circled the Brown House site as though it were the altar of a sacred flame. Serried rows of sausages in the butcher shops, United States bulldozers clearing debris for reconstruction, gluttonous women and porcine gentlemen, presented a preview of the material glitter I was to see in 1959. The lobby of a requisitioned hotel and one American brigadier provided an episode which rocked my stomach. "Of course these fellows were pretty tough on you people," the brigadier bellowed. "Like any good soldier, they obeyed orders. All the same, they're our kind. But the Russians? Whew! Different breed altogether! Can't make 'em out!"

A motley remnant of young DP's, among them tuberculous hard-core cases, had been assembled at a refugee camp in Ulm for transfer to Israel. On my arrival, the International Refugee Organization representative invited me to read an interesting mimeographed memo from headquarters. In the categories "Canadian Nurse" and "Canadian Domestic," Jewish and Armenian DP's were specifically excluded from admission to Canada. The official hoped, through indirect pressure on the Canadian immigration department, to effect a change in that policy and thus procure more help in the final liberation of surviving Jews. On consultation with Jewish Joint Distribution Committee leaders in Munich and Paris, I exposed the document at a Paris press conference. Neither the mildly anti-Jewish selectivity of Canadian bureaucrats nor their turgid and acrimonious denial when the story exploded in Canada, fortified my confidence in "tomorrow."

Dachau! The physical apparatus of genocide – sepulchral gas-chamber walls scratched with frantic fingernails, grass-grown mounds of the mass-interred dead, barbed-wire kennels of flesh-tearing dogs, a rifle-range for the lucky ones who would die with dispatch, the fetid tiers of tiny stalls (enlarged and renovated into dormitories for German refugees from the temporarily-occupied East), crematoria with long, snugly fitted, iron ladles.

Hotel clerk, cab-driver, police officer, wrinkled sausage-vendor on the corner! I talked with all! None had known what went on at Dachau, although the stench of combustible human tissues and a gentle breeze might ordinarily have been informative. I was too sick to be angry until a grape-vine rumour reached me that the government contemplated razing Dachau. And when I read a painted slogan on the main crematorium wall: *Reinheit ist hier Pflicht. Nur die Haende waschen,** I heaped silent malediction on the neat, odious German efficiency which bamboozled and bedazzled American army brass.

After the Dachau pilgrimage, I tried to forget. Remembering brought only pain to me; certainly it brought no peace to the dead, and they were beyond pity. In vain I pleaded with myself to use common sense. Like the Toronto barber who could not trust his hand to shave Germans during the Eichmann trial because of the little daughter their countrymen dragged to slaughter before his eyes, I could not expunge the noisome tombs of Dachau.

In Toronto, when delegated spokesmen of the German community invited me to attend a reception for Dr. Theodor Heuss, President of the Federal Republic, I accepted. Thus I would meet a savant who had protested against Hitlerism and meet the supreme challenge of brotherhood to rebuild a communications line with the German people. No sooner did I reach the Harmonie Club than my eyes – on their own volition – scrutinized every man in the exuberant crowd, wondering whether *he* had washed *his* hands (with soap from Jewish fat?) as a ladle-pusher of Dachau! The obsessive fantasy did not vanish with Dr. Heuss's comment that "there is no collective guilt, but there is collective shame."

A year later, I again visited Germany – not to mourn but to report. Instead, a saturnine Bavarian innkeeper who waddled like Goering and patted the blond curls of his plump daughters was transformed before my eyes into Hitler's Number Two man fondling

* Cleanliness is a duty here; be sure to wash your hands.

dogs after a grand tour of the death camps; the spick-and-span antiseptic fragrance of a Frankfurt hotelroom conjured up the wash basins of Dachau; through the shop window of a Munich art shop, I saw again the scrawled crayon sketches left behind by hollow-eyed children of the Warsaw Ghetto; at a nearby table in a swank *Kurfurstendamm* restaurant, the chignon of a richly gowned matron looked so natural it might have come from the vast storehouse of human hair in Auschwitz. The persistence of this lachrymose mood caused me deep distress. If I began to despise Germans in general, as a group, my soul would be anathematized by the Nazi curse no less than the bodies of the Dachau martyrs were powdered by it.

It is in ourselves that Albert Camus located the most rigorous resistance movement – resistance against the degradation of our passion for justice into an appetite for hatred. An overall blanket of guilt debases justice; many Germans risked, and some lost, their lives to fight Hitler and save his victims. It denies Jewish experience, in which "dirty Jew" generalizations have often preceded anti-Semitic savagery. It would degrade my own mind, which despises the superficiality of vile adjectives slapped indifferently on all the members of a group we don't like. It was not a matter of forgiving; the unimaginable vastness of Nazi criminality dwarfs such concepts as pardon, punishment, and forbearance into a sleep-walker's babble. Not for theological reasons, but from sheer default of comprehension, judgement on the Germans must be left to God – and to themselves!

My good Gentile friends admonished me to forgive – and *forget*! Did they ask and expect Jews to uproot the remembrance of martyred millions? The sacrificed are no longer; forgetting would mean that they had never been. The truth is, Gentiles were not urging *me* to forget; they wanted me to let *them, and the world,* forget! Dachau wrote a shameful chapter into the annals of a species supposedly created after God's image; let it be torn from the record.

Then a seismic disturbance shook me. It was not only "the world," the whilom observer, the sidewalk superintendent who had watched a demolition – that wanted to forget the whole thing. It was many of the Germans! They yearned to delouse, decorate, disguise the history of Hitler's Third Reich, as they had the Dachau rabbit hutches which now served as austere dwellings for Silesian refugees, with a tenderly pampered pot of geraniums on the windowsill!

My German journeys in 1959 and 1961 took me to a nation hiding from herself. A process of voluntary aphasia enabled its chromium-plated pyramidal structure, its well-padded amiability, adjustable efficiency in industrial organization, and commercial acumen to excrete the Nazi tumour, like a sick man trying to purge infection with a sound and dreamless sleep. On all levels, including, and even emphatically, the intelligentsia – silence!

History textbooks disdained to describe the Nazi era; both parents and teachers shunned 1933–1945 and the inquiries of their children; judges who had waved Jews and Socialists off to death in People's Courts still sat smugly on the bench; sub-lieutenants in Himmler's extermination squads obtained de-Nazification and juicy jobs the same day; Foreign Office diplomats served Hitler and now Adenauer with equal aplomb; concentration-camp sadists smiled at piddling sentences, strode from the courtroom, and sat out a brief interlude in prison.

Indemnity synagogues and communal centres were built with great éclat at government expense. Both German and Jewish leaders savoured the fiction of a viable, vigorous Jewry – instead of an apologetic remnant clinging precariously to the periphery or dying almost without trace save for vandalized tombstones and the dour childhood memories of the new generation transplanting itself to Israel. A corpulent public-relations functionary in Bonn crowed so lustily about reparations to Israel and restitution payments that I was sure he reckoned them sufficient to close the account.

The scintillating Director General of Krupp carried a library of data and a lively imagination in his handsome head, but gave a blank stare to my inquiry about Krupp slave labour in Auschwitz at nineteen cents a day and burlap-clad Buchenwald women staggering to drudgery in the Essen works not far from his office. And Krupp industrial production apparently was resumed where Alfried's war-crimes trial had rudely interrupted it.

When I interviewed the personal deputy of Minister of Defence Franz Josef Strauss, that rationalistic, immobile, and crisp gentleman delivered a didactic lecture. He explained why the Oriental Soviet incursion into Occidental Europe is a calamity comparable to the fall of Rome; why it must be countered by a mighty (nuclear?) rampart; why courage, unity, and strength will force Krushchov to retreat; and, unwittingly, why the United States Pentagon rearmed West Germany. Taking notes with the Olympian poise of a secretary, I reflected that his thumb-nail sketch was a soft-sell version of Hitler's volcanic pleas for capitalist subsidy to the National Socialist anti-Soviet crusade.

Vice-Chancellor Ludwig Erhard's cherubic cheeks and kindliness displayed the only official sign of humble awareness of the human condition under the enamelled texture of German society. I hoped German burghers would heed not only his sagacious expertise of West Germany's "economic miracle" which, he told me, was founded on the teachings of his Jewish mentor, Dr. Max Oppenheimer, but also the benevolent, non-flamboyant wisdom that suffused his person. At check-point Charlie, the sole aperture for two-way transport in the implacable Berlin Wall, Ruth and I saw hate-twisted faces bawling profane imprecations and threats of revenge across the line from West to East; they did not argue or augur a mellow maturation of the Teutonic psyche.

Belligerent rage against the Soviets was a conspicuous facet of post-Hitler German mentality; its obverse was maudlin pity for themselves. A month after the Wall witnessed the rage, my Temple study witnessed the pity.

"They say you hate us, Rabbi!" The startling pronouncement came from a blue-eyed young feature-writer of a German-Canadian newspaper, come for an interview. After my response that I never hated any group of human beings, he pulled out a thick wallet and placed before me, one by one, an assortment of luridly coloured photos: Berlin in flames after an Allied bomber raid.

"Look what they did to us! Is that civilized? Can you blame the German people for being disillusioned and cynical?"

Shades and shards of Warsaw, Rotterdam, Coventry, shredded swaddling-clothes on French roads of flight, fragments of bone and flesh in the London blitz! I was dumbfounded. Biting my lip, I suffered the wholesome youth to go, both of us rigid in silence, after he had pocketed the pictorialized proof of Berlin's Golgotha.

Those pictures crystallized a sense of vocation which had been gestating in me for some time. I would be gad-fly to the moribund memory of Germany and mankind. The role had to be undertaken!

I did not underrate the cost. If a Jew insists on recalling Dachau, he may be denounced for pessimism, paranoia, muck-raking, vengefulness, incitement. The world demands a blackout of Dachau; its furnaces and firing-squads mock man's avoidance of the unpleasant and contradict the dominant mood of current religious thought. Before the Dachau descent into darkness, Christian theologians had been veering away from man's irremediable wickedness, toward a cheerful, humanistic confidence in his capacity for self-improvement. With Dachau, they reverted to the ancient base: original sin and God's grace for its healing. Even the oven-tenders of the crematoria would be anointed with His atoning balm! In the meantime, let Dachau fade into the effulgence of Divine Love. . . . In such a context, a rabbi who demanded that Christendom retain the reality of Dachau might seem insensitive and inconsiderate.

Jews live in a state of conflict between the inescapable certainty that Nazi-Fascism has been blunted, not broken, and daily activities predicated on trust. Can they build a future on the patently undependable and shifting sands of human concern? In Copenhagen I spun a moiety of faith in Christendom from the yarn of a local physician who had helped systematize the heroic operation of Copenhagen citizens that spirited six thousand Jews to Sweden before the Gestapo could round them up for the cattle-cars. Those valiant, exceptional Danes can scarcely divert Jewish strategy of survival from an increasingly popular rabbinic maxim: "If we are not for ourselves, who will be for us?" In Grinkishok, the hideout of my own kin was betrayed to the extermination unit by neighbours they trusted – probably for a pound of sugar or a permit to pillage. Mental health dictates the casting out of obsessive memories of wrong. Alas, in terms of self-preservation, they are a rationally useful instrument – when others refuse to remember.

Dachau has been joined by Hiroshima in the foreground of man's fears. The two coalesce in total anaesthesia to the primal value of human life. Self-insulation from specialized crematoria for Jews begat passivity toward the cremation of mankind. Once anyone is allowed the latitude even to rant about racial genocide, the H-bomb's fuse seems less dastardly. The chimneys of Dachau rained particles of human bodies before the cloud over Hiroshima rained radioactive fallout. Both Hiroshima and Dachau must be fought: Hiroshima with rowboats to Polaris subs, sitdowns on embassy steps, pickets, Easter parades, disarmament petitions, Peace Marches across the globe such as the San Francisco – Moscow trek Ruth and I joined in Red Square; Dachau wherever its malodorous stench is detected. I would claw at Dachau with my fingernails rather than wait until anyone has to scratch an epitaph in a gas-chamber!

That day of the German newsman's visit, the soft erasing shadows of twilight were close around me when the macabre vision of Dachau's gas-chamber fingernails turned my eyes down to gaze fixedly and unseeing at my own. One after the other, episodes in my Toronto theatre of combat with German Fascism trooped across the screen of memory.

The skirmish with Walter Gieseking. What a rumpus that was! On June 3, 1952, the great pianist would perform in Toronto. He had furthered Hitlerism by joining Alfred Rosenberg's Militant League for German Culture, co-editing a Nazified musical journal and playing concerts in occupied and neutral lands to woo them with Teutonic artistry. He closed letters with "Heil Hitler" before that fraternal greeting was uniformly adopted. He even suggested the exclusion of Jewish entrants in a Brussels piano contest! During

Hitler's rise, Gieseking was emphatically a political collaborator; after Hitler's fall he reverted to the immune status of an artist "above politics."

I mimeographed a pastoral letter to my congregants under the headlined note that it was *not for publication*: "In my opinion no Jew can attend the Gieseking recital without lending dignity to Nazism's unparalleled attack on the human spirit. . . . Our world has become increasingly unmindful of the difference between right and wrong, and prone to compromise. Your absence from Massey Hall Monday evening will be a measure of self-respect and a testament of tribute – to the six million Jewish dead and to people of all lands, races, and creeds wantonly slain by Hitlerism." The letter specified that I did *not* propose to bar Gieseking from public performance.

RABBI BOYCOTTS PIANIST, the front page of an afternoon newspaper shrieked within hours of the letter's delivery to members of Holy Blossom – and the storm broke, hurling a flock of missives to the editor, orchids, mud, and anonymous obscenities via post or phone at me, and logic to the winds. The normally judicious and circumspect morning newspaper berated me for "calling a boycott," praised Gieseking for "generosity in the manner of Dame Myra Hess" – a juxtaposition not likely to win the gratitude of the British Jew – and pointed to "examples in the past of the Jewish people which have given Hitler [his] legends and myths." The pianist lamented to the press that he wished only "to elevate himself from politics to the sphere of pure art. . . ." Did Jews absent themselves from the sphere that night? A keen-eyed "plant" reckoned less than a handful present. But, in the words of a musical critic, "there was no keeping down the bravos" of a contingent of former German refugees who had fled to Canada from the Russians.

The city editor of the morning paper promised to publish a statement from me criticizing the afternoon sheet's flagrant disregard of the confidential relationship between clergyman and congregation. A reporter transcribed it word for word. The statement was deleted. I also learned that my not-for-publication letter had reached the offending journal's desk via a Jew on its reportorial staff.

The Kurt Meyer incident. A tragi-comic farce! In the first act, the SS General, nicknamed "Panzer" for adeptness in the art of mowing men down with armoured tanks, was released from Dorchester, New Brunswick penitentiary in 1954, after serving part of a life-term sentence for the massacre of Canadian prisoners.

His incarceration period, according to the rate per human life prevalent in later war-crime tribunals, could withstand criticism. Only eighteen helpless prisoners had been killed. Far more proficient executioners, some with a count of thousands, were walking the streets of quaint German villages without a hanging of heads, much less their bodies. The French would even free the "Butcher of Paris," who had merely obeyed his superiors! Why, then, did I protest the decision of Canadian top brass to release Kurt? Because he was an articulate, strong-arm fanatic who might be tempted to boost neo-Nazism in the cross-currents of his native land.

The second act took place at the magazine rack of a Frankfurt bookshop. Skimming the pages of a top-circulation tabloid, I suddenly peered closer. There was Kurt, square-jawed and authority-conscious, every inch the leader of men, scarcely a day older than he had seemed in 1954 at the time of the ruckus about the release, when his visage and mine were yoked by adjoining newspaper columns. He had climbed again – this time to the top position in an ex-SS veterans organization numbering 150,000, probably the largest in Germany!

The third act began in my living-room with the moment I saw Kurt on a television screen, being interviewed for the network by the Canadian Broadcasting Corporation, on a film taped in his home in Germany. It was a touchingly deferential "personality" chat. I reached for a pen. The next day press and radio blared my castigation of the CBC.

Newspaper accounts of Kurt's career lent my suspicions the sweet ingenuousness of a CBC lipstick commercial. Kurt had welded a veteran's force with a half-million supporters; as its spokesman, and with the prestige of a former Hitler bodyguard and his youngest SS general, he was demanding freedom for all Nazi war criminals, the readmission of SS veterans to the army with full rank, and the ejection of liberal Social Democrats from influence in politics. Many Germans labelled him "a new Hitler."

Perhaps I erred in the direction of innocence by expecting an essentially mass-entertainment medium to abjure the scoop-potential of a pleasant family *causerie* with the martinet who had ordered the execution of eighteen Canadian prisoners-of-war. The CBC subsequently televised Otto Skorzeny's "old-faithful" insistence that history might yet reckon Hitler a great man, and scheduled, before Jewish protest, the rabidly anti-Semitic barking of Adrien Arcand, Quebec's wartime *gauleiter* of the blue-shirted National Unity Party, "proud to be known as a Fascist."

Bellefeuille's Nazi cell. A minor civil employee in Quebec emerged from the night of obscurity to wear a swastika armband, rehearse the Nazi salute, and assemble a motley gang of neurotic malcontents as the chosen deputy of Lincoln Rockwell, paranoid peacock Fuehrer of American neo-Nazism. On this occasion the CBC presented not only the evangelist of Nazi salvation, but his debunkers, myself included, thereby performing a service of exposure. Bellefeuille was a pathetic creature of comedy – but I could not forget that the battlefields of Europe were strewn with the torn bodies of young Canadians who once laughed at a funny moustache. And there is no limit to the nonsense susceptible and sincere people, even in Canada, can be led to believe.

The vast majority of German newcomers want few things less than further tarring with the Nazi brush. Yet active carriers of Nazi contagion escaped from Hitler's Europe to all corners of the earth. By what special fortune would Canada be spared – especially when immigration officials might be less meticulous about Nazis than about Communists, forgetting that both are poor material for Canadian democracy?

A meeting of scientists in Philadelphia noted a primitive mental trait called "denial." It causes most North Americans to erase from their consciousness the peril of nuclear obliteration, even when they acknowledge its existence. I place the threat of Nazi-Fascism in the same context; it *can* happen again, but it bothers few who did not suffer its poison barbs in their own flesh.

"Well, dammit, it bothers me – and I just won't rest until it bothers them too!"

With that vow, I raised my head from the desk on which the Berlin photographs had been carefully sorted by the German journalist, and let my eyes roam to the thickening file of unsigned letters from cranks. On the top envelope, my name and address were meticulously traced in a huge straight-line triangular script. What kind of person takes pains with such stylized calligraphy? Beyond doubt, anyone sufficiently agitated to sit down to an anonymous scurrility has a quirk.

Practically all my self-effacing correspondents were united on one thing: I was a Communist. The accusatory epistles – and late-night home telephoners threatening my life, and early-morning malicious-mischief heroes who rang long enough to awaken me without saying a word – always spurted after I had taken aim at a Fascist target. There were three notable cases.

In May 1952 six members of the Toronto Symphony Orchestra were dismissed (with their Union's approval) when the United States Immigration Service barred them from entry for a concert engagement in Detroit, presumably because of alleged Communist sympathies. The six may have derived solace from the fact that their names were linked with a growing and distinguished list of scientists, scholars, writers, and artists – all victims of a visa-phobic "Red-tape Curtain." But the crumb of comfort would not counterbalance the loss of their daily bread.

I was a member of the TSO Board of Directors at the time and opposed the dismissal, not in militant objection to deliberate wrong but because the majority action, in my opinion, was an honest but unconscionable disregard of principle. As a Vice-President of the Association for Civil Liberties, I joined its officers and Advisory

Board (a highly respectable, and in many instances notable, roster of Canadians) in sharp protest, and affixed my signature to a further statement by a group of prominent Torontonians.

The author of the second incident was Maurice Duplessis, Premier of the Province of Quebec, who had himself empowered by statute summarily to padlock any premises under suspicion of harbouring Communist activities. His first target was the Montreal headquarters of the United Jewish Peoples Order. On the ground that the Padlock Law would replace Communism with Fascism, I mustered every device of oratory to persuade the National Executive of Canadian Jewish Congress to launch a protest; a Socialist member of the Manitoba Parliament was my sole convert. Then I resorted to the press.

Years later, Maurice Duplessis branded me an agitator bent on befouling the education of youth with atheism. Since I had never presumed to concern myself in any degree with school methods, curriculum, or objectives in Quebec, I could only assume that the Premier of that great province had been impelled by the campaign initiated by me against sectarian religious instruction in the schools of Ontario – and padlocks. My answer was swift and gloveless, that political opportunism and demagoguery had a long reach – from Quebec City to Toronto!

Finally, on January 22, 1953, the Reverend James M. Finlay of the United Church and the Reverend William P. Jenkins, First Unitarian Church, collaborated with me in an open letter to President Eisenhower asking executive clemency for Julius and Ethel Rosenberg, under sentence of death for espionage. Fifteen-hundred Protestant clergymen in the United States had not long before signed an open letter, with similar intent, to President Truman.

We urged that periodic execution of spies, for which the peacetime Rosenberg death penalty might provide an exemplar, be reserved for the Soviets and other states. The West could prove itself moderate and disciplined even under severe provocation and thus win a moral victory more effective in the war for men's minds than the electric chair.

The co-signers acceded to my proposal that we renounce the charge of anti-Semitism, which stank of hypocrisy when inspired by a régime guilty of the Prague trials and the anti-Jewish persecution currently organized behind the Iron Curtain. If anything, pro-Semitism may have exercised an impact! The presiding judge was a Jew. Did his maximum sentence originate in a consciously inadmissible need to demonstrate Jewish detestation of Communism?

The sole fruit of my intervention, in all three episodes, was an augmented load of lewd anonymous letters for the postman. A less time-worn technique of harassment – and in this instance a bon-bon of infantile malice – came to light in a series of subscription bills and dunning reminders from sundry magazines to a pair of non-existent persons, "Abe Redmann" and "Abe Redberry," at my home address!

A survey of the anti-Fascist battlefield precludes heartening prognosis. Its barometer is Franco, the squat patron of the wily art of dictatorship, who piously prates that he is "responsible only before God and to the Pope of Rome." Bolstered by the Falange version of the Nazi Party, the army, church, feudal estates, and big business, Il Caudillo imprisoned and tortured thousands of Spaniards during the war because they opposed espousal of the Axis. Yet the United States chose as its ally, with British, French, and German governmental enthusiasm, this opportunist who sent congratulations to Admiral Togo on Pearl Harbor. And all because his bases are believed to be a bulwark against Communism!

Will Fascism and its Nazi whelp be revived? There are wind-up mechanical robots of the faith, with fixed, automatic convictions, who would like to restore the eyeless, faceless, Fascist monolith to a world not indubitably lacking the conditions favourable for its re-emergence. They wrap themselves in bunting, belch stale froth in conspiratorial barns and beerhalls, and dredge up derelict hulks of demagogic omnipotence from the depths into which the storm had swept them.

During my European visit of 1961 many unregenerate riders on the Fascist tide, adapting their posture to its recession, lauded the "European" view as successor to discredited chauvinistic nationalism, and denounced Jew-baiting with an unctuous air. Yet they bear watching; the Machiavellian guile of Goebbels's graduates, their ability to dissimulate and charm, has well earned history's accolade of stout-hearted fear.

Karl Barth, the noted theologian, was expelled from Germany in 1935 for criticism of Hitler. Now he is raked over fire for a soft attitude toward Moscow. Repeatedly, and with unabating firmness, he has contended that the subtle forms of materialist atheism in the West threaten Christianity more gravely than the overt, much-trumpeted atheism of the Soviet Union, and that the danger of Nazism surpasses that of Communism, for the latter opposes Christians while the former tempts them. The pellucid cogency of the Barthian epigram is irrefutable. My small voice is not needed by the embattled, far-flung hosts of anti-Communism; anti-Nazism needs all the watchfulness and aid it can get!

Nazism's temptation is moral suicide in the name of obedience, romantic surrender to personal nihilism; the compulsory tattoo on concentration-camp inmates merely condensed into a few numerals the dehumanization voluntarily accepted by a large section of the German people. Communism, among other vital differences, has never exalted genocide into a philosophy. Its economic expression, nevertheless, is enforced collectivism; its political arm a supreme, single party; its religious symbol the deified State; and its goal for man the inert, organized atrophy of individual existence. Although my peace mission to Moscow in 1961 convinced me that Communist practice has succumbed to life, that rigidity will bend under the inexorable proddings of a consumer-goods economy, that the domain of personal freedom is bound to expand, uniformity remains its core.

A pair of socks, neither Right nor Left, epitomizes my unconditional rejection of the convenient dogma of strictly limited choice. I am *neither* – and I strongly resent the conspiracy of the poles, the ad hoc alliance of extremes, which would have me kissing Communism to fight Fascism.

My private and public feud with Fascism keeps me alive. A superannuated firehorse out to pasture? Whenever such a destiny begins to seem imminent, the bell rings, the whistle blows, someone yelps "fire," and I quiver for the harness. And when the Angel of Death comes to summon me, I hope he will croak that there are Nazis and Fascists in the realm he governs and something has to be done about them. Then I would the less reluctantly follow him!

Ritual, Righteousness, and Reform Judaism: Heart versus Mind

"YOU'RE going Orthodox! You're not Reform! You're turning backward!"

Canada, Toronto, Holy Blossom Temple, became a tripod on which I rested my sights toward the kind of rabbinical career I wanted: expenditure of one's energies for high objectives in a land undominated by the hunger for domination and unhampered by allergic reaction to ideas, in a congregation with a tradition of pulpit courage and freedom.

Within a week of my arrival, I realized why Israel Zangwill said Jews have less affinity for collective cohesion than African aborigines. I saw vivid, volatile Toronto Jewry aswarm with competitive organizations and movements, each with devotees armed for instant controversy. Even the warring camps in Zionism had their combative Toronto legionnaires. Tiny Israel's later fragmentation into more than a score of political parties was a microcosm of the internecine ferment that linked Spadina Avenue to Forest Hill.

The embattled "isms" were waiting for a sign from Holy Blossom's new rabbi. Where would he set up his tent? Each was eager to interpret any signal from him as an offer of support. And every step he took in any direction got an instant tag of partisanship.

"Going Orthodox!" That was the first label pasted on me. Why? As my first Temple project, I chose Operation Ritual.

For years Holy Blossom had been among a baker's dozen of North American Reform congregations which conducted the principal Sabbath Service on Sunday morning. It was no less sparing of ritualism than a New England Congregationalist church, with an hour-long lecture geared to public issues and open-minded Gentiles. I lost no time in forecasting a change to *Erev Shabbas*,* more Hebrew, traditional candle-lighting, wine-*kiddush*, and old-fashioned chanting.

The Sunday pulpit discourses might have been exciting. Where in the United States would a new rabbi be greeted by a weekly audience with enough patience and assiduity to listen for an hour? But revitalization of the entire ritual seemed more pressing.

The process went forward from the *Erev Shabbas* resurrection into every phase of congregational life: at the communal Seder on Passover Eve, colourful informality and songs and laughter instead of a string orchestra and stifling decorum; at Succot, a fruit-laden booth on the altar; for the *shofar*-blowing on New Year, a ram's horn and a bearded virtuoso, not a sepulchral trumpet-tone on the organ. In the religious school, kindergarten children began to lisp the blessing over bread; a voluntary weekday Hebrew School got launched; youngsters received encouragement to prepare for the

* Friday evening.

Bar-Mitzvah and, later, female Bat-Mitzvah, ceremony; Palestine, as it became a state, became an increasingly central subject in the curriculum; the whole content and mood of the classroom moved the child-mind from marginal separatistic sectarianism into the closest possible oneness with the Jewish people. I had always preened myself on iconoclasm; yet here I was in the conservative camp, extolling practices that my old-time Seminary clique would have called "compulsive flummeries"!

A trend toward ritual had been manifest among Reform rabbis for some years. To me, however, perfunctory ceremonial offered a too-convenient egress from basic dilemmas of belief. I was therefore not impressed by the drift itself, and the sovereignty of the individual rabbi relieved me of any obligation to go along with it. Jews have no papal office. If a Pope were to be chosen by the rabbis from among their number, each would receive one vote!

Was my crusade for ritual motivated by a scheme to lure into Holy Blossom the Old World-oriented majority of Toronto Jews? Had ambition for numbers energized me, a quite simple device would have come immediately to mind, namely, the reintroduction of compulsory head-covering for males at worship. As a neighbourhood Orthodox rabbi confessed to me years later, his *shule* wouldn't have stood a chance if I had restored the *yarmelke*.* "A thousand families were ready to join Holy Blossom overnight!" he exclaimed. "But they couldn't stand the sight of you standing before the Holy Ark with bare head!"

I wove my intellectual evaluation of ritual into a statement of principles, which I set down, as a somewhat revised version of the official Reform Jewish credo, in ten unequivocal headings:

One Judaism is the historic religious experience of the Jewish people.

Two Judaism welcomes all truth, whether in scripture, science, or philosophy.

* Skullcap.

Three One God rules the world by natural law and with inscrutable love.

Four The Divine Image in man makes him inviolable.

Five God's self-revelation is constant and universal.

Six Certain of the laws in the Torah have lost their validity with the passing of the conditions that produced them.

Seven The Jewish people has been held together by common history.

Eight Although Jews participate gladly in the duties of citizenship, a powerful bond, hallowed by memory and hope, links them to the State of Israel.

Nine All mankind must labour in unity for the kingdom of God on earth through the pursuit of Justice, truth, and peace.

Ten The foundation of morality is love of the ideals symbolized by God and culminating in the love of man.

What had these tenets to do with a piece of cloth on a man's cranium? Jewish males at a public dinner meeting, in lieu of a hat or skullcap, sometimes pop a handkerchief on their heads during the rabbi's recital of the *motzie,** which is frequently alluded to by the Christian term "grace" and has been elevated to formal status as a sacerdotal bow to deity. Could *I* distort faith into a fetish? Neither Scripture, logic, aesthetics, nor theology sustains the claim that what is *on*, not *in*, a male Jew's head, measures his fitness to stand before the Lord!

In a Yiddish folk-story, a pietist was confronted by the village heretic. "Why must I wear a *yarmelke* in *shule*, old greybeard?" The sage raised his eyebrows in astonishment. "How can you doubt? Holy Writ tells us that Abraham stood before God, no? Is it possible that Abraham stood before our Maker with uncovered head?" That naïve rhetorical question is the strongest argument I ever heard for head-covering!

Holy Blossom Congregation was split forty years ago by the

* Hebrew blessing over bread.

submission of a by-law about hats, which *permitted*, but did not *require*, men to worship with bare noggins, and a schismatic group withdrew to found a more tradition-loyal synagogue. Of all religious issues, cranial nudity is among the least deserving of argumentative heat and breath today – but I would not clamp a skullcap or baretta on my head for a regular service in the sanctuary. There were more valid proofs that Holy Blossom was a qualified medium of Jewish ideals. Yesterday is necessary but it cannot displace today or dictate tomorrow.

Another ready-made path to the affection of the mass of Jewry was the dietary laws. By restricting my flesh menu at home to ritually slaughtered beef, lamb, and poultry purchased from a butcher on the kosher list officially certified in Toronto after years of wrangling between two rival rabbinical "schools," by separating *milchig** from *fleishig*† dishes in the kitchen and rejecting the former within six hours of the latter, by rigidly eschewing gustatory contact with pig, lobster, shrimp, and other beasts proscribed by Bible and law codes, or the touch of any utensil polluted by them, I would earn repute for rectitude beyond a Reformer's line of duty.

A Jew, or anyone, who suffers discomfort, deprivation, the death of impulse and desire rather than surrender or subvert his ritualistic heritage, thus preserves the worth of individual conviction in a nondescript, wishy-washy world. The momentum of self-denial instigated by the dietary laws can introduce discipline into other more significant areas of conduct; uncompromising cleavage to a stomach-code may reinforce one's capacity for sacrifice to a business code. I am not unaware of the sense of *amour-propre*, of aristocratic stewardship, bred by self-abnegating adherence to restrictions on dining-room appetite – but I am neither capable of, nor drawn to it. An obligation rests on me to separate the everlasting and the transient, the essential and the expendable. The value of a regimen cannot always be reckoned by the price it imposes. Not every versifier starving in a garret is a poetic genius.

In a Maritime Jewish community I visited to collect funds for

* Dairy. † Meat.

the United Jewish Appeal, the kitchen has become chapel, shrine, and sanctuary. For years the rabbi pedalled a bicycle so that every housewife might have her chicken ritually slaughtered; meat is imported from Montreal; social acceptance hangs on the absolute banishment of non-kosher food from the home – although one might scrunch a succulent steak or sweet-savoured lobster at the hotel.

I felt a twinge of envy in that town which did not abate when the local nabobs gave niggardly response to my plea for aid to Israel. How nice to have such a commodious paradise, for which the ticket of admission was so clearly and cheaply printed! But I am spurred to wonderment, not imitation. The alimentary canal could never become my highway to God!

Do I suffer pangs of guilt? They vanished with a rectangle of ham, in the Diggity kitchen, long ago, when Bellaire's little outpost of Orthodox fealty could not support a full-time kosher butcher shop even if Baron Rothschild were to make all Jews rich enough to eat meat every day. The teacher-butcher-rabbi-cantor would slit the throat of one steer a week and dispense the permitted portions across an improvised counter in the rear of the slaughter-house. And when Mr. Pleshner or imminent starvation drove him on to another town, no animal flesh appeared on our table at all, save the chickens my father nursed in the backyard or a hard salami brought down from Pittsburgh.

If I chanced to be around at Jim's during mealtime, Mrs. Diggity invariably sat me down at the table before a platter. "Come on Abie, put some fat on those bones of yours." I steadfastly stammered that I wasn't allowed to have meat between meals.

The day it was fried ham, I "fell." Golden beads of juice dripped from a curled-up, sizzling edge, and the seductive odour of salty fat filtering through my nostrils delivered a tantalizing message to a palate which rejected the inevitable canned-salmon "goldfish" that awaited me at home.

The first bite had to be gulped; the second slid down my gullet. But that evening at supper the brown-red slab rose up from queasy bowels to become a strangling stone in my throat. Seeing the familiar greenish pallor, Mom popped a thermometer into my mouth and sent me off to bed. As I swayed upstairs I heard my father mumble, "That dreck-candy again!"

God knew, if my father didn't! I stayed away from the swimming-hole almost a week! God might give me a cramp. Ma Diggity's morsel of swine swung a flaming sword at the gate of a Jew-boy's felicity. Even when I surreptitiously consumed an ice-cream cone right after a chicken dinner, or let my cap slip off in the synagogue, or picked up a Bible from the floor without kissing it, I cowered.

I began to feel sorry for myself. Jim Diggity was poor. He could not have lots of candy and a bicycle and auto-rides either. But he didn't have to go to *heder* and he could eat what he wanted. I was not only poor, but a Jew as well! My solace came from "Jim the Bootblack" and "Tom the Newsboy." They had risen from the depths to fame and fortune. So could I!

There came a day when Horatio Alger's happy endings were stripped of surprise, when the adventures of Diamond Dick, Frank Merriwell, and Fred Fearnot could no longer count on Pop's ban to inflame my interest. For I began to read the Hebrew Prophets. At first it was the sweeping, soaring majesty of their phrases. Then, night after night, in the kitchen, while my mother, waiting up for someone, dozed jerkily into her Yiddish paper, I caught a glimpse of what the prophets meant. One meaning was unmistakable: justice and ethical conduct carried more weight with God than ceremonies in the Temple and ritual customs at home. Isaiah and Jeremiah would not have worried about what I crammed into my mouth as food, or what came out of it as words. They wanted me to be just, and to fight for the poor people of the earth! My excursions into dietary indulgence became more frequent, and the aftermath, other than gastronomic, less agonizing. Soon the tills of Gentile sandwich-stands rang with the extra nickels I gleaned from carrying baggage and collecting bottles.

The gradual attenuation of guilt-feeling about *kashrut** was accelerated by subsequent study. In ancient times, I learned, the

* Dietary correctness.

dietary laws raised a wall of self-ghettoization, adding yet another brick to the barrier of the Law. Jews could not break bread with their Gentile neighbour, thereby arousing suspicion of unclean secret rites and clannishness. In 465 a church council forbade the Christian clergy to sit down at Jewish banquets because Jews did not reciprocate.

A stand-offishness which had some reason in licentious Rome and the miasma of mediaevalism now smacks of compensatory arrogance. To reject a Rotary, Kiwanis, or Lions membership, for example, because of luncheon menus, seems palpably absurd, although the rejection may be justified on other grounds. Canada is not a feudal fief of the Middle Ages or a Czar-shadowed cluster of huts on the Russian plain. Here the Jews' self-portrait as a holy people which must safeguard its ritual purity from contamination can be turned inside out – to co-existence with Gentile civilization for the shared pursuit of a well-being neither can enjoy without the other.

I refrain from pork products at a public gathering in deference to my Orthodox colleagues and, when one of them is present, his plate of salad or fish, if he eats at all, will circumscribe my diet as well. The widespread latitude which permits conspicuously "observant" Jews to eat non-kosher food outside, for business luncheon, conference or meeting, as long as they maintain a kosher kitchen at home, answered the need for social-commercial intercourse with Gentiles; it has now extended to the entire family, evening dinners, and gourmandise. Toronto's Chinese restaurants and barbecued spareribs have become a Jewish formula for the maid's night out.

Inconsistencies and variations traverse the gamut from the enlightened libertine who flaunts a pork chop to the absolute compulsive who peers into every pot. Some Jews still gag at the slurp of raw oysters and the swallow of fresh pig; shrimp has risen to such esteem as a delicacy that an ingenious substitute similar in appearance and flavour is served to the finicky; third-generation children may vaunt their intestinal hardihood with pickled pigs feet, frogs' legs, Cantonese lobster-sauce, and *hasenpfeffer* – but "home is strictly kosher so that *zaideh* can come to us for dinner"; the Israel government having banned pig-breeding and the import of non-kosher meats, an Israeli or tourist who can tolerate and afford bacon for breakfast must patronize a *hahzer** bootlegger or slip unobtrusively into a hotel catering by special dispensation to foreign diplomats; an astonishing percentage of Holy Blossom members keep kosher out of a vague feeling for "racial" tradition, reverence for parental memory, solidarity with the scattered hosts of Jewry, ingrained childhood inhibitions, habit, or hygiene.

These rationalizations have sincerity without logic. A famous Orthodox leader found it incumbent upon him, even in the nineteenth century, to underline the only valid base for the rules of diet: "God gave them – and he who truly loves God will obey them without asking reasons." Once we accept the direct, Divine origin of the Torah, every jot and tittle explicit in that theophany or extrapolated from it is equally binding. That consistent but loftily abstract Orthodox view leaves no area for mobility and accommodation; *kashrut* then entails *total* abstinence from a Gentile cuisine *anywhere.*

Only a fragmentary segment of Jews hermetically sealed on an intellectual island in outer space would seriously claim Sinaitic revelation for the proscription of butter with meat. Apologists may summon forth medical data to prove its value for physical health, but that mundane rationale makes Moses a dietician, not a mediator of the Divine Will.

"Going Orthodox!" Did the ritualistic spree at Holy Blossom merit that solemn adjective? I did not restore all rituals in obedience to a Law allegedly proclaimed thirty-five centuries ago; I restored some, for their emotional and symbolic value today. The operation rested on personal selectivity, not on total sanctity.

Is my voice, then, the voice of God? It is the voice, rather, of the Jewish people. Always, and intuitively, my interest in a ceremony was aroused by the degree in which it incorporated the tribal feeling, the folk-sentiment and "racial" colouration of the common

* Pig.

Jew, its intimacy with the underground reservoirs of Jewish experience which, like subterranean lakes of oil, are distilled from the action and interaction of the Jew and history over centuries of time.

That pull was not resurgent nationalism via the State of Israel, nor the modern affectation for roots in the race-soul. It came from deeper regions of the heart. Even in Bellaire, my heart warmed to the lustiness and laughter of simple immigrants. Slovaks in a shambling mine-shack were little more than serfs, but the thin-lipped, straight-backed Protestant Yankees behind sheared Gravel Hill hedges got less fun out of living. How crabbed and briny in their self-esteem and station, how suspicious of pleasure were the ladies of flat chests, squared-off chins, and steel-enforced eyes! Didn't I deliver their groceries? What a difference between their vinegary silence and the full-bosomed folksiness of the Italians and Poles and Irish on Union Street! Many foreigners were hard put to learn English – but they communicated through hunch and twist of shoulder, glitter of eye, the language of muscle and bone! And who gave me a coin in sheer Christmas joy when I brought the New Year's card to the door with the newspaper – Mrs. Peyton Brown or Mrs. Giovanni Sabbatino?

Discipline and precedent channelled the anarchic surge of life into outlets conventionally classified as religious; in reality, they were folk-expressions entangled with and reflecting the long, cumulative communion of a people with the trauma of birth and fate and death.

In the Feinberg household, these folkways had the authentic tang. Pesach, Feast of Passover, for example! It could be irksome; my father leaned to stringency in enforcing the Talmudic ban on eatables touched by Gentile hands that had touched *hometz,** even forbidding peanuts which, I argued, were protected from alien fingers by shells. Jim Diggity diabolically chose Pesach to masticate gumdrops like a cow and smack his lips on a huge round sucker, store-candy being then forbidden to me. Eight days of *matzoh* left a residue of lead in my bowels. And though I liked carrying a shiny Passover pail to the dairy-farmer and watching him squirt milk into it from

* Leaven.

the udders, the inch-by-inch scouring of the house and complete change of dishes to eliminate every crumb of leaven made our beautiful Mom look and drudge like a scullion. But the Seder suppers – two, according to Orthodox custom – were a highlight of my boyhood.

Our one silver-plated dish heaped with *matzot;* a red wineglass with his own name inscribed in gold-leaf around its midriff for each child; the hard-boiled egg in salt water, so palatable I wondered why Mom didn't serve it all year; the competition in courage to bite off and chew a stick of horse-radish, symbolic of bitter Egyptian slavery; Sylvia and Sally, the youngest, slumbering blissfully into their fourth diluted cup of prescribed wine; Pop carefully tipping ten drops over the edge of his gold-rimmed tumbler while intoning the Exodus plagues, each in turn; all the siblings except the eldest searching for the *afikomon** and Pop's dime prize; the youngest boy standing erect, with protruding tummy, to chant the Four Questions that launched the reading of the Hebrew *haggadah*†; a radiant, proud sense of being together, the Feinberg family, encircling a table with song – and Pop as elfin and jovial as a leprechaun!

Appetite was sharpened by the steaming odours from the coal-stove; the *haggadah* got tiresome. I improvised a ruse that reduced it by many minutes. Pausing in my intonation of the text long enough to note where Pop was, I would shout the opening line of the next paragraph and chuckle with Mose and Jack and Sam and Allen and Dave as he raced to overtake me.

The chair and beaker set aside for Elijah who, in Jewish folk-legend, visits every Seder, unseen, as herald of redemption, stirred me to febrile dreams of Jewish glory. One year my father hid a rubber tube under the tablecloth and siphoned off Elijah's cup while the kids busied themselves with the macaroons. Sally was sure the bringer of good tidings had shared our wine! I was sure he would some day recrown a king on Zion.

Of all the festivals, the Passover supper had the brightest

* Hidden matzoh.
† Liturgy relating the story of the deliverance.

embroidery, but the others were pallid only by comparison. On Rosh Hashanah we dipped apple-sections into honey to sweeten the ensuing twelve months. During Succot a booth of slats and newly harvested fruits and corn was somehow held together with chicken-wire and annexed to the coop. The scent of grape and pear and melon mellowing in the sun, the taste of amber mead, the sound of Palestinian hymns to the largesse of nature, marble-games with hazelnuts, Pop's tales about Succot in Grinkishok, where the family sometimes *lived* in a booth, the awesome saga of a forty-year trek by the Israelites in the Arabian Peninsula – it was all "wonderful," an appraisal I diligently descanted to the Diggitys. On Purim* Pop was impresario for the drama of Esther, with crude cardboard and crayon masks, ribbons and paper crown for the Queen, and each boy begging to play the part of Mordecai, and we took *greggers*† to *shule*, and chalked "Haman" on the soles of our shoes, to raise a formidable clamour and stamp the tyrant into the dust at every mention of his name in the chanting of the *megillah*.‡ For the eight days of Hanukkah an additional candle was kindled every evening while we crowed "Rock of Ages" and carolled the Hebrew paeans to God for the storied miracle of the oil in the Jerusalem Temple; a gift – slender in cost, but a mighty fortress against the lure of one-day Christmas – came from our father's paper bag after each lighting, and the boys duelled with wooden spears to simulate the victory of the Maccabees over the Syrian persecutor.

More than anything else, the candles on Sabbath Eve flooded my heart. As soon as Dad announced in a half-whisper, addressing no one in particular, as if to himself, that three stars had appeared in the sky, our mother, in a hastily donned white calico dress, first put a match to the tapers, then fingers across her eyes, and finally her palms in benediction over the lengthening flames. For a magic moment the grinding wheels of life halted and the world stood still.

We were a singing clan. Every auspicious occasion brought Pop out of his introspective brooding to beat time and teach us the tunes of his boyhood around the kitchen table, and the jocund mood

* Feast of Lots. † Noise-makers. ‡ Scroll of the Book of Esther.

loosened his tongue for fascinating stories of Feifke Gedaliah, Grinkishok's reprobate scandalizer; maidens who threw themselves into the river and "got grounded" when he wed Mom; and how he bravely rallied a regiment of the Czar against the Japanese – until we advanced in school far enough to yell in chorus that the Russo-Japanese War was fought almost twenty-five years after he landed in Baltimore.

The indomitable folk-spirit of my father, the laughter in the lamentation, the music of raindrops in a squall, the zest of a grief-tested people beyond self-pity but compassionate rather toward the world, the rhythm of an old, unwavering heartbeat – these I wanted to introduce into Holy Blossom. True, the Seder, the last Supper of the New Testament, epitomized the fight of *all* slaves to break their chains – but it looks back for witness across thirty-five centuries to a nation that came to birth in the fight for freedom. Hebrew was the tongue of prophet, priest, psalmist, who spoke and sang for *all* men – but it is the everyday speech of cab-drivers and bankers and housewives and thieves and lovers in the State of Israel, heartland, homeland, and hopeland of Grinkishkers who did not live to hear it spoken in Tel-Aviv. The Sabbath candles were a *universal* tribute to light, as demonstrated throughout religious history from the vestal virgins of Rome to the yule-log of Christendom – but they reignite the guttering embers of fellowship for a folk dispersed around the globe. The fragility of the *succah* recited the ephemeral tenuousness of *all* human life – but chiefly the cycle of planting, fruitage, and harvest which has been woven into the biography of the Eternal Jew. Chanting by the cantor, even when overdosed with bravura, coloratura, tremolo, and falsetto, moderated the tedium of public worship – but, more significantly, its plaintive climb to the Throne links me to my father and his father before him.

Pop might well have fondled a grudge against the synagogue. He reached Baltimore at the start of the massive Russian-Jewish flight to America; religious and communal organization was less than embryonic. His livelihood rested on a stone-melting *shtimme*,*

* Voice.

a lyric spirit that would assault the gates of heaven, and the sensitivity of Jewish frontiersmen who differed from Western gunmen in that they drew a harsh tongue and economic sanctions instead of a Colt Forty-Five. He was an omnibus functionary, not an emissary to God! Presidents of overnight "congregations" plotted against the rabbi when he waved them aside as illiterates, pack-pedlars railed at the cantor for refusing to bow, clothing-store "all-right-niks" withheld the *melammed*'s fee because he would not demean himself to dun them, harridans quibbled with the *shayhet** about the three-cent rate for slitting a hen's throat – and Pop was all four of these.

Given his fierce pride, anything was preferable to such a lot, even fixing umbrellas, as long as he could be self-employed, and thus keep the Sabbath. Given his humiliating frustration by the synagogue, the intensity of his joy in ritual observance and complete abandonment to the drama of the folk were noteworthy. Whatever his sullen withdrawal or tornadic wrath on ordinary occasions, Jewish holidays wreathed his countenance in twinkling humour and placed on his brow the laurel of victory over life.

What the dramatization of the folk-saga did for Pop and for us, in the trammels of penury and defeatism, it could surely do for the householders of Holy Blossom. Therefore, I felt I must revive it. Not as a monument to my father's memory! I wanted no traffic with graveyard Judaism, a skeletal artifact of gloom and sentimentality whose fleshless bones are screwed together with *Kaddish*-prayers for the dead and with costly memorial plaques. I wanted rather to establish a line of communication between the majestic grandeur of a cathedral-synagogue, which could easily become a whited sepulchre, and the wellsprings of life. *Jewishness* – pulsating, protean, informal – not denatured Judaism!

The classical Reform I found at Holy Blossom adapted the old traditions to a new world and a new age. How could I quarrel with such a progressive pattern? Reform actually *was* tradition. Despite the lopsided portrayal of the Pharisees in the New Testament, they

* Ritual slaughterer, *shohet* in Litvak pronunciation.

were advocates of flexibility. What is the Talmud if not a seven-or-eight-century record of Pharisaic endeavour to fit the Law into life, to make it work?

Change, in response to the challenge of history, has been the Jew's immemorial genius. When Roman destruction of the kingdom of Israel scattered its people in the year A.D. 70, and terminated the sacrificial offerings, the singing of the Levites, and the elaborate rituals of worship in Jerusalem's Temple, Judaism might have vanished. Instead, it spread more widely throughout the earth. Why? Because teachers and rabbis replaced the blood of beasts with prayers of penitence and petition, a single, central Temple with humble synagogues that sprang up everywhere, and the altar with the home; every man became a priest in the household, his table a shrine, the Torah a portable and continuous revelation of God.

The French Revolution in 1791 offered political equality. Thenceforce, with intermittent retreat to oppression, the spirit of enlightment flickered across Europe, shone like a beacon in England, and then rose to a luminous torch on the North American continent. For seventeen centuries Israel had been forcibly isolated from the currents of Western thought, culture, and commerce. The Sanhedrin, which alone could authorize adjustments in the Torah, had vanished into limbo. While the world outside melted and poured itself into new moulds under the torch of the humanistic revolution, Judaism languished and congealed. Suddenly, the walls of the Bastille crashed, bringing down the walls of the ghetto – and the Jew entered the nineteenth century.

Emancipation exacted payment. A way of life suitable for segregated pariahs could not be transferred holus-bolus to a domain wherein they were equal participants. Religious observances hallowed by the reverential usage of generations bore the stigma of the outlandish and bizarre. Ex-ghetto inmates floundered between soft sentiment and hard sense, between allegiance to the past and assimilation to what they thought was the future.

That crisis begat Reform, in 1816, when a German congregation began to pray in the German language. Thenceforth, long-stiffened limbs began to move, and dammed-up streams to seek new courses. In a few decades, unshackled powers of adaptation renewed the creativity of Judaism, shaped it to the time, and showed Jews how to wed loyalty and liberty.

Reform was a child of optimism. The Occident has been released from the bondage of hate, it exulted, and wants the Jew for brother! To qualify for that privilege, the Westernized Jew severed the side-curls of piety, tore Zion from the liturgy and substituted Washington, London, Berlin, Paris, as the new Jerusalem, stylized worship into a gutless replica of decorous Protestantism, discarded most of the rituals that proclaimed Jews to be different, froze folklore and Old World wit and wisdom into ethical monotheism, summoned rabbis to specialize in Brotherhood Week, and prattled that Israel had a "mission" to conduct mankind into the kingdom of God, while withholding enthusiasm from the social measures necessary to expedite it.

G. K. Chesterton wrote that a madman is not he who has lost his reason, but he who has lost everything *except* his reason. In the beginning Reform Jews aimed at invisibility, basked in moderate, reassuring sermons, blunted their consciousness of evil, read Sokolsky columns at breakfast, nodded that Jews should be soft of speech and polite, and complimented one another on heroic refusal to join the Episcopalians or Unitarians.

Such a Judaism has no more savour than the solid-geometry propositions I sparred with in high school. It might have sufficed, however, but the Gentile world let the Reformers down. The twentieth century blasted the dreams born in the nineteenth. Around the corner, Jews bumped not into the Messianic Era, as they expected, but into the Dreyfus Case – an appropriate start for the five decades that spawned reactionary clerical-militarism in the salons of France, pogroms in the squalid villages of Russia, economic boycotts and *numerus clausus* in the schools and cities of Poland, Father Coughlin in the United States, Mosleyism in Britain and, for final grotesquerie, lampshades from Jewish skin in Germany.

Post-Hitler Jews are shorn of illusions. Survival is a do-it-yourself project. It were naïve indeed to depend on, or shape one's religion to, the good will, good faith, or goodness of Christendom Better an insurance policy with the State of Israel, which at least offers a home to every Jew who needs it and vindication of Jewish dignity, as in the Eichmann trial, than with the state of Christian morality! Better the folk-feelings of my father, and their full-bodied joy, than walking gingerly on eggs to please "friends" who desert when the bugle sounds!

"Going Orthodox?" Apart from my abhorrence of pate-Judaism, which inquires about the covering of a man's head, or pot-Judaism, which inspects what is cooking on his stove, I do not crave the cotton-batting of authoritarianism, whether the final arbitrament of truth be said to inhabit a scripture, a synod, or a sanhedrin. Not that I disdain the relaxation and security provided by a surrogate who would answer all questions! On the contrary, this incomprehensible, depersonalized, soul-crushing atomic universe frightens me, and I long for a broad bosom whereon to lay my doubts. But another human being, or a revelation he has written, does not fulfil my need. Besides, Orthodox intolerance in Toronto disturbs me more than the accustomed bigotry of Christian fundamentalists. Only affection for my father, and the recognition that Jewish fanaticism is not pandemic, restrain me from lashing out in anger at calumniators who caution Hebrew-School children against the "church on the hill," especially when they themselves ignore inconvenient prescriptions in the Torah, and defamation of Holy Blossom is the only habit that distinguishes their observance of Judaism from that of its members.

An astute Orthodox author once described an Orthodox Jew as one "whose rabbi keeps kosher." During my early years in Toronto, before planting my standard firmly with the folk-mass and thus deflating the white-plumed knights of Torah-true Judaism, I might have added a second qualification: dislike of Holy Blossom.

Any unalterable creed invites the human being to remain immature: mentally, by foregoing the right to propound the riddles that have tantalized the mind of man since his beginning; emotionally, by submerging individuality in lifelong spiritual dependence;

psychologically, by vaunting membership in a self-declared élite entitled to a celestial accolade of unshared bliss.

Lox-and-bagel, *gefillte-fisch* Yiddishkeit, on the other hand, can be perverted into ancestor-worship or biological self-idolatry, differing only in virulence from Nazi Aryanism. Christianity took hold of a Jew and made a god of him; it were arrant folly to take hold of God and make a Jew of Him.

The tug-of-war about ritual at Holy Blossom did not slacken until the rope had knotted a rosette of victory around Sabbath candles and the *kiddush*-cup. Yet this was only a skirmish in a conflict which began from the moment I began to think beyond my fingertips. Should I sit down to a drafting-board and spell out a blueprint of belief, with my mind, or should I ride with my heart on the river of folk-intuition that flows from a pristine spring in the Sinai wilderness?

Every important transaction of life is for each individual a leap in the dark toward commitment. It cannot be delegated – even to a professional clergyman trained for negotiating with the unknown. Our days are not a perfunctory plodding across a plain; they are mountain passes enshrouded in blinding mist, through which glimpses can be caught now and then of paths that may prove deceptive. Breezy self-assurance will topple us over the edge; immobility may freeze us to death; there is no alternative but to stretch a hand toward the unknown.

Two chasms flank each mountain pass: complete doubt, the only assurance being that what we wish to believe is false, and complete trust that it is true. Doubt concentrates on facts, and their absence; trust has its eyes on the faith which begins where facts end. Doubt instructs us to sit down before nature as a little child, giving up every preconceived notion and following humbly, even to a dead end; trust dares to believe man has a cosmic destiny beyond his comprehending. Doubt says, "Without science, love is helpless"; trust says, "Without love, science is brutal." Doubt summons integrity to confess that nothing can be proved; trust summons hope to kindle a light across the void.

To me, worship is an ultimately unavailing quest for union with the best we can conceive, rather than a prayer-book paginated for public convenience; salvation bids us suffuse the present world with premonition of the ideal to which it must be shaped, instead of certifying our right to heaven with a credal escape-clause in a life-contract of doom; the soul is a man's achievement, not God's endowment; religion is the thrust toward self-perfection whereby a man pours meaning into a life otherwise dismal and absurd – and Scripture culminates in Amos: "Seek Me and live."

For years, I balanced myself on a ribbon of compromise by marrying science, the realm of valid data, to religion, the realm of values. I even persuaded myself at times that the orgiastic embrace of mankind's immemorial superstitions is preferable to the intricately patterned dance of proton and electron. Often, and unhappily, I floated in a tepid pool of liberalism. First, I could not be absolutely sure about anything. Second, when society wants to discourage independent thought, it is unfortunately bound to succeed. Therefore such independence is a prime obligation. Third, every orthodox opinion was once eccentric. Fourth, peremptory dissent argues a deeper consonance with the ultimate welfare of man than passive agreement. Fifth, organized creeds have been tried for a long time with everything in their favour and have failed to crack even the surface of the conduct of mankind. Sixth, the majority is often wrong.

Behind the liberal half-faith on the façade of my mind, however, lurked some needling suspicions. Liberalism exalts ambiguity and ambivalence. How can I ever take a stand? Openness to the convictions of other people is only a truce between the least common denominator of innocuous generalities I can espouse and the bold odysseys of the mind it bids me avoid. The liberal credo declares, "There is no God, and man is his prophet." A liberal clergyman hovers between the protective haven of a tradition he doubts and the uncharted ocean of a nihilism from which he recoils. Like Volstead gin, his mixed-drinks potion is diluted beyond the power to inebriate.

During my Temple Sinai days in New York, liberal religion's universalism, rationalism, social idealism were a resonant tocsin-call. The 1929 débâcle which ended the roaring 'twenties devitalized that challenge into a string of catchwords; despite intravenous injections by the dwindling devotees of Ethical Culture and humanism, it was emasculated beyond the power to arouse passionate controversy. Can a doctrine of no-doctrine allay the anguish of an age again affluent, but apprehensive, whose today cries havoc and whose tomorrow may never arrive?

Not for the patronizing pseudo-religion of the psychologist do the 'sixties thirst, however well he may understand the trauma of man alienated from nature, from himself, and from God. The sociologist's concept of religion as the highest social aspirations of collective man rubs no balm on a soul whose science-oriented Utopia evaporated at Hiroshima. Preachers no longer draw easement from the Einsteinean cosmos, which awes the intellect, has the impeccable symmetry of the Parthenon, and leaves the heart in ice.

But the claims of reason? Dare we dismiss them? Extravagantly pretentious parochialisms – national, ethnic, religious – imperil the very existence of the human species in an H-bomb world. "There is something in all of us that yearns not for penetrating clear thought but for the whisperings of the irrational," Karl Jaspers cautioned. That "something" now descends into a twilight of the mind, an anti-rational Couéism retooled in the "positive thinking" of Norman Vincent Peale. Better use God's gift of reason to deny Him, I say, than indulge the sham ecstasy of unreason to cheapen and degrade Him! And we dare not forget that mystic intuition and romanticism helped Hitler seduce Germans to idolatry of race and folk!

The stiff-necked, hard-headed rabbis of old had contempt for flights into unreality; they despised deliberate anti-intellectualism. Bachia ibn Pakuda invested the endeavour to comprehend God with the status of a God-ordained commandment; Saadia startled tenth-century scholasticism with the insistence that even without revelation the human mind would have ultimately apprehended God's existence; Maimonides, greatest of all the giants, denied the necessity of supernatural aid, for men can arrive at truth through their own quest. In other words, if we cannot know all the answers to religious riddles, we are bound to know all we can.

Man's endowment with reason, nevertheless, does not prove that he lives by it. Overwhelming evidence discloses him to be a thinking animal only when driven to it for survival; confronted by the unprecedented threat of nuclear extermination, he has still not "put on his thinking cap." Like love and rapture, religion does not seem at all to require the ratiocinative faculty.

Reason alone has led man into inhumanity and doubt; religion alone has led him into inhumanity and illusion; together they may lead him to a full realization of his humanity. Mind is not enough in a species which already has gained sufficient scientific knowledge to destroy itself; heart is not enough in a world which has lost the spiritual anchor of supernaturalism and needs to be convinced that such an anchor is available elsewhere. Interpenetration, peaceful co-existence, a nuptial flight of the soul, is the desideratum of this new "ice age."

The civil war in religion will never proceed beyond shadow-boxing. Orthodoxy is blind, groping truth *plus* numbers; heterodoxy is blind, groping truth *minus* numbers: If I must choose between heart and mind, however, give me heart! At least it places a taper in my hand; I am not able to advance on my way when a logician comes up and blows it out.

The only beliefs immune to the sandpaper of doubt on my escutcheon are uncerebrated, instinctive affirmations. By these I live. One of them is the Jewish folk, the centrality of its saga, dramatized in ritual, and directed toward social righteousness. The others are:

MY CREEDLESS CREDO

I believe in God – beneath and beyond all else I believe in.

I believe Judaism, like other religions, may have the

truth about God, the soul, and death, in addition to a miscellany of minor truths demonstrable by logic and evidence – but the larger truth cannot be proved, to myself or to anyone else; therefore it behooves me to be humble.

I believe that *all* truth is *very* difficult to come by; therefore I must be skeptical.

I believe life has significance, even though I can't prove it.

I believe men display more cleverness now than in the days of Moses – not more wisdom.

I believe personal happiness to be good, and there is no special virtue or charm in doing without it.

I believe democracy is less prone to folly than dictatorship.

I believe unauthorized opinion is vital to a world which already knows so much it must learn more to survive and that in-between neutrality is intellectual eunuchism.

I believe we are animal in much the larger part – but the rest can redeem us from becoming wholly so.

I believe in "probably," "perhaps" – and also in "Thus says the Lord."

I believe the fatal disease of our nuclear age is hate.

I believe God is love – but love is not a god.

I believe in one world at a time; if my soul lives on after death, I hope to enjoy the change of residence.

I believe the worth of an idea is unrelated to the martyrdom of those who proclaim it; in fact, the two categories may have inverse relationship.

I believe the most obnoxious human frailties are a thick skin, a thick skull, and the itch for a thick wallet.

I believe a saint who knows he is occupies a lower rung on the ladder of humanity than a sinner who knows he is.

I believe the rotten fruit of our educational system is the habit of unquestioning obedience.

I believe in heaven and hell – on earth.

I believe in praying as though God were all and then doing as though man were all.

I believe in the final, inviolable dignity of human life – and that no one is unimportant.

Christianity Goes to School

On June 19, 1944, the postman brought me five textbooks on the life and times of Jesus. Colonel George Drew, Ontario Premier and Minister of Education, had imported them from England for the public-school religious teaching he had pledged in his Speech from the Throne.

A Gallup Poll registered coolness toward the Drew Plan. The Inter-Church Committee cautioned against unseemly haste. Career officials in the Department of Education noted that high-school religion classes might spark Roman Catholic pressure for extension of the Separate School system from elementary to secondary grades –

and, inevitably, a Protestant counter-attack. That war-torn June, nevertheless, saw sanction given for the teaching of religion by the regular classroom staff, two half-hour periods every week, with revised British texts, for elementary grades. Specific pupils would be exempted on written request by parents, teachers on their own request, and entire schools by petition of Education Boards.

In a spirit of "good will," the original texts had been submitted to me for recommendations within two weeks. I would not undertake the analysis in such a brief time, but my reply made one cursory comment: the textual material revealed a strong Christological slant and a version of the Crucifixion story whose "cumulative effect on pliable minds might be disastrous."

On July 19 and 26 I received galley proofs; again, the government invited suggestions. The deadline? August 7!

Now my answer was categorical. Any participation on my part in preparing textbooks might be construed as acceptance in principle of public-school religion. This I would not concede. Furthermore, I was disturbed by a statement in the preamble.

> *The Scriptural interpretations are to be non-sectarian. . . . They will be confined to those expressions of the Christian faith upon which all Christian denominations are in substantial agreement.*

Apparently, the educational authorities regarded that statement as an assurance; to me, it contained a flagrant contradiction. "Non-sectarian" in one sentence was "confined to the Christian faith" in the next. Were the terms interchangeable? Was I to believe that "non-sectarianism" can be achieved within the borders of Christendom, by a concordat among Presbyterians, Methodists, and Anglicans? Then Buddhists, Moslems, or Jews need not be considered or consulted. In the view of the Ontario Department of Education, they had no status. Therefore, "Religious Instruction in the Public Schools" is actually "*Christian* Instruction in the Public Schools." Calling it that would free the classroom majority from the temptation to see themselves as the exclusive defenders of religion, and would be more honest.

The attempt to establish a universal Christian interpretation of Scripture for the school children of Ontario, in which endeavour, I presumed, Catholics and Unitarians had been invited to share, was laudable, and I appreciated the opportunity given me to help the Department implement its stated objective to teach the "Christian way of life." In justice to my colleagues of the Christian clergy, however, I begged leave to express confidence that a rabbi was extraneous; they were quite competent. . . . The letter mailed, I sat in the sun, at a rented Sturgeon Point cottage, to study the textbook for Grade Four.

The mood and content of the original English base had been scarcely touched. Not a single verse from the Hebrew Bible headed a chapter; Pilate became a Roman patrician driven by Jewish vindictiveness and chicanery; the Nazarene's tenderness was contrasted with the bitter legalism of his people; gratuitous and unwarranted slurs were heaped on his ancestral faith.

I asked myself if Christian trust and love *had* to be indoctrinated by calumnies against Judaism that encouraged distrust and hostility. On Hallowe'en the year before, a ten-year-old Jewish boy had been robbed of his apples and pelted down the street with "Christ-killer" ringing in his ears. I found him sobbing on my doorstep. Could not the life of Jesus be inspiring without a luridly inciting account of his death? Jews – as well as Unitarians, Buddhists, agnostics, and atheists – contribute tax levies for the maintenance of public education. Surely a minority need not pay to have itself defamed!

The symbiosis of church and state seemed too cozy! Zealous churchmen would obtain from the state large captive audiences inaccessible to the ordinary Sunday school, and an efficiently operated, adequately financed machinery of religious training; the state would have the gratification of doing something for God. And Christian superiority would be authenticated by the massive prestige of a public teacher turned Christian apologist, whom the child exalts as repository of truth.

Jewish parents were being forced into a choice of two images; their children squirming in classroom for two half-hour weekly periods, or spotlighted as wilful, lost dissenters. In the current obsession with emotional adjustment, many might prefer the squirm – although its effect can be worse. Undoubtedly many Jewish youngsters, above all when they are an impotent minority, would beg parental consent. Will an impressionable Christian youngster rationalize the technical right and moral duty of a non-Christian to skip the half-hour? Will his impressionable Jewish counterpart be unassailably immune to indoctrination?

The Drew Plan, I reflected, was born centuries ago, with an established church, when pre-Christian Rome exacted conformity to its state divinities as a safeguard of the state's internal order. Christian Rome, forgetting the catacombs and its own martyrs in the Coliseum, continued the pernicious notion that political stability required an official creed. One of the first laws of the Christianized Roman Empire visited death on Jews who penalized back-sliding converts to Christianity and on Christians who dallied with "that evil sect" or attended its assemblies.

In the United States the age-old coupling of church and state had been broken by a clear Constitutional prohibition. Canada, in that respect at least, was not a carbon copy of the United States, either in law or precedent. It had never really relinquished the British tradition of Establishment. What I had read about the history of Ontario's public-school system led me to fear that Anglican churchmen in Toronto nursed the dream of a state alliance already enjoyed by Catholicism in Quebec – and I could not have foreseen that, years later, the Anglican General Synod, without a dissenting vote, would reaffirm its demand for the use of public schools to teach the Christian view of life and God, or that the most widely heard individual voice in the United Church, the Reverend J. R. Mutchmor, would wonder whether much attention need be paid the two-or-three hundred thousand Canadian Jews in regard to statutory observance of Sunday.

On completing my perusal of the Grade Four textbook, I wondered whether an American newcomer to Canada could ardently espouse the principle expressed by the Baptist Churches of Virginia in a memorial against public-school Bible reading: "If the conscience of the majority is to be the standard, then there is no such thing as the right of conscience at all. There are some rights even the majority cannot take away; of these, the most sacred is the right of conscience."

The Baptist statement was succinctly written, and cogently reasoned. Once a dominant denomination reaches into the schools against the wish of weaker faiths equally taxed for their support, the power of right is replaced by the right of power and the primacy of conscience by an adding machine. *That* manifesto could be planted on *both* sides of the border!

What was the role of school in a democracy? To help the young learn, think, and understand, not to indoctrinate. Even in the prosaic domain of verified data the teacher merely indicates that such is the way to spell, or count; the pupil may be *expected* to give assent, he does not *have* to. How much the more does this principle apply to the unverifiable abstractions of religion?

The public school functions horizontally to level children of every faith – and none – into a fellowship demonstrated at the very moment of the Drew Plan's inception by Canadian youth in overseas combat; church and home operate vertically, to root the child deep into the sub-soil of his own religious heritage. "Fraternity" emerges from "liberty" and "equality." Under the Drew Plan the morals of the in-group that takes the course are jeopardized by smugness and the morale of the out-group by insecurity.

I recalled the answer of a schoolmaster to a question put to him by L. P. Jacks, the noted British author and educator: "Where in the timetable do you teach religion?" "All day long!" the master replied. "In arithmetic, by accuracy, in language by learning to say what we mean, in geography by breadth of mind, in astronomy by reverence, in the playground by sportsmanship – in kindness to animals, courtesy to servants, good manners to one another, and truthfulness in all things."

Sometimes I suspected the most lethal ruse in the Communist campaign against religion would be to encourage its definitive classification as a school course. When chemistry, for example, is only a lab-exercise and a dry textbook, the pupil fails to perceive its ceaseless ferment in the cells of his own body. If religion must have a place in the curriculum, let the teacher expound the basic tenets of *all* faiths, accurately and dispassionately, and emphasize that the individual's choice is an unassailably private prerogative. To convey the idea, even unintentionally, that a prescribed textbook Scripture has the *imprimatur* of God, while the doctrines of others, not only of stubborn Jews, but of the benighted hordes in Asia and Africa, are false, is not only exploitation of the schoolroom, but an affront!

This was not the first time I had encountered clerical misuse of public education. In 1942 I helped circumvent a legislative attempt to include Christian teaching in the school curriculum of Denver – and was rewarded with a warning from Monsignor Hugh McMenamin. Catholics are "the greatest defenders of your people throughout the world," he wrote me; actions such as mine would provoke them to "retaliate"!

The priest was a distinguished leader of the church, and the founder of Brotherhood Week; he and I enjoyed a warm and cordial friendship. The recollection of his scowling letter – an unwarranted and unwonted gesture of intimidation – should have alerted me to the dynamite-potential in Christian feeling.

On March 12, 1944, nevertheless, I flung a burning brand into the study halls and vestries of staid Toronto by denouncing sectarian public-school religion. Although initial hurrahs came from anti-Catholic societies which sought allies to further a fierce campaign against Roman Separate Schools, private education-experts, albeit gingerly, soon joined me; Unitarians shouted "infringement of religious freedom" and the English and History Teachers' Association condemned the Drew project as "contrary to the spirit of free inquiry" and conducive to the "sinister growth of religious and racial prejudice"; Protestant pastors vehemently defended it, with the exception of two Baptist Conventions, a Lutheran Synod, and a United Church General Council whose resolution against "State control of religion," after heavy support, was subsequently reversed. An Association for Religious Liberty improvised to underscore the threat to democratic institutions was summarily tagged as "Communist-inspired." The Honourable Mitchell Hepburn, Opposition leader in the Provincial Legislature, sufficiently overestimated the strength of my crusade to make it the spearhead of a lack-of-confidence motion which the Conservative government beat down with the aid of half the CCF contingent, that party having decided in caucus to effect a neat straddle.

After the political brouhaha, I submitted the matter to the Canadian Jewish Congress. The more pacific element in Jewish communal leadership – among them the elders who had no children in school – shook its head. "Our position here is not strong enough for your American brand of militancy, and this business is explosive," it explained. "If they want Christianity in their schools, let 'em have it!"

Jewish spokesmen in the United States were dallying with a proposal to release children from classrooms for religious instruction in their respective churches and synagogues, and other devices, not to prevent sectarian privilege, but to ensure equal teaching privileges. Even New York's organizational brass leaned toward co-operation, not controversy, and braced itself for a homeopathic dose of public-school religion. Within a year after I had sounded the trumpet in Toronto, American Jewry realized that even "Released Time," resembled a little bit of pregnancy. Since then the battle has engulfed the country.

My retort to conservative counsel plumbed deeper than considerations of strategy: "Compromise will earn only contempt from the *goyyim*. If you *want* to be treated second-class, act that way. I trust the Canadian people. Besides, we owe something to our kids!"

On September 19, 1945, as Chairman of the Public Relations Committee of the Canadian Jewish Congress and B'nai B'rith, I appeared before the newly created Royal Commission on Education armed with a brief, which combined the research of a Congress leader, Archie B. Bennett, Edward E. Gelber, and experts in Canadian history. The brief listed a random sampling of the spate of errors in the textbooks and quoted British ecclesiastical bodies, among them the Church of England, against government interference in religion. Printed copies were made available to many American groups who requested the guidance it offered in their expanding struggle. Along with the brief, I presented a pamphlet on the widely heralded Springfield Plan to foster religious and ethnic brotherhood in the schoolroom, and *One God*, a handsome book which described with meticulously balanced enthusiasm the respective doctrines of Catholic, Protestant, and Jew.

My address prior to the brief surveyed the areas of conflict between school religion and democracy; it went unchallenged. The verbal exchange after the brief unleashed a barrage from the Chairman's dais so inquisitorial that a Gentile waiting in the wings to make a submission on art classes phoned to apologize for Christians and the Canadian people.

The Chairman took occasion to "remind" me that the province of Ontario had been hewn from the pioneering piety of Christians who were determined to transmit their treasure trove to future generations despite the interference of "newcomers." His thrust almost pinned me helpless to the wall. I rallied my resources. It was parry, or be bulldozed into impotence! The piety of his forbears, I assured the Chairman, was all the more notable since their religious nurture had been limited to home and church, without the edification provided by public-school half-hour classes in textbook Christianity.

The Chairman "informed" me that Canada was a Christian nation under the Crown. I countered that Jews would never need to defend their children in a land whose policy matched its Christian preachment. For a technical demolition of his reference to the

Crown, I summoned to my side the Research Director of the Canadian Jewish Congress. His lecture on the Crown in Canada and its irrelevance to an official religious establishment was so brilliant and conclusive that the Chairman withdrew the "Crown" allusion, even denying that he had voiced it.

The Chairman drew analogy between my charge of segregation and the absence of Jewish boys and girls from class during their Holydays. "They segregate themselves! If being different is proper on those occasions, why not for two half-hours a week of religion?" There is another form of "difference," I replied, between voluntary occasional absence in deference to personal religious commitment and government-compelled, morally compulsive, regular absence from sectarian teaching installed for the benefit of the majority. In one case, a child stays home to practise his own faith there and in synagogue, where it belongs; in the other, he must be tough-minded enough to stay away from religion in the classroom, where it does *not* belong.

The Chairman was "astonished" to hear me quote the sayings of "imaginative" children who tell mummy that Gentile classmates accuse them of not believing in God because they don't "go to religion." I conceded that pigtail reporting might fall short of unimpeachable validity. But no adult could impugn the validity of the observation that non-Christian children were being subjected to psychic pressures which a Commission representing all the people of Ontario should wish earnestly to examine. Therefore, a panel of psychological experts might analyse the effects of the religion course on all the children exposed to it. I would abide by its findings!

The brief had alleged that religious instruction would create a moral dilemma for teachers by luring them into unintentional presentation of personal bias and experience. The Chairman "congratulated" me on the brief's lachrymose solicitude. He was "quite confident" in the teachers' ability to take care of themselves without rabbinical paternalism.

I emphatically disavowed mistrust of the teaching profession – but realistic estimate of clashing theological pressures, and my frequent conversations with teachers who had exacted a promise of secrecy, pinpointed many areas of inner tension. As Dr. W. E. Blatz, an expert acclaimed by all Canada, reminded us, "Teachers are only human, and inevitably inject personal views into Scripture interpretation." Some had already manifested inability to resist ingrained missionary fervour. Jewish children are still prize candidates for salvation. Suppose an instructor is an agnostic. The Drew Plan strews stumbling-blocks on the path of any teacher who believes much more, or much less, than the text prescribes. Increase in newspaper ads for Protestant teachers illustrated the inevitability of a doctrinal test. (Seventeen years later, a General Synod of the Anglican Church would call for "more Christian teachers," to counteract the non-religious who might "pervert a pupil for this life and beyond!")

The Honourable Chairman can scarcely deny, I ventured to predict, that religion is not a scientific technique; its realm is the impalpable world of faith. To deal with it in a single individual, as every clergyman knows, requires tact, kindliness, patience. All the pedagogical paraphernalia of normal school would not arm a teacher for the diverse family backgrounds and creeds of an entire class. The Ontario Education Association repeatedly deplored the inadequacy of many teachers for the three R's, due to personnel shortage, lowered academic requirements, and the constant proliferation of new subjects. Misgivings about the complex and delicate subject of religion are not a reflection on the teacher's competence.

The Chairman found it "unbelievable" that a Jewish rabbi aimed to deprive the public schools of their character-building value, in view of Nazism's corruption of German youth. I called history to witness. The *Hitler-Jugend* who grew up to swagger in SS uniforms and bash out the brains of other children had received generously subsidized religious indoctrination from government-paid clergy in a state-supported church. Had that church not been integrated for years in the state's orbit, Hitler's seizure of the educational system, keystone of his entire paganizing program, in all likelihood would not have met with such easy success. The schools of Fascist Italy and Spain were steeped in religion!

I surmised that the Chairman would find similar government subsidization enchanting also in Ontario, albeit the sectarian beneficiary would be synthetic Protestantism rather than Catholicism. Would religion be strengthened by such dependence? And if one faith receives help from the state, why not others? Jewish parochial schools, I confessed, were anathema to me – but Protestant public schools could make them attractive.

A school dedicated to neutrality need not be atheistic. There are basic truths common to all creeds which can be conveyed without violating anyone's scruples. Collaboration to define them might set a better example for youth than strife about classroom propaganda!

The Chairman cocked no more avid ear to this proposal than to my previous one anent a panel of psychologists. Instead, he challenged me to deny the usefulness of religion in the war on juvenile delinquency. I accepted! That was precisely my contention. If the Honourable Chairman meant formal religious training, there was ample evidence of its futility. Psychologists and social workers can discover no link between Sunday school and behaviour, between Biblical knowledge and conduct. Academic sessions in religion would produce not a God-centred generation, but a gaggle of grinning savages who identified God as a classroom bore. And a barrier between home and school, parent and teacher, one kind of pupil and another, would not engender the belongingness and brotherhood that bulwark youth against anti-social attitudes.

Besides, should the moral anti-toxin concocted with public funds be earmarked for Christians only? Are not Buddhists, free thinkers, and Jews entitled to safeguards for *their* children? It would be discriminatory to let minority youth flounder in a morass of wickedness – unless the Commission at the outset tacitly assumed that non-Christians are unworthy or incapable of redemption.

The duel between the Chairman and me never descended from a plateau of urbanity; it was sword-play rather than scuffle. Despite the undercurrent of contentiousness, we manoeuvred according to the Queensberry-Chesterfield code of lethal courtesy. The following

Saturday, Ruth and I attended a reception given by the French Ambassador. Several times, as we casually cruised around the ballroom, Ruth noted that a slight, impeccably groomed "diplomat" seemed to be drawing closer by slow and almost imperceptible degrees. At last I ended the encircling tactic so that the hesitant hunter might "accidentally" apprehend his quarry.

"Ruth, meet Mr. Justice Hope, Chairman of the Royal Commission. I presented that brief a few days ago, remember?" A courtly bow, a smile – and the Chairman turned to me.

"I gave you a rough time, Rabbi. Sorry!"

"Perhaps! Although I didn't have the benefit of a public-school course in Christian ethics, Mr. Justice, we can overlook it." And the Chairman grasped my hand.

Camouflage and persiflage are not normal weapons in religious strife. Snarling about God can be bare-fanged to the degree of one's devotion to Him. The two contestants about public-school religion bristled like two scorpions in a bottle. Both camps ostensibly regarded the spiritual health of Ontario's school children as their supreme concern, for which no sacrifice was excessive – except the passion of a hectoring, rancorous hand-to-hand fight which gave youth more ribald amusement than edification.

At a supine Home and School convention the Chair peremptorily closed debate on a resolution upholding the Drew religion program after I had begun to ascend the platform. In announcing the completion of a textbook for Grade Seven on the Life of Jesus according to St. Mark, the Department stated that the teacher would be expected to use "the full power of imagination" – although strict control through rigid adherence to the text had been repeatedly promised. During a Holy Blossom panel discussion, the former Chairman of the Inter-Church Committee on Religious Education in the Schools, whose roster for some reason was never widely disseminated, after eliciting my readiness to help work out a *non*-sectarian school project *about*, not *in*, religion, exclaimed, "Of course, it would be based on Jesus!" – and thereby touched off such a contagion of audience-tittering that I blushed for him. The Gideon Bible

Society, with the Principal's hearty sanction, distributed free Bibles to all the children of a Toronto school, with each pupil's name on the flyleaf in advance, followed by a printed pledge "to lead a life in Christ," and asked them, during a presentation ceremony, to raise hands and promise to read it.

Pastors on a tour of Holy Blossom's magnificent educational building hinted at the advantage accruing to the Jew's alleged wealth, which enabled him to buttress the young soul with the "most modern facilities." Actually, the (overestimated) accomplishments of Jewish youth-training programs rest not on radiant-heated, air-conditioned classrooms but on the creative, constant concern of the best Jewish brains with teaching methods and materials. The average church Sunday school has been mired in the horse-and-buggy age. Only a thorough overhauling can rescue it from the doldrums and preclude the temptation to strangle the church's freedom with a government lifebelt.

"Why not divert some of the money you collect for Home Missions to Sunday school salaries for trained pedagogues?" I sportively badgered an old pastor friend. "You're not catching many Jews anyhow!"

"In your country Israel all pupils are compelled to study religion!" he replied. My chagrin at this oft-repeated charge was a measure of its falsity. Israel inherited ethnic-based schools from the Ottoman and British régimes. Yet it has instituted a public-school system which bars religious dogmatizing of any kind. If Christians, Moslems, or any of the sub-divisions in Jewish traditionalism wish religious instruction, they may set up their own schools with government subsidy. Furthermore, Israel is *not* my country; it is a sovereign nation to which only Israeli citizens owe allegiance, and for which they alone are responsible!

Throughout the latter years of the high-voltage controversy, the Canadian Jewish Congress made numerous constructive proposals, such as postponement of the half-hour religious sessions to the final period of the classroom schedule and a shift of initiative from parents who refuse them to those who want them. Let the written request come not for exemption but for participation – a procedure no more dramatic or complex than petition for a course in Greek or tap-dancing, and entailing no psychological burden for the secure majority.

To every scheme which envisaged a workable agreement, the response from school and church leaders was negative, save one conspicuous proposition: to supplement public-school Christmas observance with Hanukkah. A growing segment of Jewish opinion welcomed the Christmas-Hanukkah axis as a promising augury. In my mind, it was rank opportunism!

I undertook quiet research into the history of Christmas. It dredged up interesting data. To the early Christians birthdays were a sacrilegious pagan rite, unthinkable for man or God. December 25 waited until the year A.D. 354 to be chosen by the Bishop of Rome as the Divine natal anniversary. Thirteen centuries later the Puritans deplored its joyousness, damned the wanton frivolity of carollers, and made December 25 a market-day on which it was forbidden to close up shop or consume mince pies and plum pudding.

Western Christendom has forgotten these austerities or, remembering, dubs them perverse. Christmas is light and laughter, holly and "holyness," cheer and charity. My garrulous Italian barber, in reply to a conversation-making question I put to him, told me one wintry day that he was "not a drinking man" and consequently did not know just what he would be doing come Christmas! Like Bar-Mitzvah, the manger has sunk into a carnival of conviviality.

As Christmas moves from a spiritual to a social nexus, Jews inch toward it. Jerome Weidman, proclaimed by his clique "one of America's finest Jewish novelists," advised American Jewry to celebrate Christmas because "it is a non-sectarian oasis free from the shackling bars of race, religion, poverty, or even strict analysis." That superficial, pontificating indulgence is an insult to Christians who regard the birthday of Jesus as the veritable seed of a religion which portrays and propagates his divinity. Were I a Christian, I would resent cavalier de-Christianization of a pivotal sanctity by one without any prerogative, either in birth, belief, or belonging, to speak in its name, unless I conceived the sanctity to be all things to all people, and I would deem it a doubtful compliment that Jews exchange Christmas cards, cases of Scotch, and congenial office parties.

Synchronized dates make the Christmas-Hanukkah schoolroom partnership convenient; it is also blessed with good intentions. For the Christian, it sticks a thumb in the dyke, to contain the floodtide of secularism. Children in public school can be lassoed by the aura of the Nativity. On the other hand, public-school glorification of the militant Maccabees may counter-balance the glamour of the Christ-child for the children of Abraham. Guerilla commandos slinking down from the hills at Judah's signal, God-inspired spears of a few Jews scattering phalanxes of the tyrant and his vaunted elephants, the exultant cleansing of the Temple, and a miracle – holy oil for the lamps of rededication! What can outstrip *that* child-appeal? Jewish parents could send Bruce and Brenda cavorting off to school during Yuletide with equanimity; Judah Maccabee had sheathed them in armour-plate! The Gentile playmates my own youngsters brought into our home to see the Hanukkah lights and share the eight-fold presents had been thrilled by the Maccabeean legend. Why not bring it to the classroom?

A bedrock principle, however, is not shaken by blandishments. The classroom houses Buddhists, Moslems, non-believers, to whom manger *and* Maccabee meant the psychic disturbance I deplored in Jewish children. Hanukkah puppetry and pageants, cutouts and costumes, streamer ribbons and storytelling would compound the evil. I had opposed religion in the schools – *all* religion!

On Friday evening, December 1, 1950, at Sabbath Service, I delivered a sermon of which every word had been written with candour tempered by care.

Are Jewish pupils embarrassed by massive Christmas observance? I asked. They deserve the benefit of the doubt. One recognizable proof of good will is concern for the plight of minorities too weak for any claim save justice. If a lone non-Christian sits among a thousand who describe themselves as Christian, he must be shielded against spiritual segregation on grounds of religion, which is even less supportable than physical segregation by race. The classroom's distortion into a prize and pawn of competitive clerical interests makes it an agent of cruelty, and of hypocrisy as well, when perpetrated in the name of one who suffered little children to come unto him.

In my boyhood I sang Christmas carols, often substituting words or mere sounds under my breath. That was scarcely an apprenticeship in heroism, but it caused no permanent traumatic injury. In most popular carols, nevertheless, Jesus is the Christ-Messiah, Son of God, Word Incarnate, adored, worshipped and bowed to as King. This constitutes Christian dogma – in song.

Some dedoctrinate schoolroom Christmas by lowering it to a secularized, inter-faith folk festival; others defend it by raising Canada to the level of a "Christian country." If I understand Christmas at all, it is a day hallowed by and for particularistic religion, or nothing – and the most erudite historian would hestitate to defend or define the legal and political ground for affixing "Christian" to Canada. In a world trembling under the premonition of a Third World War, the application of that adjective to *any* nation is meretricious obeisance to the Prince of Peace!

Will Hanukkah in schools cancel Christmas? Not at all! *What is wrong for Christians is not right when shared by Jews!* I would unswervingly resist it! Thus ended the sermon of December 1, 1950.

Members of the Presbyterian Youth League were guests that evening and accepted my invitation to an open forum after Service. I assured them of my desire to hear their views in the same spirit of open-mindedness which prompted them to hear me. The young church people were a balm to my soul. One after another arose to voice appreciative pleasure, despite disagreement, in the sermon's insight and honesty. A Sunday school marm even confessed misgiving about her ability to inhibit an attempt at conversion if presented with Jewish children in a public classroom. We exchanged views about the difference between Hanukkah, which commemorates a national event whose historical import all might endorse, since Maccabeean defeat would have left Judaism too anaemic to beget Christianity, and Christmas, a theological concept alien in essence and context to deep-set Jewish belief. During coffee and cake, Christian and Jew mingled with frank, free-flowing cordiality. It was almost midnight before our Presbyterian visitors took their leave.

"We must do it again!" "A wonderful evening, Rabbi!" "A new path to fellowship, sir!" "Thank you for a happy experience we'll never forget!" "God bless you and your people!" Hours after the stimulation had worn off sufficiently to send me to bed, the ring of those parting words echoed from the Temple corridors into my fitful sleep.

It was the voice of a new-found Presbyterian friend – I recognized it at once – that awakened me. "Excuse me, sir, for calling at this hour. I leave home early for work." I hastened to thank her instead; I had almost overslept an appointment, out of weariness after a memorable evening.

"That's what I'm calling about. I just read the morning paper. Please don't feel badly. Everybody knows what reporters do!" I repeated my thanks and pattered to the front doorstep.

CELEBRATION UNDEMOCRATIC. KEEP YULE OUT OF SCHOOL: FEINBERG. The front-page headline's crisp rhyme was its only excuse, since the demand accredited to me therein bore little relationship to the fair, circumspect digest of my sermon that followed. A bit sensational, I thought, but hardly worth the shy solicitude of that nice girl!

She was more perceptive than I. The afternoon papers rounded up comments, with results dear to any city editor's heart. A clergyman said the rabbi is "shooting off his mouth"; a school trustee was "disgusted with this sort of thing. Canada is a Christian country. If we were to go into Israel or Russia we would not expect them to take their festivals and observances out of the schools because we were there"; another trustee condemned it as "nothing less than nerve for Rabbi Feinberg, who has been treated very well in Toronto, to demand that we drive Christmas out of the schools"; a third and a fourth were "surprised that so intelligent a man should make such a suggestion we live in a Christian democracy"; a Jewish alderman thought I was "ill-advised and unfair"; an Anglican educator ascribed the practice of carol-singing to the explicit and implicit Christian basis of the Ontario school system.

The following Monday three Orthodox rabbis dissociated themselves, in a press release, from "Rabbi Feinberg's personal opinion," deemed the "majority . . . free to operate schools for the best advantage of the greatest number," and dubbed it "absurd to eliminate Christmas from its rightful place in our schools," promptly bringing on themselves the scornful wrath of Yiddish columnists throughout the United States; a synagogue President, who years later sought my endorsement of his provincial Parliamentary candidacy on an *anti*-school-religion platform, predicted that the "ninety-five per cent" (his estimate!) of Toronto Jewry which is Orthodox "will regard this latest outburst of the Reform Rabbi as a joke" and ventured a verdict that "Toronto Jewry has no more right to dictate to the Gentile majority than a Gentile majority would have to change the practices of schools in Israel"; the Rabbi of Toronto's largest Orthodox congregation pronounced Judaism's emphasis to be "appreciation of and respect for the thought and feelings of other peoples"; a prominent Rabbi-official of the Canadian Jewish Congress, with "great concern," designated Congress the spokesman for the Jewish community and promised to have it issue a statement.

In less than one hundred and fifty words, Congress valiantly proclaimed that Jews "look to their Christian brethren in the spirit of this season to wage incessant war on prejudice and discrimination in those areas where they still blight our social and economic life."

During the next few days a turgid stream of smut flowed through the post office to my desk and, with Bowdlerized language and tenderized blood thirst, to the letter columns of the press, while invective and threat hissed through the telephone wires to my home and family. A newspaper editorial deplored the Rabbi's "extraordinary error of judgement," condemned "anti-Christian" as no less reprehensible than "anti-Semite," invested the majority with "an absolute right to hold its own beliefs and express them in its own way," doubted whether "any word or act in years will have done more to stimulate the religious prejudice we all wish removed," described it as "both significant and encouraging that other leaders of the Jewish community have repudiated Rabbi Feinberg's suggestion" – and detoured the entire point of my sermon. Throughout those days of fury not one commentator asked me for a copy of the full text of the sermon, which I had mimeographed in the expectation that critics would want to read it before they ran into print.

The editor of the *Canadian Jewish Standard* did not indulge in hyperbole when he defined the general condition as a "seething cauldron of Christian fury and Jewish fear." Had racial memory been brought into play, it might have led Spadina Avenue back retroactively into terror-crazed Rhineland ghettos during the Crusades. My friend Bill Jenkins, the Unitarian minister, said the lynching lacked only a tree and a rope.

Ride out the storm? I might have succeeded, save for desertion by colleagues, Jewish communal leaders, and panic-stricken co-religionists who regarded my injection of the issue into the Christmas period, perhaps correctly, as impolitic, ill-timed, and tactless. One would have thought my sermon had created – instead of merely revealing – anti-Semitism! The Board of Trustees of Holy Blossom did not at any time exert coercive pressure; on the contrary, the Temple left me to fight it out with my own conscience, in fidelity to a free pulpit and with comprehension of the principle involved.

It had been a laggard Christmas shopping-season. A disenchanted reporter divulged his opinion that "a Jewish storekeeper or two was worried about the fray's influence on his commercial prospects." I observed no direct evidence of such venery. The drama was not complex at all! A considerable number of Christians were infuriated by an apparent attack on Christianity, the feral clamour stampeded Jews – and I stood alone.

"Call it off! Put an end to it!" parents began to implore. And they told me of Jewish children mocked, shunned, occasionally struck and running home in fright. At the Forest Hill Village

School, the loudspeaker announced to all classrooms that carols would be sung in the assembly, but those pupils who did not wish to participate could stay behind – and Jonathan Feinberg was the only one who stayed. . . . I could not bring myself further to entangle the very children in whose behalf I had girded myself for battle, or to thrust my own into the maelstrom.

On December 8 "An Explanation," which I read at Temple Service that evening, appeared over my signature in the Toronto newspapers. Both afternoon papers published laudatory editorials; one declared that "An Explanation" indicated the "fine spirit of the man . . . who had been noted for his advocacy of fellowship among the creeds," the other predicted that "in the spirit of Christmas" which I had "invoked," my position would be "viewed with understanding." The *Jewish Standard* said the Explanation "gave evidence of a humility which would better have become those Christian clergymen who pilloried the rabbi without making any effort to understand his remarks or their religious background."

It was from men to whom I might have looked for support that I received the final coup de grâce of disillusionment. Ugly words – "Retraction!" "Recant!" "Weakness!" "Surrender!" – began to filter in to me through the circumambient haze. Usually they were dispatched on their errand of moral compensation by fair-weather liberals and Jewish nabobs who had fled the fray at the first smell of smoke.

I had spent an entire night formulating the statement – after a chat with a Gentile publisher whose friendly advice I importuned. Not a syllable spelled surrender! It expressed regret, not at believing what I continued to believe about Christmas and religion in the schools, but at believing what I could not continue to believe, namely, that the issue might be rationally debated in the current atmosphere of a laboriously Christian city. It was not retraction, but retreat from the immediate front – to fight again! In any case, "An Explanation" exorcised the demons of disputation like magic; overnight the tempest ended.

The "carol affair" chalked up an impressive list of wounded. Among them were "inter-faith brotherhood," shockingly fragile under stress; "first-class Jewish citizenship," with enough self-respect, and respect for Canada, to presume that rights must be defended; the vestigial hope that Christmas rites will be banished from public schools in North America, *l'affaire Feinberg* having already become a classic example, for Jewish defence agencies in Canada and the United States, of romantic quixoticism; my own reputation for perspicacity and foresight; the power of the Christian spirit, temporarily overcome by the spirit of Christian power.

All three Toronto papers which pounded the tom-tom for my carol execution and upheld public-school religion now look askance at the Drew Plan. In the United States the Jewish dalliance with cavalier disregard of church-state separatism which gave my 1945 brief a radical tinge has given way to consistent, courageous attack.

Did the carol crisis irreversibly pervert my pro-Canadian bias? Not at all! The Gentile man-in-the-street did not let me down; it was rather the man in the pulpit and at the editorial desk – the whilom keepers of his spiritual and intellectual conscience. Christian misleadership profaned Christianity in defence of Christendom against a one-man protest necessitated by Christ's teaching. The clerical sin lay in omission; I did not hear a pastor anywhere admonish his flock to practise tolerance of error – much less understanding of its origin. Inasmuch as Greek Orthodox and Roman Catholic priests hurl imprecations and fists at each other in Bethlehem's Church of St. Catherine on Christmas Eve, I should not have been overwhelmed by the passive indifference of clergymen to the tide that surged against a solitary unbeliever. . . .

A decade later, just before Christmas, I chanced to read an article by the columnist Max Lerner which reopened the sluice gates of that fateful week and released its full impact again upon me. Lerner contrasted the humble passion of Jesus for the defeated with Christmas – New Year orientation around victory.

I looked about me in Toronto. Lights, tinsel, Yuletide trees, the birth of glad tidings, the entrance into history of a promise of salvation! They are surely an authentic paean to the Christmas message of man triumphant. But Lerner was right! Occidental adulation of success has blended the Nativity with Horatio Alger. Around New Year's Day, I reflected, there will be blurbs about the successful: man of the year, woman of the year, the most this and the biggest that, the best-dressed, the richest, the prettiest – prize-winners in a society which has eyes and ears only for the fleet-footed after fame and scarcely a nod for those not brash enough to seek it. . . . The truth then burst on me like fireworks. *There* lies the abnormality of the 1950 carol *shlimazl*!

The antithesis between Christmas, glorious efflorescence of personality, and Jesus, consort of the submerged who hunger even for a name! The birthday has supplanted him who was born.

During the Yule season of blue-ribbon awards, I salute the broken ones with broken dreams, the sensitive *shlemiels* incapable of soldierly discipline or ruthlessness, the absentminded misfits more interested in a chat with a nobody than a charm-school exercise with Mr. Somebody, the "queer ducks" despised and pitied by the organization-man jingling his fringe benefits and pension certificate, the fool who could not schedule his time and make every hour count and practise the rules and learn how to make the right friends and say the right things to the right people.

Does my mind turn toward the defeated every Christmas because my memory turns back to my own defeat at Christmas in 1950? Be that as it may, at every Yuletide fireside of tinkling glass and togetherness I would drink a toast to those whom Jesus would have honoured because they are unimportant, "for they shall inherit the earth"; who don't amount to anything, "for they shall be comforted"; who are naught in the sight of their fellow men, "for theirs is the kingdom of heaven"; who are segregated by colour or creed from the haunts of the respectable and the righteous, but united indissolubly with all mankind in Divine Love.

Will the little people inherit the earth? Will it be worth inheriting if the big people continue to rule it? I don't know. I *am* sure, however, that Jesus did not exclude little people from compassion, that he would protest the public-school observance of his birthday according to the majority-minority guide line of politics, and that, had he been in Toronto during the carol affair, "the Rabbi" would *not* have stood alone. . . .

Death

IN Quebec City, at the start of an auto-jaunt to the Gaspé Peninsula, I received a phone call: Sally, my youngest sister, had cancer.

Only two weeks before, Ruth and I had visited her little family in Pittsburgh. Under a special ex-soldier's mortgage plan, they had scrounged enough to buy a tiny house, even on Al's modest salary as lawyer in the Veterans' Administration. And Sally had just given birth to a second son. But the rouge did not hide her pallor or stifle an involuntary groan. The young doctor said it was all post-parturition and hypochondria after a difficult confinement.

Sylvia's report to the Chateau Frontenac was terse. Yellow

jaundice in our sister's complexion finally lodged her in hospital for surgery. Too late! "It" had metastasized to the liver. The prognosis in such cases was usually about eighteen months. I slammed down the receiver and gritted my teeth. "Car-ci-no-ma! Lilting Latin syllables! It could be one of those love songs I used to croon on the radio!"

Fate disdains the brave dreams we thrust into the void like infantry slogging in the mud against a lava tide. Nothing dramatizes our tragic helplessness like the malignant cells that crouch unseen and sinister in human vitals, and multiply until they overrun and smother and throttle the bastions of life. Before Sally, the principal figures in my version of the drama were stricken friends and members of my congregation; I had sympathized, tried to divert and encourage. In a trice the clichés laden with anodyne for others echoed like the mocking chatter of monkeys I remembered from a childhood storybook.

The cosmic playwright's grisly opus had the authentic ring: Prometheus-man chained on a rock and struggling to soften a blow he cannot deflect. We contrived feather darts of futility to aim at the black engulfing zero: conversations muted, letters intercepted, medical explanations manufactured, massive, stupefying sedation administered so that she wouldn't know; a specialist brought down from New York's Memorial Hospital, "if only to relieve the pain"; David and Norman housed with a neighbour when their prattle and gurgling could no longer ignite a smile in a mother's eyes.

On a harried visit to the bedside, I found Sally deep in motionless brooding. Did she know? Her eyes probed mine for a clue to the never-ending misery, their fixed stare haunted my sleep. The native, irrepressible alertness of her perceptions twisted a devastating screw, as moaning subsided to a barely audible whimper, and limbs grew slack with weariness. When I saw her face shrivelled with mental and physical suffering, I buttonholed the surgeon.

The wrinkles around Dr. Sternberg's eyes were a character reference. He seemed to realize why I had come. Couldn't he do *something*? Wouldn't a copious swift needle end her agony and the demoralization of those who watched and wept? Suppose he were to operate? "Rabbi, I feel for all of you, believe me!" His hands flapped out in a racial gesture. "But I can't take out her liver!" From that day, I could never negotiate a "righteous" posture against euthanasia. It is not a theological question to be resolved by priests alone, but a human problem, for the psychologist, physician, poet, and involved family!

When nature lowered the curtain at last, love outspoke prudence, and I conducted the funeral service. In Pittsburgh, at a brief ritual of courtesy for Sally's suburban neighbours, I had the assistance of a young colleague. In Bellaire, I sought an emotional brake in draughts of whisky.

Our parents had been buried from home and synagogue – both bare of pain-muffling adornment. The mortuary parlour was bathed in a soft haze that blurred the sharp edges of consciousness; it seemed to undulate with dulcet-hued draperies, alcoves for meditation, a memory book for solace-bringing signatures, and the expertise of kind Christian men to whom comfort was commerce and art. But no anaesthesia could blind me to keening, shawled crones, faces carved and furrowed by the thrice-told dolour of the poor – my mother's friends who had gathered to sorrow with her children. Abe, "the Rabbi," had returned home to add a postscript. My abdominal muscles heaved and jerked, and I signalled brother Dave for the brimming cup he held for me. Then Birdie stood with uplifted hands before the coffin. "Why wasn't it me?" Her cry brought me down. Wracked with sobbing, I thrust my face into the brocade backdrop.

At the wind-blown, freshly dug sod of a grave in Agudas Ahim cemetery, the Feinbergs squeezed a drop of comfort; Pop and Mom were already buried there and did not see their youngest die!

The next day swam in Indian summer. Nature's timetable does not do handsprings for a man's mood! I plodded glumly along Winding Hill Road, glance riveted downward on withering grass and swirling dust, but thoughts directed to the Inscrutable One Up There who withers dreams and turns man to dust.

"Rebel against what can be changed, resign yourself to what

can't, and be wise enough to know the difference." A fine sermon text – and I had often used it! There were other placebos! Spinoza names no theme less amenable to rationalization than death; Buddha turned from a funeral cortège to meditate himself into Nirvana; George Babbitt turned every frenzied second to practical account; a Chinese proverb warns us to keep the birds of sorrow from building nests in our hair; Cyrano shrugged, and commended to our attention the falling leaves: "a little way from branch to earth, a little fear of mingling with the dust, yet they go down gracefully"; the Talmud cautioned against an overdose of grieving. All very pretty – but Sally's descent from the tree of life made no sense, no whit or tittle of contact with a merciful God.

How often I had tried to console others! In New York it was psalm and prayer between the potted palms on a well-padded platform, sundry hypodermic phrases from a card-index file, treacle poems, stock gobbledygook in preachers' anthologies. What else could be done, since in most situations I had never seen deceased or mourners? When I could visit the "late residence" of a Temple member, I sought a key to the person of the "dear one" who had left it: a book with pencilled notes in the margins, an armchair with a sitter's imprint, a gold-handled comb, a tricycle, kewpie-doll – to retouch a portrait for the eulogy.

Unreined tears and ritualistic minutiae could be a vent for guilt no less than grief, I knew. Yet there was no health nor healing in repression; capping the spring of sorrow as though it were a wild oil-gusher made the lifestream a stagnant pool of self-torment. As to the traditional observances of mourning, I abhorred a necrophilic theology which forsakes reason and common sense to embrace auto-intoxicating and bromidic balderdash at the death-gong. Turning mirrors to the wall, cutting the garment (later reduced to the symbolic snip of a tie, then to a pinned black ribbon), sitting unshod and unshaven (for sackcloth and ashes), placing stones on the grave (or pennies on the eyes), a primitive pine box and "holy" shroud, could no more alter the destiny of the deceased than a bronze coffin, blanket of roses, concrete vault, or marble mausoleum. Both were hollow artifacts – one of fear, the other of vanity. Sometimes I was almost harsh with people who belittled ritualism and yet begged to be told the exact minute for candles and mourning-periods, how many males were required for a quorum at the home services and whether neglect of daily *Kaddish* would doom their dear one's soul. My answer was both honest and evasive: "Whatever you feel in your heart – is right!"

Now I realized that death's presence permits no one to be sophisticated. All need the therapy of the deed, a cleansing act, something to do other than be petrified into a Job on a dung-heap. Like the specialist from New York's Memorial Hospital whom I entreated to see Sally in Pittsburgh, the ritualistic trivia were puny penetrations into the void – but they might loosen and lessen the tyranny of pain.

Long-range planning in the post-bereavement period is bootless; one should aim at each day as it comes. Such a limited objective can utilize a tallow candle in a glass calculated to burn twenty-four hours. My brothers and sisters fled the cell blocks of their individualized grief into the more spacious courtyard of past generations, where they clasped hands with our parents. It was the ancient rituals of mourning that linked them all, and Sally, into a fellowship of faith. Even Birdie, the eldest, who had been assistant mother to Sally, unwound the tight, strangulating coil by busying herself with the mourners' meal. But *my* plight was irretrievably personal, between the Mystery and me – and I had recited the routine so often, for others, that it bore no balm. *Shiva* and the liturgy of memorial left me untouched. Sally was not an "old story" from the past; she was a young mother robbed of present and future; no analgesic emollient could dull that fact!

I reached the place of burial on the sloping crest of Winding Hill that overlooked the Ohio Valley. The brush and tangle of the woods below me now became part of a broad encompassing canvas, forest, sky, river, hills, took each its place in an interrelationship of form and plan. My heartbreak also slipped away from the centre of me and sought place in a grand Design.

Jacob's dream! I had always loved that Bible episode. Alone in the desert, fleeing from Esau, impinged upon by darkness, he made hard stones his pillow and beheld in sleep a ladder to God's throne. Jacob fathered a long procession. Jeremiah, for example, carved Israel's captivity into immortal verses by the waters of Babylon; Dante drew the *Inferno* from the loam of a hopeless love; Beethoven begot the *Fifth Symphony* out of torment; and countless lesser men and women have shaped stress into strength and cross into crown. They did not let the Adversary go without his blessing!

Shall I waste time, I asked myself, devising idle argument to explain the inexplicable or whitewash a world in fief to whim? Better that I should transmute bereavement into some grace of character! My body absorbs things profane – protein, carbohydrates, fat – and they become the play of sinew, curve of bone, hue of hair. Cannot the soul demand a nutritive function and transform the cruel, the agonizing, into noble mood and passion? Even the angels cannot guide blundering earth-children as can one earth-child broken on the wheel! The human spirit of which I am a feeble ray penetrated the distant depths of space to warm them with a God of mercy, and peered into the emptiness of the grave to irradiate it with immortality. But at Sally's day-old grave, I thought the sun and stars had gone, and bottomless nothing stretched above, about and within me. I was desolate.

My mind detached itself in cold appraisal and propounded questions. Does Judaism posit an afterlife? The Pharisees, being human and enamoured of personal identity, specified physical resurrection as a basic article of faith, in a faith not predisposed to supernatural dogmas. Without that tradition, the miracle of the third day would have been spurned by the disciples whose trust made it the rock of the Christian faithful. But normative Judaism never shifted its focus from this world to the next. Death came as despoiler of the life we have, not as escort to life everlasting. Jews don't celebrate wakes, or even dream, much less try to believe, that a child crushed by a truck was wanted "home" by God the Father. Byron's

Cain, who bellowed a curse on him "who invented life that leads to Death," more accurately echoes the Hebraic mood.

The same regard for the life at hand which made Jews preeminent in medicine from mediaeval centuries when Christendom was exorcising demons until today, convulses them in bereavement. Our sages did not draw maps of golden stairs. They categorically affirmed *Olom Haba** – and also that we may not describe or comprehend it. If they feasted their fancy on leviathan, the great celestial fish to be savoured by the righteous at God's table, it was play, not prediction. The *Kaddish* prayer of memorial says nothing about mortality and man's triumph over it – and everything it says is about the majesty of the God of life and our acceptance of it.

Somehow, somewhere, Sally and Mom and Pop and all the others live. What if only like vapour drawn from the sea, that falls on the mountain peaks and flows down to the sea again in rivulets, or like fireflies of a summer night that flit and flame and merge with the Source that spawned them, or like the irreducible energy of the universe that changes form and feature endlessly through time, peradventure in a series of reincarnations, each according to the virtue of its predecessor, until finally at One with the All?

Somehow, somewhere! I exclaimed to my grief-benumbed spirit. If there be nothing after now – why live? Is it enough simply to *be*, on earth, a little while, and try to leave it better than I found it? I cannot know the answer. Am I privy to God's secrets, when the sun is thirty thousand times larger than the earth, and Betelgeuse, a spark in the Milky Way, three hundred thousand times the sun? Birth was a travail-secret between Mom and me; death will be a secret between God and me. I cannot recall the one nor reveal the other! Science weighs no evidence on either side; Copernicus removed immortality from the realm of evidence; microscope and mathematics are powerless to detect or disprove the chance of man's survival anywhere except on earth. Needing to believe, therefore I may choose.

If the unseen, immeasurable atom can produce the monstrous

* The World to Come.

miracle of nuclear energy, why cannot the vast, immeasurable universe come up with the miracle of man's immortality? But do I really believe that it will preserve the personal trivia by which men are men and not mere clods of chemistry – a spatulous nose, a lisp, a flush among the freckles, the way Sally had of softly crooning? Outside the nature of man I find no clear trace of compassion, and in the cosmos no sensitivity to the human person; only in himself can the human animal find comfort.

Sally wanted desperately to hold on to hope. When beset by high fever, abdominal oedema, debilitating weakness or pain, she accepted every medically false, but morally true, "reason" advanced by her humane physician for the symptoms. The will to believe led her mind to occupy itself with new chintz curtains, a coffee table, a college for David and Norman, Al's promotion – until coma cancelled all. Something unquenchable by the hosts of darkness remained, and whispered, as on the first day of Creation, "Let there be light."

That soul-spark in Sally is Everyman's, and convinces him that he is a citizen of two worlds: the one he loses, of noise and nastiness and dreams deferred, and the one of eternal light – or night, he can't be sure. I was unspeakably *proud* of my species! Of man the creator, who fashioned the Divine Love after the image of his need and cast It into the teeth of the whirlwind and defied the universe to make him snivel! Of man, who called forth courage from his bowels and named it God! . . . Yet, not inconceivably, there may be More!

I gazed down into the ribbon along the river, which was Union Street. I picked out our house, and that of Isabelle Thompson across the road. Yes, that was her name! Her father was a brakeman in the freightyards. One day, almost four decades ago, they brought him home, mangled by a runaway engine. I watched the people walking in and out shaking their heads, the wreaths of flowers, the crêpe hanging on the door, which Jews don't ever have. The gang moved away to the next corner for its game of run-sheep-run, and we were afraid to breathe. The next afternoon after school I tiptoed into Isabelle's parlour and stood thumbnail in teeth before the coffin.

He wore a black suit and looked like a plaster dummy in Herschman's store window, pink and smooth, with an empty sleeve neatly pressed at his side.

For weeks I could think of nothing else. What happens to people when they die? How did we come to be born? Was there ever a time when nothing existed? Where is heaven? Was Isabelle's father looking down and watching all the people and the goings-on and the nice things they said about him? That would be wonderful! I'd like that!

The same questions I asked then I am still asking. Grade school, high school, college, books, the intervening decades – they taught me nothing. Maybe I should stop the yammering, and leave the business to God and concentrate on one world at a time!

My very ignorance may be the seedbed of faith. Suppose I did know! Then God's mind and mine would be of the same substance, on the same level, in the same frame of reference – and the Cosmic Intelligence in charge of things would be itself governed by my limitations. Would I be heartened by the knowledge that the Plan behind the Veil is visible to my ignoble sight, determined by a wisdom comprehensible to my snippet-brain, directed toward a purpose so strait that it can mesh with the ego-centrism of man? To consort with God, I must needs be God. The fact that His mind conceives and plans beyond my ken gives me the right to hope it has something in store for me beyond this life and beyond me.

Divine Design with Divine Deed – must they be equated? Is God's omnipotence essential? Does the significance of the human maggot on the terrestrial crust depend on his Father's almightiness? The Father's earth-domain is a mess! Because he *would* establish love throughout, and can't – or because he *can*, and would not? The ingenuity of man was never more industrious than in the brain-convolutions that devised answers to that one!

From my college days, I have been tempted by illicit liaison with a finite God unable to do everything He wants – not the Lord of Hosts, but a Captain who marches *with us* into a war of the spirit against injustice, barbarism, and non-existence. At the centre of every struggle He stands, unfurling the banner He has inspired us to weave from the fabric of our hopes; every outreach for goodness, truth, and beauty is His to share; when we descend into the pit of agony we are joined by God; as we work, He works with us and, in that work, suffers the sweat of labour, the grime of strife, and the scars and stripes of the wounded. Such a One is more congenial to my need, and perchance to my vanity, than an All-Supreme Emperor on his cloud-canopied throne. His incompleteness reaches out to me more than mine reaches out for immortality.

Do mouldering decay and dissolution entice me? He who fears them dies a thousand times – and I am a coward. Death, after all, is only a piece of the world's order, I remonstrate. Who knows whether it be evil? But in my heart of hearts, a starkly naked intuition lies curled up like a foetus: death is total unconsciousness, dreamless sleep. When humble Socrates said that twenty-five centuries ago, he ascribed his perception to others. "*Some* say," he told disciples. And, being urbane, and yoked to a shrew, he deemed a dreamless sleep "far pleasanter than most of our days." I have neither his humility nor acedia. Every morning, however, when I awaken, I suspect that I have tasted the nihilism of death – and resurrection. Shall I seek confirmation of this truth from other men? I live it nightly. Shall I shout hosanna for that endless sleep to come, "pleasanter" than life? Such a heroic greeting were an empty gesture, bravado without risk, since a day will dawn of no awakening, and without my leave.

Isaiah, Lincoln, Gandhi, Pope John XXIII – did they set the date of their leave-taking? What these endured surely must not make *me* cringe or cavil! Life hereafter? I do not know. But unto him who, like these, has built with a generous spirit, comes weariness, and repose were sweet. I hope I shall be tired enough from fruitful quest, fullness of life, heat in this handful of dust, to lie down without much futile fret.

To live on through illimitable time? That eventually would be brutish boredom, a state of elementary being no more zestful than the inanimate and similarly infinite rock and sand of the desert. I am more concerned with the quality of life than its quantity. It is the transiency of our span that gives it savour. A perpendicular penetration of the self into the marrow before the long horizontal yawn!

Would downgrading death portend the death of religion? It would indubitably lose its bargaining position. The transaction offered by salvationist doctrine, of starry bliss for the ache and hazard of this world, of Divine Love beaming its effulgence in paradise throughout eternity for a few paltry decades of fidelity on earth, can scarcely be scorned by any sentient person – once he believes its major premise, that the doctrine "saves."

Passion for personal physical survival, if not in complete corporeal form, then in some nondescript equivalent, is the concomitant and apotheosis of human egoism filtered through the altruism of Christianity. Eastern religions, Buddhist and Hindu, idealize absorption into an impersonal, timeless, all-pervasive Absolute to which this wretched tellurian abode is only a prelude of training. The death-wish thus is legitimized. In Christianity, the individual is denied liberation from the confines of personality even in death; he sits saved and separate, under the benign gaze of the Father.

Yet, is not every happiness a little death? Felicity arrives with self-erasure, a dimmed-out sense of separation. What is spiritual love if not self-forgetting in contemplation of an adored object or sacrificial service of a cause? What is carnal love if not the mutual annihilation of two egos in a crescendo of togetherness? The tribute to an experience of awe or beauty, that it "took me out of myself," has a profound root in the psyche.

On the other hand, the pursuit of immortality as reward vouchsafed by a supreme All-Powerful One who must be placated and whose Will we must obey, can be an anxious and neurotic affair – particularly when we also itch to postpone the verdict by living as long as possible. And an alert church, to compound the worry, warns us that a final favourable reckoning can be jeopardized by any one of countless peccadillos, despite our meticulous perfectionism.

Pragmatists who reject the proposition of bartering three-score-years-and-ten on earth for an everlasting niche in heaven appear to enjoy no less serenity than a high proportion of clerics who, physicians report, die in fear. The bankers and lords of Victorian England permitted themselves to be beguiled into believing that enthusiastic delight in material success here may be a normal preliminary to, or advance instalment on, an exalted status there, thus striking a favourable bargain with both worlds. It is always risky and nerve-wracking to invest quite everything in the unknown and unknowable.

I am not even sure that the effort to lift oneself across the frontier of eternity is morally healthful. Into whatever realms of fervour and abnegation it may lead, the starting-point is one's self. I have seen fine souls totally preoccupied with their own salvation, prepared to consummate it at any cost to others as well as to themselves, bedevilled by the essentially irreligious obsession with virtue as the price of viability beyond the sepulchre, and progressively devastated by niggling anxiety for the future.

The mediaeval age of faith trifurcated the cosmos into heaven, earth, and hell, like geological strata in downward succession; this "forked radish," man, was the sole ward of the Divine Arithmetician, who reckoned the merit of each of His children and consigned them to the upper or lower realm in accord with strict justice – and mercy, when properly mediated. If mass docility, political stability, and social rigidity are ranked in hierarchical order among the higher virtues, the age of faith can be credited with superb accomplishments. Church and state, having both emanated from the Throne, left no loose threads or rash individual freedom.

The breakup of that rudimentary monolithic structure was a bid to moral chaos, and a crucial watershed in human history. The Christian world displayed the berserk responses of deceived children. No longer scared into reverential obedience by Satan and the threat of losing heaven, rudderless man now repairs to Satanic demagogues and nostrums in the hope of gaining the world.

Personal immortality Beyond may be logically authenticated

by theologians armed with dialectical skill and erudition. Let those who can, retain it as cornerstone and vindication of life! In my opinion, the sooner we scuttle the hell-heaven dichotomy as the basis of morals, the sooner we shall build the desperately needed foundation of a positive, effectual ethics for man.

Strange to say, the fatalism of death was later symbolized, for me, by a bullfight I once witnessed in Nogales, Mexico. A bullfight is a unique sport (or art), in that one of the protagonists, nearly always the bull, must die.

That sunlit afternoon, a snorting half-ton of virility and black flame charged into the ring, on his haunches a rosette in the colours of the ranch he had freely ranged. Within a few minutes, his relentless push toppled horse and picador to the sand. He stood over the prostrate bodies, his horns probing for the horse's soft belly under the padding, while the hapless rider stretched out frozen until frantic cape-waving lured the beast away.

I bled for the bull. The picador's lances weakened neck muscles and brought his head down to help the matador get a sword over the horns; darts were plunged into the shoulders to prevent hooking; he was baited into furious, exhausting charges.

The matador risked death. A sudden gust of wind, by shifting the cape, might expose him; a minute miscalculation of the horn, as he inched close until it ripped the gaudy shirt, could leave him bloody on the turf. Waving the scarlet muletta, the matador goaded his prey as red rivulets trickled over the glistening black hide and eerie screams filtered through dripping saliva.

A deft matador will insert the sword between the shoulder blades and sever the aorta. That day his hand blundered. Instead of falling with appreciative promptness, the wretched bull swayed in bewilderment for several minutes while subordinates on the matador team tried to shove the sword deeper into his vitals. After acutely embarrassing delay, he keeled over, sank to his knees, and lay piteous and panting until one of the gaily bedecked flunkies plunged a dagger into the brain. I was bored and sickeningly self-degraded by the inglorious end of a beast noble in dimensions of power and courage.

Suddenly, under that blazing Mexican sun, a suspicion blazed into my mind like an acetyline torch: the bull may have been the embodiment of man – not of his sexual potency, as the ancient Egyptians thought, but of his impotence! We human beings also engage in proud combat with the unappeasable enemy which has willed our obliteration; we also are lured by the scarlet baubles of hope manoeuvred by a superior intelligence; we also perish, perhaps, for the entertainment of cosmic onlookers who foresaw and savour our predestined doom.

When the bull of Nogales, an iron chain around his horns, was dragged inert out of the arena, a scene from my college reading began to plague me. In Thomas Hardy's *Tess of the d'Urbervilles* it was – a hanged young girl's body and the novelist's comment: "The President of the Immortals had ended his sport with Tess." To stem my maudlin tears, I teased Ruth about the moisture in *her* eyes, and shouted to the attendant for a bottle of beer.

The spectacle harassed me. A bullfight could terminate only in the defeat and death of the inferior animal; that was the rule, and I must needs accept it. But the shame of his degradation, the matador's bumbling ineptitude, which denied the victim a shred of dignity and left a brave warrior-knight naked to ridicule, a dazed and witless hulk slowly sinking under its own weight? That was gratuitous! A bull – and a man – have the right to die with dignity!

I resolved never to see another bullfight; I could refuse to sit among the titillated gods. But what of man? Are we impotent to dignify *his* death? I began to prod myself for an answer.

Does that answer reside in the purveyed dignity of the mortician? As if with ironic intent, a book emerged from the press during the very period of my soul-searching. Four-and-a-half pounds of data on funeral and mourning-rites, past and present, over the world, entitled *The History of American Funeral Directing*. One would conclude that humans have more concern with death than with life. Every culture has accumulated sacred rites of exorcism, placation, and purification to guarantee safe passage for the dead and safety for the living. Mongols anoint the cadaver's head with butter and place a yellow leaf on a prescribed spot seventy-two times; Dahomeans in West Africa dance with the deceased before throwing it into the grave; Tibetans chop it up for the vultures, Sioux Indians bury it in trees, Hollywood deposits the cosmeticized Beloved One, with stylized sentimentality, in a grave-grove coiffured to preview the peace of paradise.

Hocus-pocus for blunting the blow of death is an improvement on the horses-and-chain technique of the Nogales bullring. Flowered scent in a funeral parlour, soft speech of the striped-pants professional, pride-sustaining coffin (when it does not empty the cupboard of an impecunious widow), transfiguration by an agile-fingered embalmer – all are a velvet glove on the iron hand of bereavement. The less confidence the sophisticated have in eternity, the more camouflage they require at interment.

These outer accoutrements provide a slack-jawed drug; dignity for the dead, as for the quick, comes from within and is a radiation of respect for our common humanity. Even the final Silence cannot deafen us to the saga of our race's ascent from the primordial ooze to primate, from fire-worship to nuclear fission, from crude drawings on a cave wall to Shakespeare and Spinoza.

Every rouged corpse is humanity rising out of an oceanic swamp, crawling across the barren earth, climbing underbrush and trees, walking upright on the ground – a biped beast with outsized brain who lost his prehensile fingers to gain memory and hope, whose will to the Perfect began in protozoic scum on a pre-historic stream. Of course there was a master-script by the Life Force, inspirational prompting by the Divine Director, but the dynamic thrust got delivered by the Urge-to-Become inside the little guy on the stage. A blob of decaying flesh need not be cast as the "late deceased" or consigned for heaven to be endowed with dignity. The rabbi's eulogy cannot always make us charitable enough to forget its earth-life faults; the story of evolution *can* make us remember that they are but the clinging residue of skins not quite outgrown, the scars of battles not yet won.

In the beginning all the principal life forms were biologically immortal. A single cell reproduced by dividing into two identical cells, and each half went on dividing. The substance was literally imperishable. When the one-celled organism developed bi-sexuality, the genetic male-female material mingled and produced individual variations which, becoming more diversified, sped up the evolutionary process. Progeny also grew in number, thus enabling nature to widen mutations and hasten the chain of change. Creatures soon appeared that could reproduce not two for one, but millions for two – and death was pressed into the service of life to prevent overswarming and riotous instinctual anarchy. Thus it was sexuality that brought death that in turn brought man the chance to become what he is.

"This is all very interesting in the vast context of biological development," I can hear my friends say. "You wax eloquent, Rabbi! But rhapsodies about man don't help men who have to die. Tell us what just ordinary creatures of clay can do!"

Within limits, a man can make himself death's master. For one thing, he might choose it! Suicide is an expression of this choice declared impermissible by a society which reserves for itself the right to confiscate lives in war and destroy them in legal execution. Self-determined surrender of life for a cause held dearer than life is another expression: on the battlefield for one's country, at the stake for one's faith, in the marketplace or prison cell for one's social ideals. Even Judaism, celebrated for its addiction to the priority of life, counsels voluntary death in preference to idolatry, incest, or murder. Martyrology is a highly creditable shelf in ecclesiastical libraries. On Remembrance Day, what institution tops the church in tribute to those who made the supreme sacrifice?

Also, a man may stretch himself into the future by creating objects of beauty, ideas of truth, artifacts that glow in the cumulative stockpile of human culture, and by founding a family that bears his imprint. He may be mortal; humanity is not. To the degree that what he was and did survives in human memory, he will be renewed.

In the nuclear age, however, this armament against death can be shrunk to a stone hatchet.

The martyr is an identifiable individual – Leonidas at Thermopylae, Socrates drinking hemlock, Jesus on the cross, a Jew burned in the Inquisition. They met death by an act of will and invested it with meaning. How can meaning be drawn from the atomic obliteration of fifty-million Americans and a like number of Russians, and innocent spectators, all reduced by the twist of a key to the same undifferentiated atomic ashes?

What about the permanence of man's works after nuclear holocaust? That which has been fashioned for inheritance will vanish and "leave not a rack behind." The very names of men and women will disappear with the monuments whereon they were inscribed. Historians – if any remain alive and sane – will have no records to explore; the past will dissolve in flame and the future retreat to a start from scratch in a remote radioactive cave. As for freedom and honour, in defence of which men once opted to die, there will not be an ordered society even to mouth them. Nuclear armament, when the spiral race for it bursts out of control, would banish not only life but the testimony of our triumph over death. Under its Damoclean sword we dwell in fear, and die for futility.

All this, however, relates to the big world. My private ingathering back to the Source will be a detail of little import to the mighty forces which make the globe their recreation room. With each aging day my personal involvement in atomic desolation becomes more unlikely; the hour approaches when I shall be released from all anxiety.

What may I presume, nevertheless, to think about *myself* and the "great scandal" (as a grim eschewer of illusions once defined death)? The poet Swinburne celebrated a dour mood by thanking "whatever gods may be That no life lives forever, That dead men rise up never, That even the weariest river Winds somewhere safe to sea." Will the fitful fever of life within me have ebbed enough to share his gratitude? Then only a farthing can be taken from me, namely, the present – the past having gone and the future not yet come to being. If intuition serves me truly and death be dreamless, endless sleep, there can be no pain. If there is Something behind the curtain, I confide it to the Unknown God, in the assurance that He will permit me to explore it, and not punish me for hesitating to foretell His design and fit His unknowable truth into a tidy doctrine. However thickly veiled the attributes or acts of the God I cleave to, He has not built a hell for my penitential torment, and I hope I shall have led a reasonably decent life without its lash.

Should the Harvester dispatch a herald of bad tidings to my flesh and give me time to effect a gradual transfer of residence, I hope I shall use it not for ritual confession like a criminal awaiting the noose, but instead like Harry Cassidy, a University of Toronto professor who employed a cancer-harassed reprieve before his appointment with eternity to counsel students, converse with friends, cogitate about plans for his Department and conserve the morale of his family.

Darkness? I had a foretaste of it during months of confinement at home, when both eyes were covered to trick that corneal virus. Ruth read aloud to me every day. One news story I never forgot was an interview with a twelve-year-old boy blind since birth which she gleaned from the *New York Times.*

"I have darkness around me all the time. I must learn to know that darkness. I think I do know it very well. Sometimes as an enemy, sometimes as a friend." The boy said that – and more. "If I only had one wish, I wouldn't waste it on wishing I could see. I'd wish instead that everybody could understand one another, and how a person feels inside."

When the fight for sight immobolized me in a hospital bed after the corneal transplant and it was dark again, I first whispered that blind lad's astringent courage toward the ceiling, and then a prayer.

In Thy hand, O God, is mine.
Through the shadows I follow after
Thee with perfect trust;
lead me to Thy light and love.

Help me to meet adversity with courage,
to greet humanity with compassion and
to glorify life with the inner vision
which reflects Thine eternal spirit.

Liberate me from fear that I may walk with firm step,
renew my faith that I may work for the brotherhood
of man to whom, as equal children all,
Thou art Father.

Open these eyes to Thy countenance, that I may see the
path whereon to tread, and face each unknown morrow
with head bowed to Thee alone.

Shall I be strong enough to summon such resources for the Eternal Darkness? I wonder! That brief collision with the blackout led me at least to one resolve: if and when I got back to the light of day, I would think and write and speak as I please, without fear or favour. Life is too short for anything else!

In the meantime, the cost of living is seeing others die. Abe Willinsky, a physician friend of mine, once made that translucently wise comment to me after a funeral service. Perhaps the trauma of watching death come to one we love is more painful than our own. Mom, Pop, Sally, Birdie, Jack, Sam, Sylvia, Ruth's parents and Frances and Harry and Joe – the death of each was death in life for me.

For such a crisis, an old Jewish parable may be the prescription. A king owned an exquisitely pure diamond which, by mishap, was badly scratched. None of his diamond-cutters could remove the blemish until a gifted lapidary appeared at court and promised to make the stone more beautiful than before. The man kept his word. He used the scratch to form a stem and engraved around it a lovely flower. . . . The Biblical story of Jacob! After philosophies are drained of solace, it is to Jacob's dream that we repair. With the hand of need, he chiselled from the stone faith and courage – to live!

At the rate of 186,000 miles per second, light rays from the sun reach earth in eight minutes. To travel across the entire "abysm of time" to our galactic shore, they take eight billion years. In one swift severance of a cord, *I* shall have touched the other shore. Shall I then whimper that the universe note my journey more than the flash of sunbeams which move so fast and far? May I only be, like them, a bearer of light – brief, but a candle – and let me but know the darkness as a friend.

Epilogue

THIS book began in a New York hospital room – my own – after a corneal transplant; it ended in a Toronto hospital room – my sister Sylvia's – a few hours before she died. Knowing her death was imminent, and that many days would pass ere I could chisel words again, I drew the floor lamp over a dresser and drove my mind into final revision of minor flaws in the text, while her wasted body heaved with tumultuous breathing.

Like my two other sisters and Ruth's sister and two brothers, Sylvia was taken slowly and painfully, by cancer. Her gentle loveliness deserved such a fate no more than they. But who am I to submit a bill of particulars against a universe that seems to ape Francis Thompson's "City of Dreadful Night," wherein "None can pierce the vast black veil uncertain Because there is no light behind the curtain"? – wherein the most cogent evidence for a next world is the brutality of this one?

I remember a poem by Thomas Hardy warning the souls of infants about to be born against over-eagerness to enter this dismal realm. Yet disaster heroically confronted, rather than tame bliss, may be man's true destiny.

Granted, the Talmudic rabbis said yes, valiantly and vigorously, to life. Also, they conceived it as the shadow of a bird in flight. The rival schools of Shammai and Hillel debated for years whether the creation of man was good or bad, and the outcome was a compromise: it were better had he never been created, but, since he is here, let him do his best.

Perhaps the secret of so sorry and ambivalent a matter lies in detachment; whoever would yield ardour and high expectations to a transient itch on a peripatetic planet, to a journey he did not choose on a rugged road beset with tragedy for a dubious span toward a goal about which he can be sure only that it is dark and enigmatic – had best have a care to his wits.

Maybe life is an end in itself, and the only question is whether I have enough. Then the joys might offer one reason for living, and the sorrows an even better one, since they compel me to live more intensely.

On October 8, 1963, when the family grouped once more at the edge of a gaping grave on Winding Hill and released Sylvia into the growing community of the dead, I might have vibrated like a tuning-fork to the immedicable pain of man's existence. Instead, the shattering trauma of heartbreak was blunted, bitter reflections were banished, and I ceased picking at psychic sores. Why?

The previous day, in the funeral home, a hundred children had raised in my heart the first level of a dyke against the engulfing waters. A hundred children – white, brown, black, big, little, Italian, Slovak, "American," often with mother or grandmother! Sylvia had taught and loved them all, three generations, in Grade One of public schools from one end of town to the other, planting their feet on the path to knowledge of themselves and the world, later guiding them on the tight-rope to maturity. Singly, in tiny clusters, an older sister holding the hand of a younger, they approached her recumbent form that day, whispering how sweet Miss Feinberg looked, and wrote or drew their names in the visitors' book, carefully, so that she would be pleased with their writing, and some moppets so small they had to be lifted up.

The evening after the funeral, Agudas Ahim congregation, in a trim, bright, modern synagogue, shored up the dyke by mustering almost its entire male membership, now barely a dozen, to make a *minyan* for *Kaddish,* and reminisce about Mom once taking in a whole family during a flood, and Pop chanting the all-day Yom Kippur liturgy without a *mahzor* (Holyday prayer-book) – while the surviving "Feinberg boys" sang some of the Hebrew melodies he had taught them.

For almost seventy years our family headquarters was Bellaire. All the cumulative strands of homespun kindliness and affection woven in a small town had coalesced in Sylvia, the last of us to dwell there. During the post-funeral week I mourned not only her loss, but the end of an era – at the moment of its ripe burgeoning and bitter-sweet fruit. The link had broken, the ancestral shrine was desolate.

Then a historic fact fell from somewhere into my mind. Nineteen centuries ago, the Jewish nation was bereft of its Temple sanctuary in Jerusalem. Instead of turning inconsolably toward an emptiness that held no hope, scattered Jewry turned into their local synagogues, which had grown up in the very shadow of the Temple, accompanying the people everywhere, a bastion of faith and beacon of wisdom. The spiritual and moral foundations of the Temple did not totter; they were transferred intact, strengthened, to a new site and to a new, viable form of expression.

Gradually a luminous truth was kindled within me. The far-off sanctities of the past, inherited from my fathers can best be preserved by and in the close-by sanctities of the present, fashioned with wife and children. Ruth has shared every twinge of grief, from the day my mother died until Sylvia sank into the silence, augmenting, with mine, her own familial reverences, and yet walking and working with me toward a future, a fate, a family, exclusively our own. For decades she, then Jonathan, Sarah Jane, and Jerry, with the mortar of loyalty and love, had been building a rampart to stem loneliness and alienation. On its parapet, I can warm the memory of that dyke raised in Bellaire, and gather sustenance, in Toronto, wherever I may dwell, for the continuous struggle against blind circumstance and the blindness which afflicts mankind and me.

Like all men, I am a part of nature, subject to her physical laws, and also apart from nature, no longer in animal harmony with her. Between the poles of that dichotomy I swing – between a mind which visualizes impotence and extinction and a body chained to the common earth-home of all creatures. There is, *au fond,* one dignity and triumph: to welcome this temporary loan from the vast reservoir of vital energy animating all things, from Arcturus to the beastie-virus which will likely kill me – to welcome it courageously, rejoicing in the struggle, and with the comradeship and love for God and man which is but an extension of the comradeship and love with wife and children. Love! Just that simple – and that difficult!

Glossary

Explanatory Note: Based on the Germanic tongue in use at the time of the Jewish migrations from Western Europe during the thirteenth century, Yiddish, itself a colloquialism from the German *Judisch,* became the language of Central and East European Jews. With considerable enrichment from ancient Hebrew, and a smattering of words borrowed from the immediate environment, it is still the common speech of the decimated Jewish folk surviving in Central and Eastern Europe, of immigrants from those lands, and of the older generation in the Soviet Union. Many second-generation American and Canadian Jews, like myself, find their Jewishness invigorated and enlivened by knowledge of this colourful tongue.

Except at the end of a word, the German guttural *ch* has been replaced by *h,* for greater ease of pronunciation.

Afikomon (Heb). *Matzoh* hidden from the children at the Passover supper. The finder was awarded a prize.

Bal-Agoleh (Heb). Wagon-driver, or drover.

Bar-Mitzvah (Heb). "Son of the commandment." A Jewish lad who, on reaching the age of thirteen, may be called to the Law in synagogue, and is thenceforth regarded as an adult responsible to God. The term also has been applied to the initiatory public ceremony at which he traditionally proves his religious competence. Today it is often misused to name the social function subsequent to and celebrating the synagogue ceremony.

Bat-Mitzvah (Heb). "Daughter of the commandment." Induction ceremony for girls, identical with Bar-Mitzvah. A modern innovation, as yet unacceptable to rigid Orthodoxy.

Bes-hamedrash (Heb). House of study. The basic, educational bastion of the Old World synagogue.

Deitschen (Yid). Germans, or German Jews.

Eili, Eili, Lomo Azavtoni (Heb). "My God, my God, why hast Thou forsaken me?" A verse from Psalm 22 spoken, according to the New Testament, by Jesus on the cross.

Erev Shabbas (Heb). Sabbath Eve, or Friday evening.

Etz Hayyim (Heb). "Tree of life." The beginning of a Scriptural passage incorporated into the synagogue liturgy which glorifies the Torah as "a tree of life to those who lay hold of it; its ways are ways of pleasantness, and all its paths are peace."

Fleishig (Yid). Pertaining to meat. Food containing, prepared with, or touched by meat products. Rabbinic Judaism centuries ago interpreted one particular Biblical verse as a ban on admixture of meat and dairy dishes.

Galach (Heb). Priest.

Gefillte-fisch (Yid). Filled, or stuffed, fish. Well-known feature of Jewish cookery, usually associated with Sabbath Eve, Passover repasts, and other social occasions.

Goldene medina (Yid and Heb). Golden land, America.

Golem (Heb). Clod or inanimate clay. One of the numerous terms employed by Old World Jewry to pillory the stupid. Also, an automaton.

Goyyim (Heb). Nations, or Gentiles; adjective, *goyyische*.

Haggadah (Heb). "Account." Home liturgy of ritual and prayer, centring around the Exodus narrative, recited at the Passover supper, or *Seder*.

Hahamim (Heb). Wise men, or sages.

Hahnosas orhim (Heb). Welcome of strangers. Charitable activity in behalf of non-residents, usually the transient or homeless.

Hahzer (Heb). Pig. All food in contact with any pork substance is forbidden by Orthodox Judaism.

Hanukkah (Heb). Dedication. Festival of Lights, commemorating the Hebrew victory, under the Maccabees, over the Syrian ruler Antiochus in 165 B.C., and the rededication of the Temple to the worship of God, thus preserving Judaism. It is marked by the kindling of lights for eight days, and gifts, often of *Hanukkahgelt* (money) to children. The close similarity of date between this Jewish feast and Christmas, according to some scholars, reflects the connection of both with the winter solstice.

Hasidim (Heb). "Pious ones." A Jewish sect which developed in Eastern Europe during the early eighteenth century in reaction against Rabbinic legalism. It exalted emotional expression, enthusiasm, joy, fellowship, saintly leadership, and a pantheistic sense of holiness in all things. Its greatest modern interpreter is Martin Buber. Singular, *Hasid*.

Hatikvah (Heb). "The Hope." Title of a song regarded as the national anthem of the State of Israel.

Hazzan (Heb). Cantor.

Hesped (Heb.) Eulogy at funeral rites.

Hillul Hashem (Heb). Profanation of the Name (of God).

Hometz (Heb). Leaven. Banned during Passover.

Humash (Heb). Five. Here it refers to the first five books of the Hebrew Bible, from which a portion is read at every synagogue service on Sabbaths and holidays.

Huppah (Heb). Canopy under which the bride and groom stand in the traditional marriage ceremony.

Kaddish (Heb). Sanctification. Memorial prayer for the dead recited at every synagogue service, traditionally by mourners only, but increasingly by the entire congregation.

Kashrut (Heb). The principle of adherence to dietary regulations.

Kehillah (Heb). Community, or council.

Keter Torah (Heb). Crown of the Law. Linguistic symbols of the obeisance given the Law, which had royal rank.

Kibbutznik (Heb and Yid). Worker in a *kibbutz*, co-operative colony, in Israel.

Kiddush (Heb). Sanctification. Blessing of Sabbath, with prayers and sacramental wine, on Friday evening.

Kiddush Hashem (Heb). Sanctification of the Name (of God). Term used to signify martyrdom for religion's sake.

Kleib nahas (Yid and Heb). Gather joy. Colloquialism for parental pride and gratification.

Kol Nidrei (Heb). All vows. Chant sung in a synagogue on the eve of Day of Atonement.

Kosher (Heb). Clean, proper. Ordinarily applied to foods not banned in the Bible or in the dietary minutiae prescribed by later rabbinical authorities and supposedly derived from it.

Lamden (Heb). Learned man or scholar.

Lantsmann (Yid). Man of (our) land or town.

Litvak (Yid). Lithuanian Jew.

Mahzor (Heb). Holiday prayer-book.

Matzot (Heb). Cakes of unleavened bread. Singular, *matzoh*. Prescribed, in lieu of leavened bread, during Passover, in symbolic commemoration of the Biblical Exodus from Egypt.

Mazl tov (Heb). Good luck.

Megillah (Heb). Scroll. In synagogue parlance, it refers to the Book of Esther, read in synagogues on Purim, Feast of Lots.

Melammed (Heb). Teacher.

Menorot (Heb). Candelabra. Reminiscent of the ancient Temple in Jerusalem, and part of the sacred furniture of every synagogue.

Meshugass (Heb). Insanity, madness. Often categorizes any action regarded as foolish and ill-advised.

Meshuggener. One who is insane, a madman.

Mezuzot (Heb). Door-posts. Receptacle, about the size of a small cigar, affixed to the threshold of most Jewish homes, containing a tiny parchment of certain paragraphs from the Hebrew Bible. Singular, *mezuzah*.

Mikvah (Heb). Public bath. In every Central and East European Jewish community, an instrument of hygienic and ritualistic cleanliness; often built today as an adjunct to the synagogue by strict Orthodox congregations in the West.

Milchig (Yid). Of dairy products. Food containing, prepared with, or touched by, milk products. The Orthodox regimen bars the consumption of such edibles within six hours after meat.

Minyan (Heb). Count. Quorum of ten males – the minimum requirement for Orthodox Jewish worship, no longer observed by Reform Judaism.

Mitzvah (Heb). Commandment. Expanded to mean, in common usage, not only a Biblical mandate, but any good deed in keeping with Jewish tradition.

Nudnik. An onomatopoeic Yiddish word for bore.

Olom Haba (Heb). The world to come. Realm beyond the grave, of the other life.

Pesach (Heb). Festival of Passover. In the spring, for eight days, among Orthodox Jews; Reform Judaism has reduced the period to seven, in accord with Scripture. It celebrates the deliverance of the Children of Israel from Egyptian bondage.

Pilpulism (Heb). Aramaic *pilpul*, hair-splitting. Has been incorporated into English usage.

Purim (Heb). Lots. Holiday celebrating the deliverance of Persian Jewry from Haman by beauteous Queen Esther. As related in the Biblical scroll of that name, lots were cast to determine the date on which all Jews would be killed.

Pushke (Yid). Little tin box nailed on the walls of exile-conscious Jewish homes as repository for coins collected by the Jewish National Fund for the purchase of land in Palestine on behalf of the Jewish people.

Rachmonut (Heb). Compassion.

Rav (Heb). Master or rabbi.

Rosh Hashanah (Heb). New Year. First day of the Hebrew month Tishri, observed with a solemn service and blowing of the *shofar* (ram's horn) in the synagogue.

Seder (Heb.) Order. The home meal and service of prayer, song, and symbol which inaugurated the Festival of *Pesach* (Passover).

Selihah (Heb). Pardon. Penitential prayers, often psalms.

Shabbas (Heb). Sabbath.

Shadhanim (Heb). Match-makers. An important intermediary when marriages were arranged by parents; champion of the practical, rather than the romantic. Singular, *shadhan*.

Shayhet (Heb). Litvak pronunciation of *shohet,* ritual slaughterer. Even the flesh of permitted animals may not be eaten by Orthodox Jews unless the slaughtering is done by a licensed functionary with meticulous training in centuries-old rabbinical rules of procedure.

Shehinah (Heb). Divine Presence.

Shlemiel. Derivation obscure, but meaning clear and universal: a pathetic figure doomed to failure by inadequacy – the poor guy who always gets it in the neck.

Shlimazl (Yid and Heb). Hard luck. The harsh blows of destiny, or the little man who receives them. A *shlemiel* may be defined as a waiter who spills the soup, a *shlimazl* as the customer whose lap is doused with it.

Shmoos (probably Heb). Gossip, trivial talk.

Shnorrers (coll. Heb). Beggars.

Shtetl (Yid). Diminutive form of *shtot,* town. Plural, *Shtetlach*.

Shtimme (Yid). Voice.

Shule (Yid). Synagogue. Use of the original German word for school emphasizes the educational function of the synagogue.

Shuster (Yid). Shoemaker.

Succot (Heb). Booths. Feast of Tabernacles, or harvest festival, which occurs in early fall, soon after the Day of Atonement. Singular, *succah*.

Talmud (Heb). Learning. Vast, all-inclusive compendium of laws, ethical precepts, ritual observations – and the debates about them – compiled from the records of rabbinic conversations and conferences over a period of six centuries, roughly, from 200 B.C. to 400 A.D., and based on the fundamental laws of Sinai as believed to have been revealed in the Bible; regarded for centuries as the authoritative code of Jewish life.

Teitching Humesh (Yid and Heb). Translating the Pentateuch, or Five Books of the Torah.

Tephilin (Heb). Phylacteries. Placed on forehead and arm by an observant male Jew, with prayers and ritual at the start of each day, every morning except the Sabbath; largely obsolete among Jewish youth in Western countries, except in strictly Orthodox circles and as a temporary aftermath of Bar-Mitzvah training.

Torah (Heb). Teaching or Law. Originally applied to the first five books of the Hebrew Bible, or Mosaic code; as here used, a general term for the entire body of Jewish religious precept and practice.

Tref (Heb). Literally *trefah,* torn. Food banned as non-kosher by Orthodox regulations.

Tzitzit (Heb). Fringes. A garment worn by extremely pious Jews under the outer clothes, in accordance with ancient interpretation of Biblical law.

Yarmelke (Yid). Skullcap.

Yeshiva (Heb). Sitting at the feet of the wise. Rabbinical seminary.

Yetser-harah (Heb). Impulse or desire of evil, carnal passion.

Yidden (Yid). Jews.

Yom Kippur (Heb). Day of Atonement. Most sacred day in the Hebrew calendar of religion; devoted to individual self-judgement and penitence as the path toward forgiveness by and reunion with God, and marked, traditionally, by fasting from sunset to sunset, and all-day prayers in synagogue. Concludes the Ten Days of Repentance that follow *Rosh Hashanah.*